GO MATH! FLORIDA

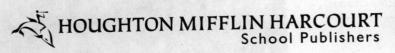
HOUGHTON MIFFLIN HARCOURT
School Publishers

GREEN EDITION

GO MATH!
FLORIDA

**HOUGHTON
MIFFLIN
HARCOURT
School Publishers**

ISBN 13: 978-0-15-380261-4
ISBN 10: 0-15-380261-8

1 2 3 4 5 6 7 8 9 10   073   19 18 17 16 15 14 13 12 11 10 09

Dear Students and Families,

Welcome to **Go Math! Florida,** Grade K! In this exciting mathematics program, there are hands-on activities to do and real-world problems to solve. Best of all, you will write your ideas and answers right in your book. In **Go Math! Florida**, writing and drawing on the pages helps you think deeply about what you are learning, and you will really understand math!

By the way, all of the pages in your **Go Math! Florida** book are made using recycled paper. We wanted you to know that you can Go Green with **Go Math! Florida**.

Sincerely,

The Authors

Planet Friendly Publishing*
Made in the United States
Printed on 100% recycled paper
By using this paper in a typical run, we achieved the following environmental benefits:
· Trees Saved: 406
· Air Emissions Eliminated: 35,782 pounds
· Water Saved: 148,189 gallons
· Solid Waste Eliminated: 19,076 pounds

* Learn more about our Planet Friendly Publishing efforts at greenedition.org

* Environmental impact estimates calculated using the Environmental Defense Fund Paper Calculator. For more information, visit www.papercalculator.org

GREEN EDITION

Authors

Thomasenia Lott Adams
Professor of Mathematics Education
University of Florida
Gainesville, Florida

Juli K. Dixon
Associate Professor of
    Mathematics Education
University of Central Florida
Orlando, Florida

Matt Larson
Curriculum Specialist for Mathematics
Lincoln Public Schools
Lincoln, Nebraska

Joyce C. McLeod
Visiting Professor, Retired
Rollins College Hamilton Holt School
Winter Park, Florida

Miriam A. Leiva
Founding President, TODOS:
    Mathematics for All
Distinguished Professor of
    Mathematics Emerita
University of North Carolina Charlotte
Charlotte, North Carolina

Consulting Author

Jean M. Shaw
Professor Emerita of
    Curriculum and Instruction
University of Mississippi
Oxford, Mississippi

Number and Operations

BIG IDEA

Represent, compare, and order whole numbers and join and separate sets..

1

Teaching Benchmarks for Depth   Pacing School Days: 7–8

MA.K.A.1.1: Lessons 1.1, 1.2, 1.3, 1.4, 1.5, 1.6, 1.7

Model, Read and Write Numbers 0 to 5

2

Teaching Benchmarks for Depth   Pacing School Days: 7–9

MA.K.A.1.2: Lessons 2.1, 2.2, 2.3, 2.4, 2.5, 2.6, 2.7

Compare and Order Sets to 5   37

Big Idea 1

Math Story

Connect • Science

Look for these:

H.O.T.

Higher Order Thinking
(see Teacher Edition)

Use every day for Florida Benchmarks Practice.

v

Look for these:

REAL WORLD

H.O.T.

Higher Order Thinking
(see Teacher Edition)

GO MATH! FLORIDA

Use every
day for
Florida Benchmarks
Practice.

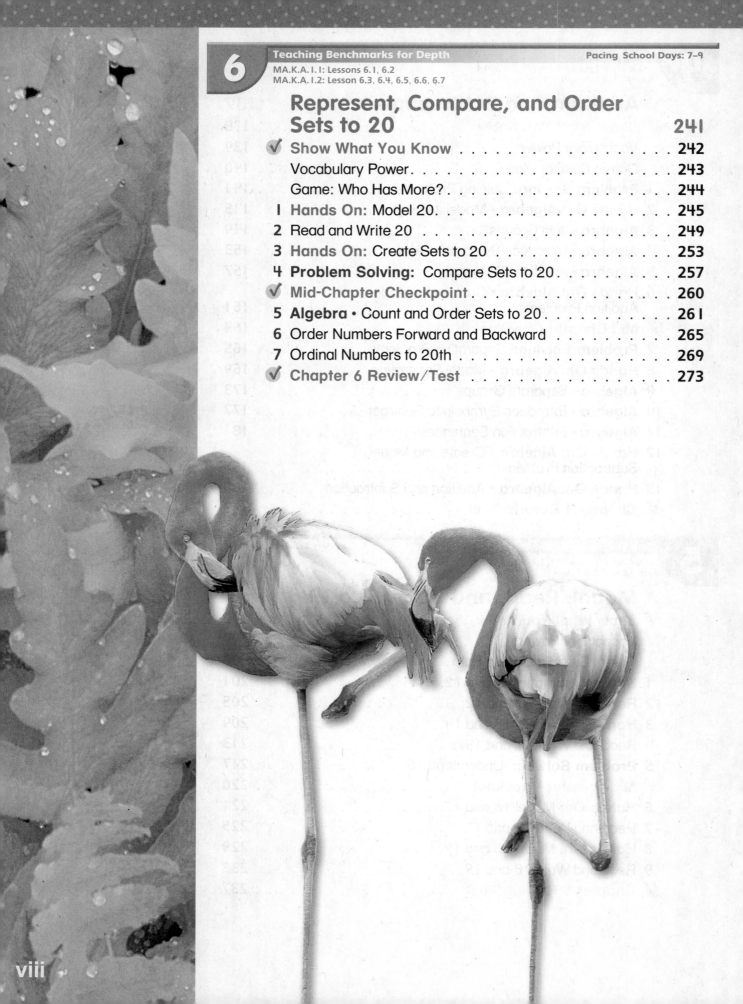

Geometry and Patterns

BIG IDEA Describe shapes and space.

Big Idea 2

Geometry and Patterns

BIG IDEA Describe shapes and space.

Literature: Back to School Fun . . . . A–H

Look for these:

REAL WORLD

H.O.T.
Higher Order Thinking
(see Teacher Edition)

GO MATH! FLORIDA

Use every
day for
Florida Benchmarks
Practice.

Big Idea 3

Math Story

Plants all Around

Science

Connect · Science

Look for these:

REAL WORLD

H.O.T.

Higher Order Thinking
(see Teacher Edition)

Use every
day for
Florida Benchmarks
Practice.

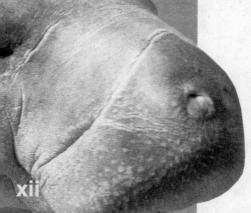

Measurement and Time

BIG IDEA Order objects by measurable attributes.

Fall Festival!

written by Alison Juliano

BIG IDEA

Represent, compare, and order whole numbers and join and separate sets.

A

Fall is here! What do you see?

One big apple tree.

Science

What season is this?

B

Fall is here! What do you see?

Two pumpkins, for you and me.

Science

What do you know about fall?

C

Fall is here! What do you see?

Bales of hay — 1, 2, 3!

Science

What do people wear in fall?

Fall is here! What do you see?

Four leaves falling from a tree.

Science

What changes in fall?

E

Fall is here! What do you see?

Five stalks of corn. Do you see me?

Science

What is different about fall
and other seasons?

F

Write About the Story

Vocabulary Review

one	four
two	five
three	

DIRECTIONS Look at the picture of the fall scene. Draw a story about fall using the numbers you have learned. Invite a classmate to count the objects in your story.

G

How Many Do You See?

 1

1 2 3 4 5

 2

1 2 3 4 5

 3

1 2 3 4 5

 4

1 2 3 4 5

 5

1 2 3 4 5

DIRECTIONS 1–5. Look at the picture. Circle how many you see.

H

Model, Read, and Write Numbers 0 to 5

Name _____

Colors

Count Forward to 10

1   2   3   4   5   6   7   8   9   10

Explore Numbers

DIRECTIONS 1–3. Name the color. Then color the star to match the crayon. 4. Point to the numbers and say them in order. 5. Circle all of the sets that show the same number.

FAMILY NOTE: This page checks your child's understanding of important skills needed for success in Chapter 1.

Name _____

match

set

DIRECTIONS Draw a line to match a set of chicks to a set of flowers.

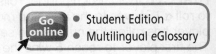
- Student Edition
- Multilingual *eGlossary*

Game Bus Stop

START
0

1

3

2

FIRE STATION

4

POST OFFICE

5

END

© Houghton Mifflin Harcourt

DIRECTIONS Each partner rolls the number cube. The first player to roll a 1 moves to the bus stop marked 1. Continue playing until each player has rolled the numbers in sequence and stopped at each bus stop. The first player to reach 5 wins the game.

MATERIALS game marker for each player; number cube (0-5).

Name _____

Model 1 and 2

Essential Question How can you show
1 and 2 with objects?

MA.K.A.1.1 Represent quantities
with numbers up to 20, verbally, in
writing, and with manipulatives.

Listen and Draw REAL WORLD

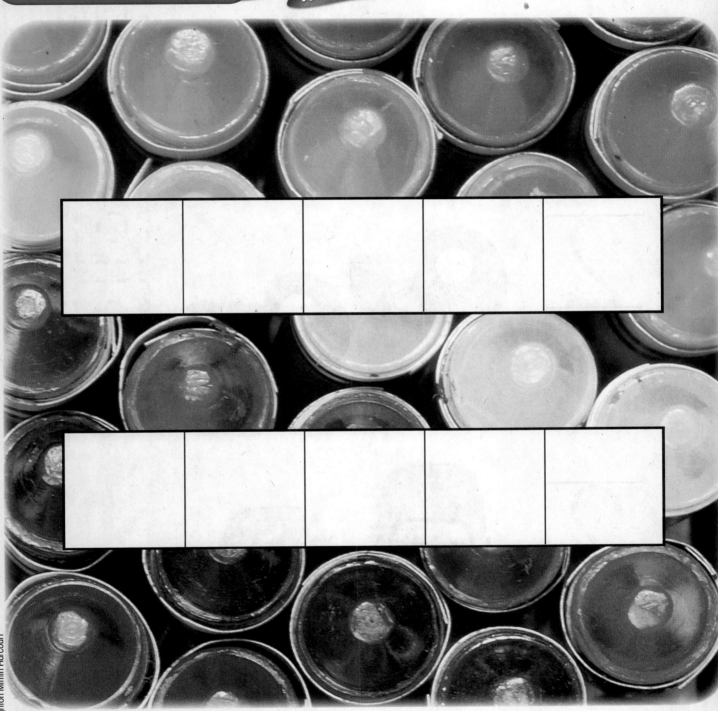

DIRECTIONS Use cubes to show the number 1 in the top five frame
and the number 2 in the bottom five frame. Draw the cubes.

Chapter 1 • Lesson 1

five **5**

Share and Show

1

I

one

2

2

two

3 ☑

2

two

DIRECTIONS Use cubes to show the number of objects. **1–2.** Say the number. Trace the cubes. **3.** Say the number. Draw the cubes.

Name _____

4

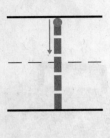

one

5

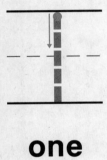

one

6

two

DIRECTIONS 4–6. Use cubes to show the number of objects. Say the number. Draw the cubes.

PROBLEM SOLVING REAL WORLD

1

2

DIRECTIONS **1.** Circle the set that has two objects. **2.** Draw to show what you know about the numbers 1 and 2. Tell about your drawings.

HOME ACTIVITY • Ask your child to create a set that has one or two household objects, such as books or buttons. Have your child point to each object as he or she counts to find out how many objects are in the set.

8 eight

© Houghton Mifflin Harcourt

FOR MORE PRACTICE:
Florida Benchmarks Practice Book, pp. P5–P6

Name _____

Read and Write 1 and 2

Essential Question How can you show 1 and 2 with pictures, numbers, and words?

MA.K.A.1.1 Represent quantities with numbers up to 20, verbally, in writing, and with manipulatives.

Listen and Draw REAL WORLD

DIRECTIONS Count the cubes. Tell how many. Trace the numbers and words.

Share and Show

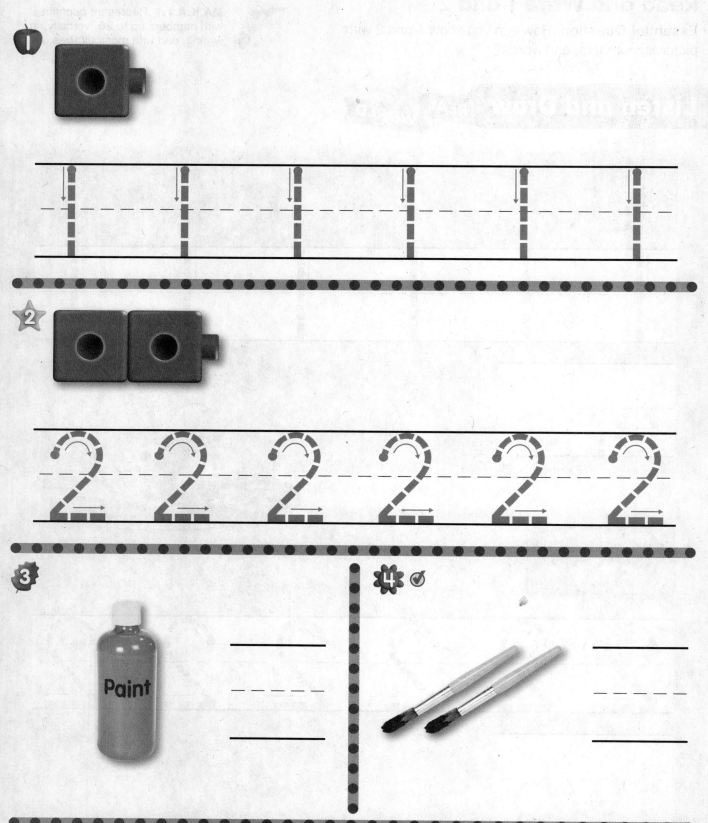

1

2

3 Paint

4 ✓

DIRECTIONS 1–2. Count the cubes. Say the number. Trace the number. 3–4. Count and tell how many. Write the number.

5

_____

- - - - - - - - -

_____

6

_____

- - - - - - - - -

_____

7

_____

- - - - - - - - -

_____

8

_____

- - - - - - - - -

_____

9

_____

- - - - - - - - -

_____

Paint

10

_____

- - - - - - - - -

_____

SCHOOL GLUE

SCHOOL GLUE

SAFE. NON-TOXIC

SAFE. NON-TOXIC

DIRECTIONS 5–10. Count and tell how many. Write the number.

Chapter 1 • Lesson 2

PROBLEM SOLVING REAL WORLD

_____

- - - - - - - - -

_____

_____

- - - - - - - - -

_____

DIRECTIONS Draw to show what you know about the numbers 1 and 2. Write how many objects are in each drawing. Tell about your drawings.

HOME ACTIVITY • Ask your child to create a set that has one or two household objects, such as books or buttons, and write the number.

FOR MORE PRACTICE:
Florida Benchmarks Practice Book, pp. P7–P8

Name _____

Model 3 and 4

Essential Question How can you show 3 and 4 with objects?

MA.K.A.1.1 Represent quantities with numbers up to 20, verbally, in writing, and with manipulatives.

DIRECTIONS Use the five frames and counters to show several ways you can make 3 and 4. Draw one way you showed the counters for each number.

Chapter 1 • Lesson 3

thirteen **13**

Share and Show

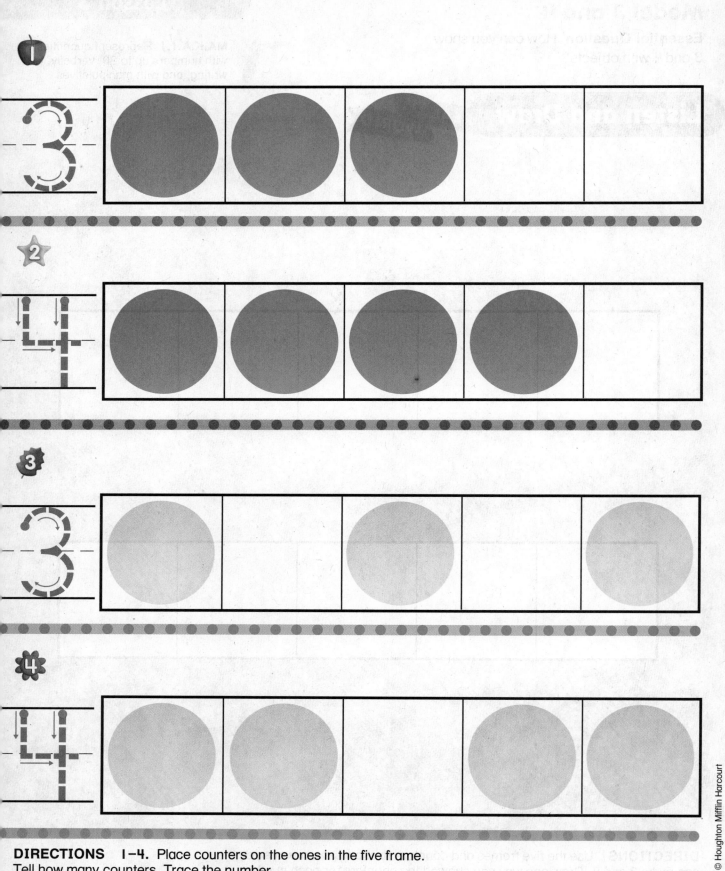

DIRECTIONS 1–4. Place counters on the ones in the five frame. Tell how many counters. Trace the number.

5 ✓

3

6 ✓

4

7

4

8

3

DIRECTIONS 5–8. Place counters in the five frame to show the number.
Draw the counters. Trace the number.

Chapter 1 • Lesson 3

DIRECTIONS **1.** Circle the set of 3 objects. **2.** Draw to show what you know about the numbers 3 and 4. Tell about your drawings.

HOME ACTIVITY • Draw a five frame or cut an egg carton to have just five sections. Have your child create a set of up to 4 objects and place the objects in the five frame. Then have your child write the number on paper.

16 sixteen

FOR MORE PRACTICE:
Florida Benchmarks Practice Book, pp. P9–P10

Read and Write 3 and 4

Essential Question How can you show 3 and 4 with pictures, numbers, and words?

MA.K.A.1.1 Represent quantities with numbers up to 20, verbally, in writing, and with manipulatives.

Listen and Draw  REAL WORLD

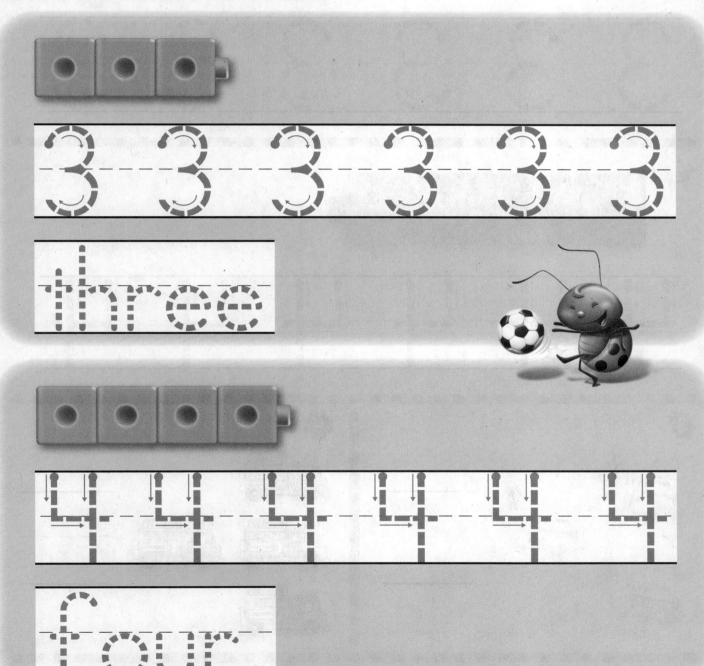

DIRECTIONS Count the cubes. Tell how many. Trace the numbers and the words.

Chapter 1 • Lesson 4

Share and Show

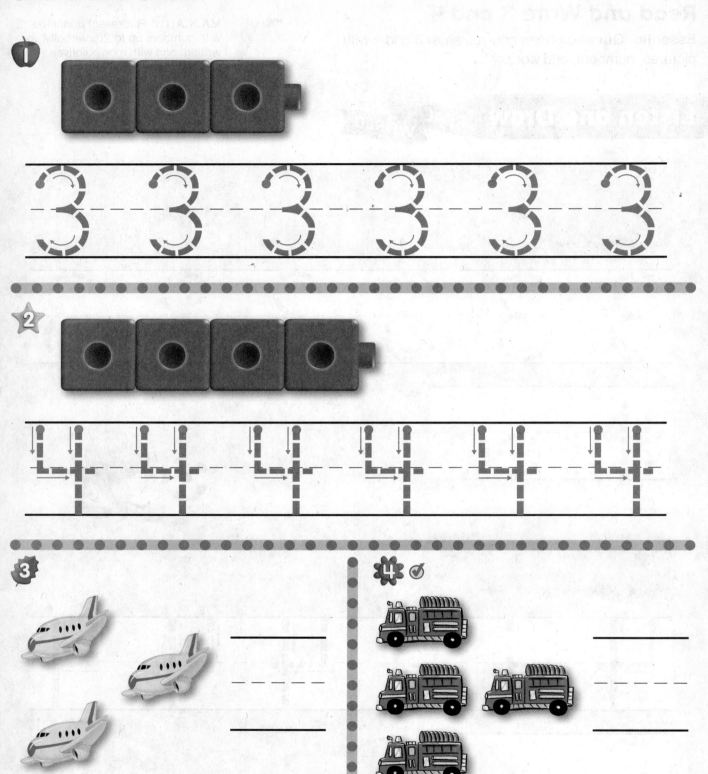

1

3 3 3 3 3 3

2

4 4 4 4 4 4

3

_____

- - - - -

_____

4 ✓

_____

- - - - -

_____

DIRECTIONS 1–2. Count the cubes. Say the number. Trace the number. 3–4. Count and tell how many. Write the number.

Name _____

  _____

 6

 _____

   _____

   _____

    _____

 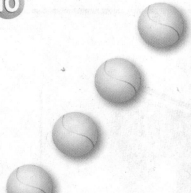 _____

DIRECTIONS 5–10. Count and tell how many. Write the number.

HOME ACTIVITY · Ask your child to create a set of three or four household objects, such as books or buttons, and write the number.

© Houghton Mifflin Harcourt

Concepts

1	2	3	4
○	○	○	○

DIRECTIONS **1.** Place counters on the five frame to show the number 3. Draw the counters. Write the number. (MA.K.A.1.1) **2–3.** Count and tell how many. Write the number. (MA.K.A.1.1) **4.** Mark under the number that shows how many books. (MA.K.A.1.1)

Name _____

Model 5

Essential Question How can you show 5?

MA.K.A.1.1 Represent quantities with numbers up to 20, verbally, in writing, and with manipulatives.

Listen and Draw REAL WORLD

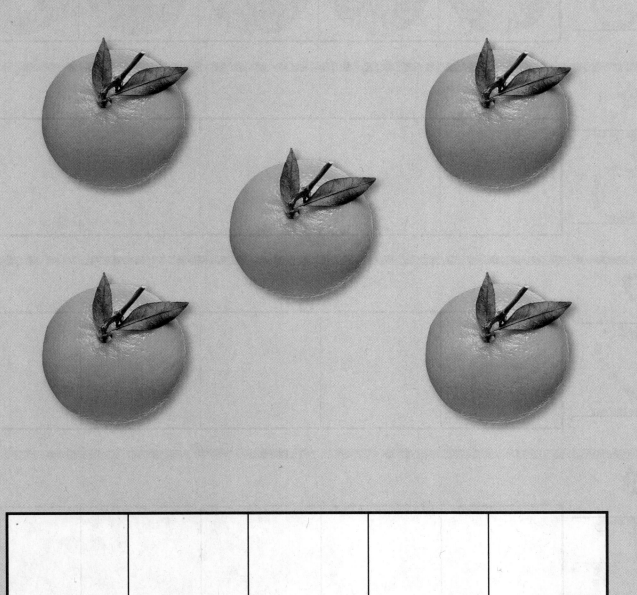

DIRECTIONS Place a counter on each orange. Move the counters to the five frame. Draw the counters.

Chapter 1 · Lesson 5

twenty-one **21**

Share and Show

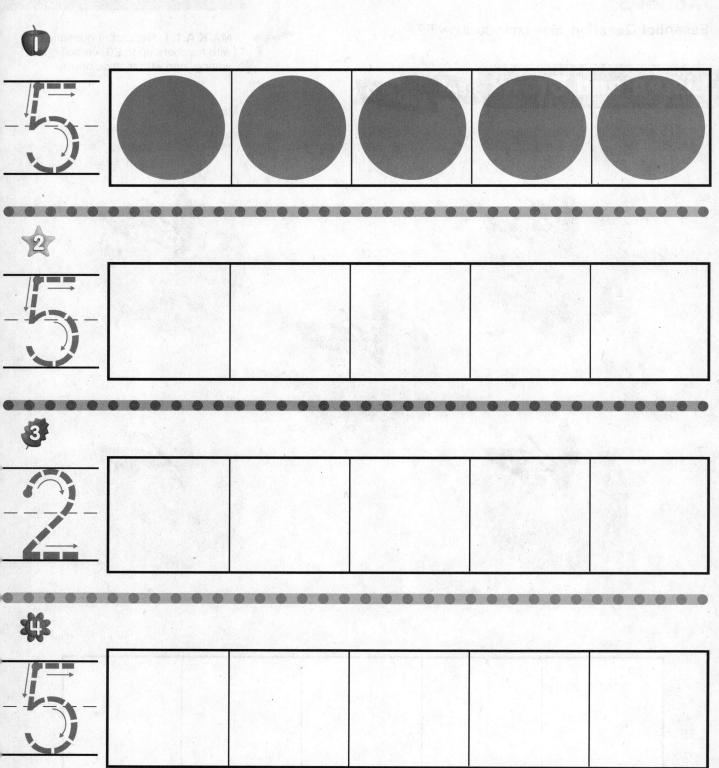

DIRECTIONS **1.** Tell how many counters. Place counters
on the ones in the five frame. Trace the number. **2–4.** Place
counters in the five frame to show the number. Draw the
counters. Trace the number

22 twenty-two

5 🦋

_____

- - - - - - -

_____

6 🌰

_____

- - - - - - -

_____

7 💜

_____

- - - - - - -

_____

8 🐟

_____

- - - - - - -

_____

DIRECTIONS **5.** Place counters to show five. Draw the counters. Write the number. **6.** Place counters to show four. Draw the counters. Write the number. **7.** Place counters to show five. Draw the counters. Write the number. **8.** Place counters to show three. Draw the counters. Write the number.

PROBLEM SOLVING REAL WORLD

1

2

DIRECTIONS 1. Circle the sets of 5 objects. **2.** Draw to show what you know about the number 5. Tell about your drawing.

HOME ACTIVITY • Draw a five frame or use an egg carton with just five sections. Have your child create a set of 5 objects and place the objects in the five frame. Then have your child write the number on a sheet of paper.

FOR MORE PRACTICE:
Florida Benchmarks Practice Book, pp. P13–P14

Name _____

Read and Write 5

Essential Question How can you show 5 with pictures, numbers, and words?

MA.K.A.1.1 Represent quantities with numbers up to 20, verbally, in writing, and with manipulatives.

Listen and Draw  REAL WORLD

5 5 5 5 5 5

 five

5 5 5 5 5 5

DIRECTIONS Count the cubes. Tell how many. Trace the numbers and the word. Count the apples. Tell how many. Trace the numbers.

Share and Show

 1

5 5 5 5

five

 2 ✓

DIRECTIONS 1. Count and tell how many. Trace the number.
2. Circle the sets of 5 apples.

Name _____

3

_____

– – – – –

_____

4

_____

– – – – –

_____

5

_____

– – – – –

_____

6

_____

– – – – –

_____

DIRECTIONS 3–6. Write the number that shows how many apples are in the set.

Chapter 1 • Lesson 6

twenty-seven **27**

PROBLEM SOLVING REAL WORLD

_____

- - - - - -

_____

DIRECTIONS Draw to show what you know about the number 5. Write the number. Tell about your drawing.

HOME ACTIVITY • Ask your child to create a set of five household objects, such as books or buttons, and write the number on paper.

FOR MORE PRACTICE:
Florida Benchmarks Practice Book, pp. P15–P16

Name _____

Understand 0

Essential Question How can you use objects to show 0?

MA.K.A.1.1 Represent quantities with numbers up to 20, verbally, in writing, and with manipulatives.

🔑 Unlock the Problem

DIRECTIONS Listen to the problem. Place one counter in the fish bowl. How many counters will you have when you take that counter away? Trace the number. Tell what that number means.

Chapter 1 · Lesson 7

twenty-nine **29**

Share and Show

 1

_____

- - - - - - - -

_____

 2

_____

- - - - - - - -

_____

 3 ✓

_____

- - - - - - - -

_____

 4 ✓

_____

- - - - - - - -

_____

DIRECTIONS **1–4.** Which tanks have 0 fish? Circle the
tanks that have 0 fish. Write how many fish.

Name _____

5

_____

6

_____

7

_____

8

_____

DIRECTIONS   5–8. Which tanks have 0 fish? Circle the
tanks that have 0 fish. Write how many fish.

Chapter 1 · Lesson 7

On Your Own

1.

2.

DIRECTIONS **1.** Bryce has two fish. Chris has none. Circle to show which fish bowl belongs to Chris. **2.** Draw to show what you know about the number 0. Tell about your drawing.

HOME ACTIVITY • Draw a five frame or use an egg carton that has just five sections. Have your child create a set of up to 3 or 4 objects and place the objects in the five frame. Then have your child remove the objects and tell how many are in the five frame.

FOR MORE PRACTICE:
Florida Benchmarks Practice Book, pp. P17–P18

Chapter 1 Review/Test

Vocabulary

1	•	•	two
2	•	•	one

Concepts

_____
- - - - - -
_____

_____
- - - - - -
_____

_____
- - - - - -
_____

_____
- - - - - -
_____

DIRECTIONS 1. Draw a line to match the number to the word. (MA.K.A.1.1)
2–3. Count and tell how many. Write the number. (MA.K.A.1.1) **4.** Place counters on the five frame to show 1. Draw the counters. Write the number. (MA.K.A.1.1) **5.** Place counters on the five frame to show 4. Draw the counters. Write the number. (MA.K.A.1.1)

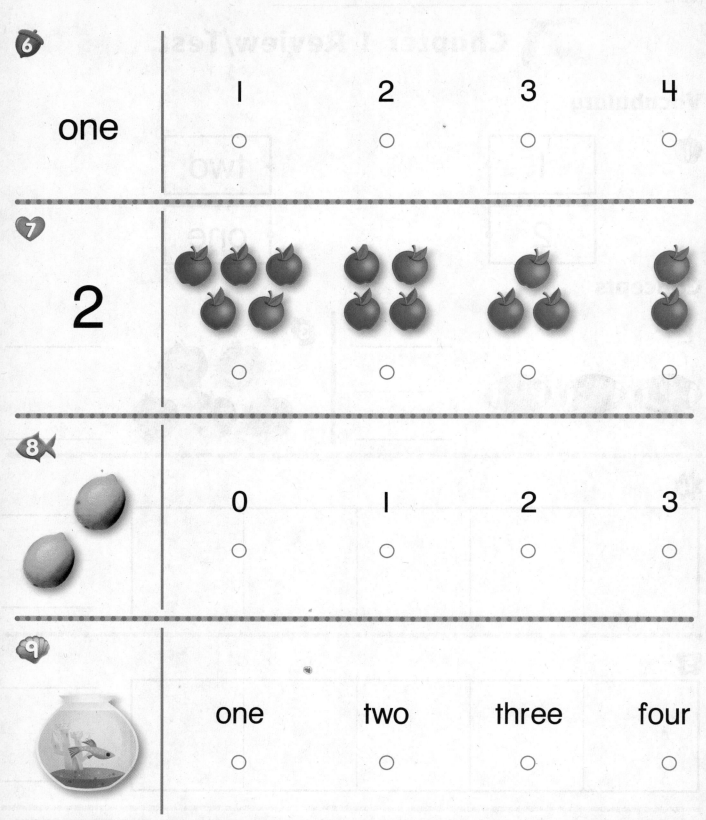

6 🌰

	1	2	3	4
one	○	○	○	○

7 ♥

2

○   ○   ○   ○

8 🐟

	0	1	2	3
	○	○	○	○

9 🐚

one	two	three	four
○	○	○	○

DIRECTIONS 6. Mark under the number that matches the word. (MA.K.A1.1)
7. Mark under the set of apples that shows the number at the beginning of the
row. (MA.K.A1.1) **8.** Mark under the number that shows how many lemons.
(MA.K.A1.1) **9.** Mark under the word that shows how many fish. (MA.K.A1.1)

34 thirty-four

Name _____

10

2	3	4	5
○	○	○	○

11

3

○	○	○	○

12

4	3	2	1
○	○	○	○

13

2	3	4	5
○	○	○	○

DIRECTIONS **10.** Mark under the number that shows how many fish. (MA.K.A.I.I)
11. Mark under the set of limes that shows the number at the beginning of the row.
(MA.K.A.I.I) **12.** Mark under the number that shows how many airplanes. (MA.
K.A.I.I) **13.** Mark under the number that shows how many balls. (MA.K.A.I.I)

Chapter 1

thirty-five **35**

© Houghton Mifflin Harcourt

14

5	4	2	0
○	○	○	○

15

two	three	four	five
○	○	○	○

16

0

○	○	○	○

17

5

○	○	○	○

DIRECTIONS **14.** Mark under the number that shows how many fish. (MA.K.A.1.1) **15.** Mark under the word that shows how many apples. (MA.K.A.1.1) **16.** Mark under the nest that shows eggs to match the number at the beginning of the row. (MA.K.A.1.1) **17.** Mark under the set of balls that shows the number at the beginning of the row. (MA.K.A.1.1)

Compare and Order Sets to 5

Show What You Know

Same and Different

  |

  |

Model Numbers 0 to 5

Write Numbers 0 to 5

   _ _ _ _ _ _ | _ _ _ _ _ _

DIRECTIONS **1–2.** Circle the object that is exactly the same as the one at the beginning of the row. **3.** Place counters on the five frame to show the number. Draw the counters. Trace the number. **4–5.** Count and tell how many. Write the number.

FAMILY NOTE: This page checks your child's understanding of important skills needed for success in Chapter 2.

Name _____

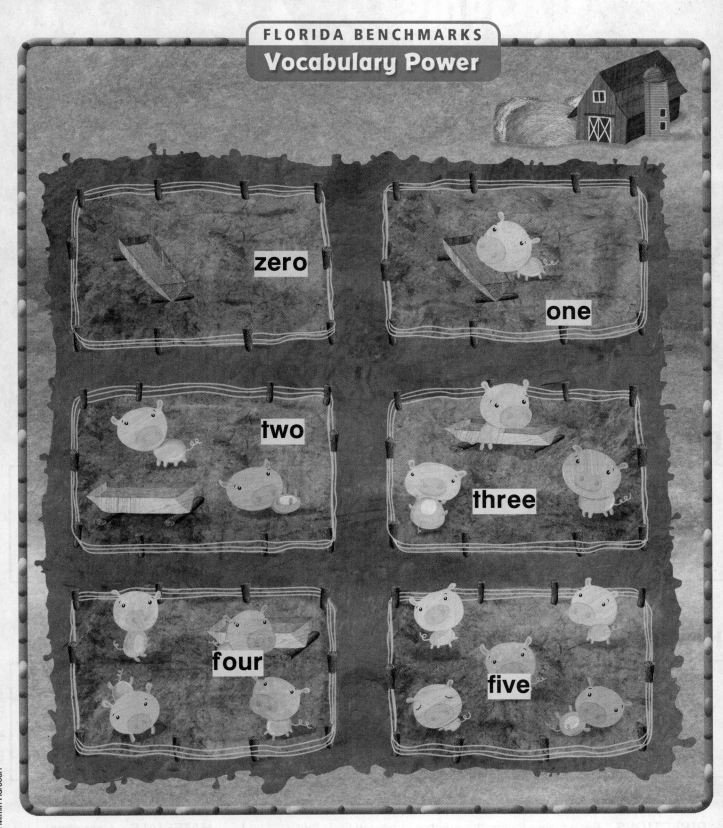

DIRECTIONS Circle the set with 2 pigs. Mark an X on the set of 5 pigs.

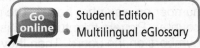
Go online
• Student Edition
• Multilingual eGlossary

Game

Counting to Blastoff

Player 1

5	4	3	2	1	0

Player 2

5	4	3	2	1	0

DIRECTIONS Each player tosses the number cube and finds that number on his or her board. The player covers the number with a counter. Players take turns in this way until they have covered all of the numbers on the board. Then they are ready for blast off.

MATERIALS 6 counters for each player; number cube (0-5)

Name _____

Same Number

Essential Question How can you create sets that have the same number of objects?

Listen and Draw REAL WORLD

MA.K.A.1.2 Solve problems including those involving sets by counting, by using cardinal and ordinal numbers, by comparing, by ordering, and by creating sets up to 20.

DIRECTIONS Use the five frames and cubes to create sets that have the same number of objects. Draw the sets of cubes.

Chapter 2 • Lesson 1

Share and Show

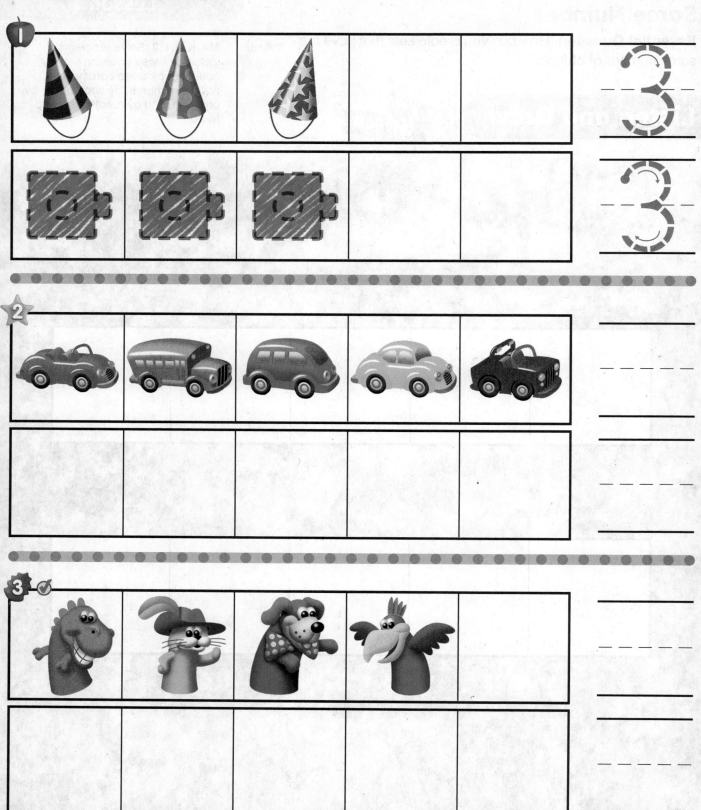

DIRECTIONS 1–3. Place a cube below each object to show the same number of objects. Draw and color each cube. Write how many objects are in each row.

Name _____

_____

- - - - - - -

_____

- - - - - - -

_____

_____

- - - - - - -

_____

- - - - - - -

_____

DIRECTIONS 4–5. Place a cube below each object to show the same number of objects. Draw and color each cube. Write how many objects are in each row.

PROBLEM SOLVING REAL WORLD

DIRECTIONS 1. Which set has the same number of objects in each row? Circle that set. **2.** Draw to show two sets of objects that have the same number of objects. Tell about your drawing.

HOME ACTIVITY • Show your child a set of household objects that has between 1 and 5 objects. Have your child create a set of objects that has the same number of objects as your set.

44 forty-four

FOR MORE PRACTICE:
Florida Benchmarks Practice Book, pp. P25–P26

Name _____

More and Fewer

Essential Question How can you solve problems by using sets with more and fewer objects?

MA.K.A.1.2 Solve problems including those involving sets by counting, by using cardinal and ordinal numbers, by comparing, by ordering, and by creating sets up to 20.

Listen and Draw REAL WORLD

DIRECTIONS Use the five frames and counters to create sets that have different numbers of counters. Draw the counters. Tell how you know which set has more counters and which set has fewer counters.

Chapter 2 • Lesson 2

forty-five **45**

Share and Show

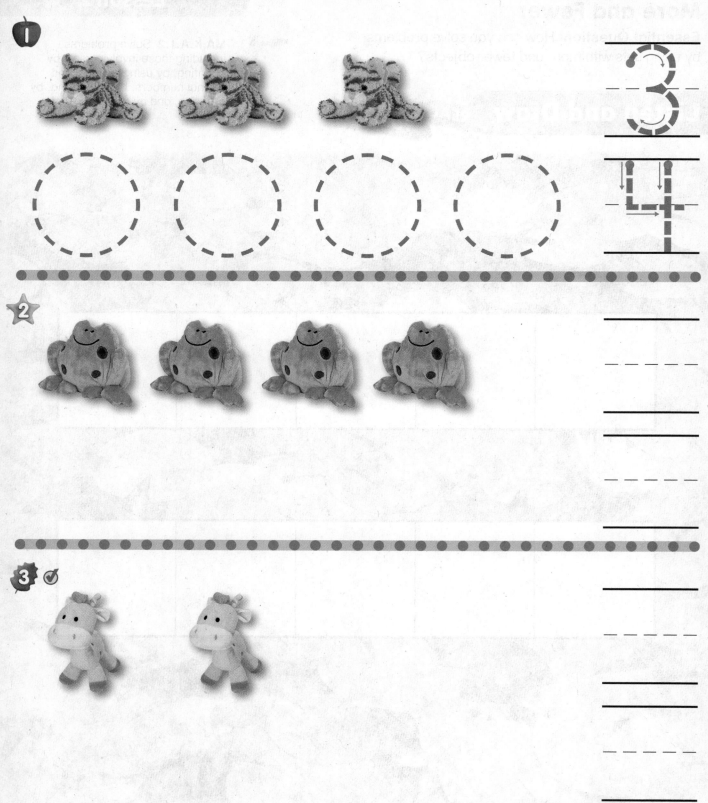

1

3

4

2

3 ✓

DIRECTIONS 1–3. Count and tell how many stuffed toys. Write the number. Use counters to show a set that has more counters than the set of stuffed toys. Draw the counters. Write how many.

Name _____

4

_____
- - - - - - - - -
_____
- - - - - - - - -
_____

5

_____
- - - - - - - - -
_____
- - - - - - - - -
_____

6

_____
- - - - - - - - -
_____
- - - - - - - - -
_____

DIRECTIONS **4–6.** Count and tell how many stuffed toys. Write the number. Use counters to show a set that has fewer counters than the set of stuffed toys. Draw the counters. Write how many.

Chapter 2 • Lesson 2

forty-seven **47**

PROBLEM SOLVING REAL WORLD

DIRECTIONS There are 3 people at a picnic. There are more plates than people. Draw the plates. There are fewer cups than plates. Draw the cups. Tell about your drawing.

HOME ACTIVITY • Show your child a set that has between 2 and 4 household objects. Have your child create a set that has fewer objects than your set.

48 forty-eight

© Houghton Mifflin Harcourt

FOR MORE PRACTICE:
Florida Benchmarks Practice Book, pp. P27–P28

Name _____

One More

Essential Question How can you create a set with one more object?

MA.K.A.I.2 Solve problems including those involving sets by counting, by using cardinal and ordinal numbers, by comparing, by ordering, and by creating sets up to 20.

Listen and Draw REAL WORLD

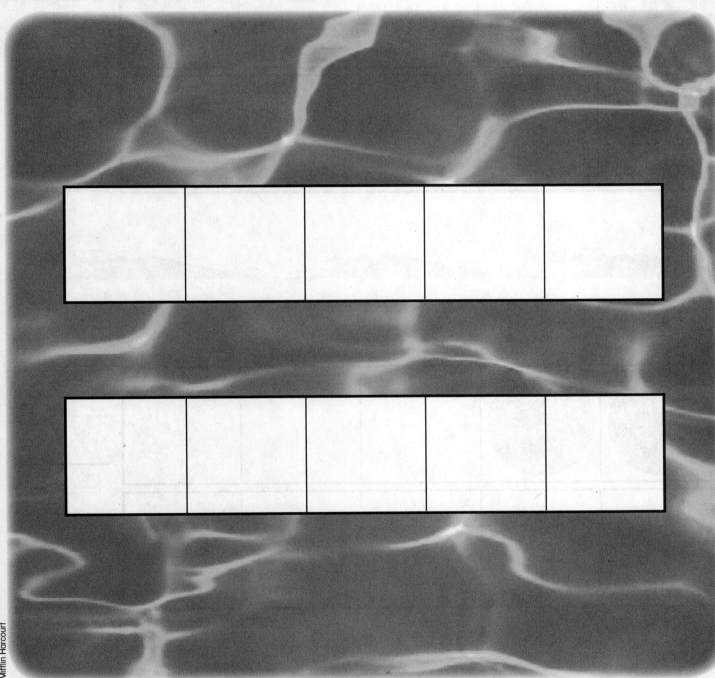

DIRECTIONS Use the top five frame to create a set that has up to 4 counters. Use the bottom five frame to create a set that has one more counter than the set in the top five frame.

Chapter 2 • Lesson 3

Share and Show

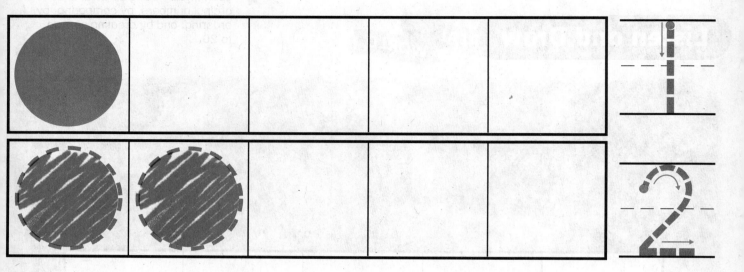

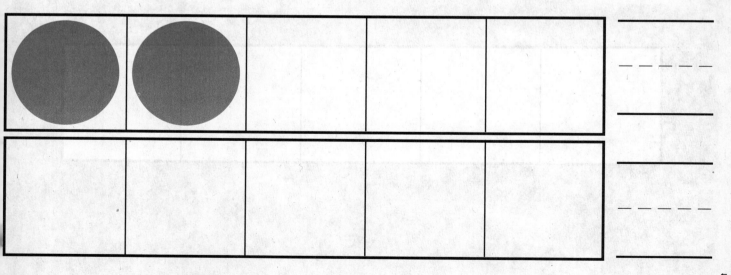

DIRECTIONS **1–2.** Count and tell how many. Write the number. Create
a set that has one more counter. Draw the counters. Write how many.

50 fifty

3

⬤	⬤	⬤	⬤	

_ _ _ _ _

_ _ _ _ _

4

⬤	⬤	⬤		

_ _ _ _ _

_ _ _ _ _

DIRECTIONS   3–4. Count and tell how many. Write the number. Create
a set that has one more counter. Draw the counters. Write how many.

PROBLEM SOLVING REAL WORLD

DIRECTIONS A set of 5 objects has one more object than another set. Draw to show what you know about the other set of objects. Tell about your drawing.

HOME ACTIVITY • Show your child a set of household objects that has between 1 and 4 objects. Have your child create a set of objects that has one more object than your set.

FOR MORE PRACTICE:
Florida Benchmarks Practice Book, pp. P29–P30

Name _____

One Fewer

Essential Question How can you create a set with one fewer object?

Listen and Draw REAL WORLD

MA.K.A.1.2 Solve problems including those involving sets by counting, by using cardinal and ordinal numbers, by comparing, by ordering, and by creating sets up to 20.

DIRECTIONS Use the top five frame to create a set of counters. Use the bottom five frame to create a set that has one fewer counter than the set in the top five frame. Draw the counters.

Chapter 2 • Lesson 4

fifty-three **53**

Share and Show

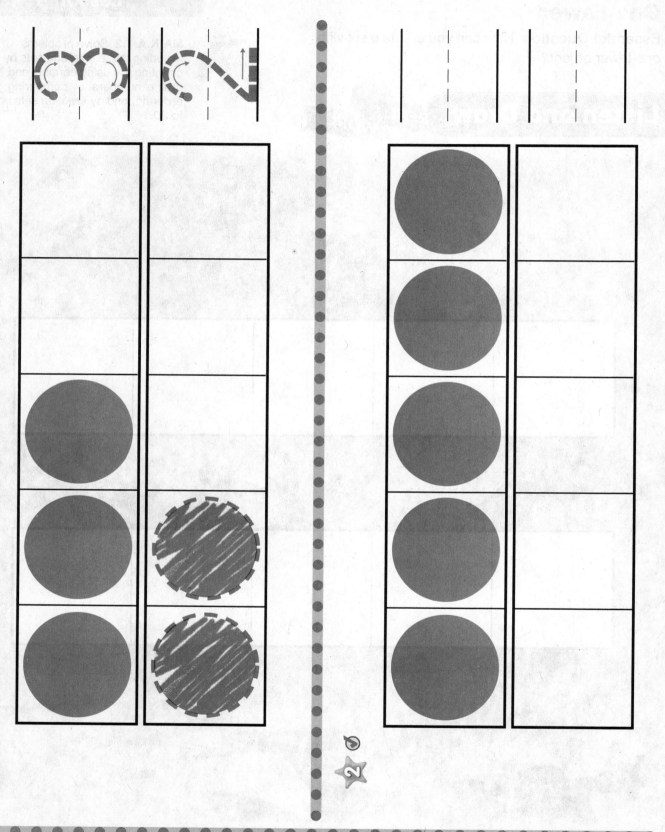

DIRECTIONS 1–2. Count and tell how many. Write the number. Create a set that has one fewer counter. Draw the counters. Write how many.

3

4

DIRECTIONS **3–4.** Count and tell how many. Write the number. Create
a set that has one fewer counter. Draw the counters. Write how many.

Chapter 2 • Lesson 4

fifty-five **55**

DIRECTIONS A set of 3 objects has one fewer object than another set. Draw to show what you know about the other set of objects. Tell about your drawing.

HOME ACTIVITY • Show your child a set of household objects that has between 2 and 5 objects. Have your child create a set of objects that has one fewer object than your set.

FOR MORE PRACTICE:
Florida Benchmarks Practice Book, pp. P31–P32

Name _____

Compare Sets to 5

Essential Question How can you solve problems by using sets that have more or fewer objects than a given set?

Unlock the Problem REAL WORLD

MA.K.A.1.2 Solve problems including those involving sets by counting, by using cardinal and ordinal numbers, by comparing, by ordering, and by creating sets up to 20.

DIRECTIONS Brandon has 1 more toy car than Joshua. Which set of toy cars belong to Joshua? Circle Joshua's set.

Chapter 2 • Lesson 5

Share and Show

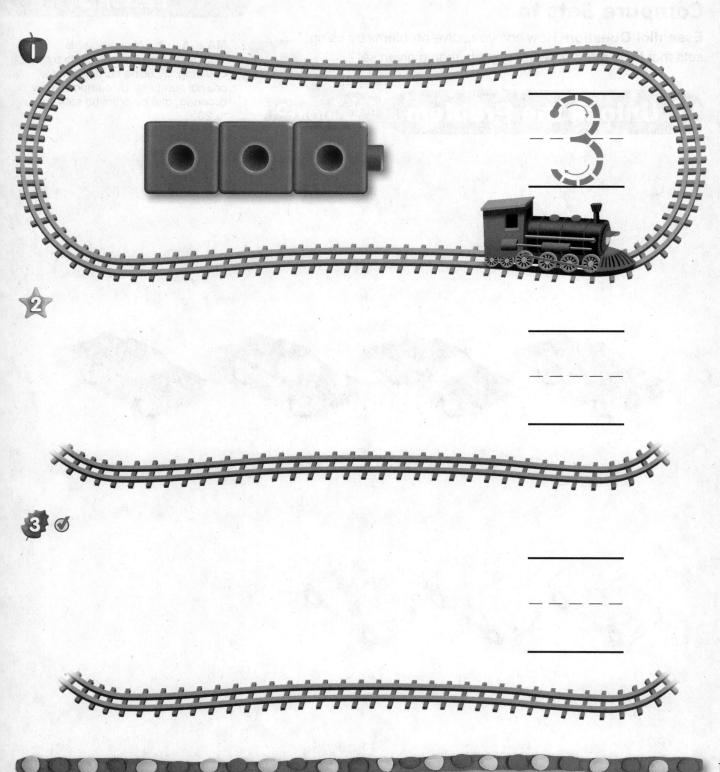

1 ``3``

DIRECTIONS **1.** Count and tell how many cubes. Trace the number. **2–3.** Create a cube train that has more than 3 cubes. Each cube train must have a different number of cubes. Draw the cube train. Write how many. Which number is greater? Circle it.

4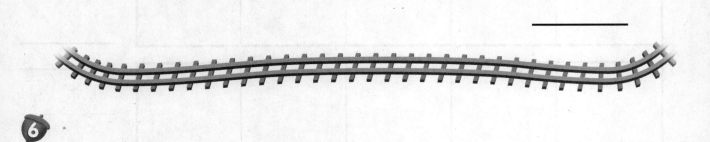

_____
- - - - - - -
_____

5

_____
- - - - - - -
_____

6

_____
- - - - - - -
_____

DIRECTIONS **4.** Count and tell how many cubes. Write the number. **5–6.** Create a cube train that has fewer than 5 cubes. Each cube train must have a different number of cubes. Draw the cube train. Write how many. Which number is less? Circle it.

HOME ACTIVITY • Draw a domino block with up to 3 dots on one end. Ask your child to draw on the other end a set of dots that has more dots than the set you drew.

Chapter 2 • Lesson 5

FOR MORE PRACTICE:
Florida Benchmarks Practice Book, pp. P33–P34

fifty-nine **59**

Concepts

_____

- - - - - - - - -

_____

- - - - - - - - -

_____

- - - - - - - - -

_____

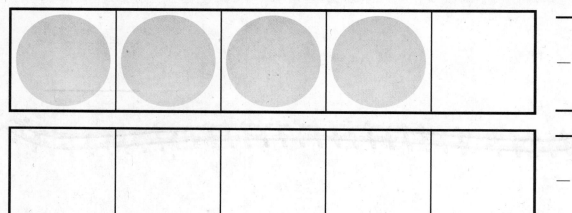

_____

- - - - - - - - -

_____

- - - - - - - - -

 Test Prep

    ◯   ◯   ◯   ◯

DIRECTIONS **I.** Place a counter below each object to show the same number of objects. Draw and color each counter. Write how many objects in each row. (MA.K.A.1.2) **2.** Count and tell how many. Write the number. Create a set that has one more counter. Draw the counters. Write how many. (MA.K.A.1.2) **3.** Jade has 3 fish in her bowl. Mark under the bowl that has fewer fish than Jade. (MA.K.A.1.2)

Order Numbers to 5

Essential Question How can you order numbers to five using objects?

MA.K.A.I.2 Solve problems including those involving sets by counting, by using cardinal and ordinal numbers, by comparing, by ordering, and by creating sets up to 20.

Listen and Draw — REAL WORLD

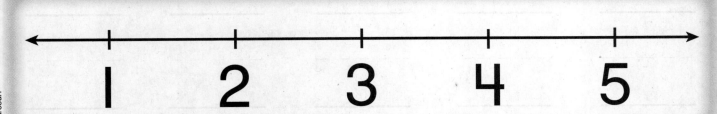

DIRECTIONS Use cubes to make cube trains that have 1 to 5 cubes. Place the cube trains in order from 1 to 5. Draw the cube trains in order.

Share and Show

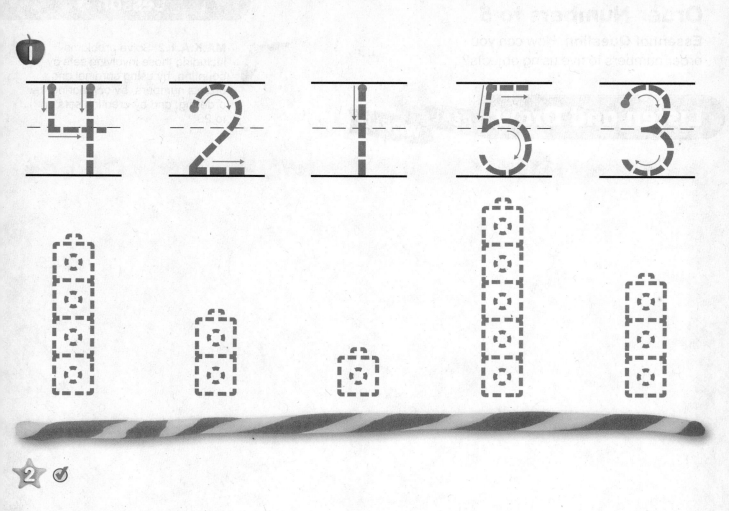

1 4 2 1 5 3

2 ✓

DIRECTIONS 1. Trace the numbers. Make a cube train to show each number. 2. Place the cube trains in order. Draw the cube trains. Write the number of cubes for each train.

3

4

DIRECTIONS 3. Write how many windows are on each rocket.
4. Write those numbers in order on the number line.

PROBLEM SOLVING REAL WORLD

1

| 1 | 3 | 5 | 2 | 4 |

| 3 | 2 | 4 | 5 | 1 |

| 1 | 2 | 3 | 4 | 5 |

2

DIRECTIONS 1. Which set of blocks has the numbers in order? Circle that set of blocks. 2. Draw to show what you know about putting numbers in order from 1 to 5. Tell about your drawing.

HOME ACTIVITY • Show your child number cards for 1 to 5. Have him or her place the cards in order from 1 to 5.

64 sixty-four

FOR MORE PRACTICE:
Florida Benchmarks Practice Book, pp. P35–P36

Ordinal Numbers to 5th

Essential Question How can you solve problems by using ordinal numbers to fifth?

MA.K.A.1.2 Solve problems including those involving sets by counting, by using cardinal and ordinal numbers, by comparing, by ordering, and by creating sets up to 20.

Listen and Draw

first

first

DIRECTIONS   Use different colored cubes to fill the five frames. Draw and color the cubes. Start with the first cube in the top five frame. Tell the ordinal position of each cube by color. Now start with the first cube in the bottom five frame. Tell the ordinal position of each cube by color.

Share and Show

first

First

STOP

first

STOP

first

DIRECTIONS **1.** Trace the circle around the first child. Trace the line under the fourth child. **2.** Circle the first person. Draw a line under the third person. **3.** Circle the fifth car. Draw a line under the second car. **4.** Circle the second truck. Draw a line under the fourth truck.

66 sixty-six

DIRECTIONS **5.** Circle the first child in the blue lane. Circle the third child in the purple lane. Circle the fifth child in the brown lane. Mark an X on the last child in the race.

DIRECTIONS **1.** Look at the number on each shirt. Circle the set that shows children in ordinal position from first to fifth to match the number on their shirt.
2. Vera is fourth in line. Draw to show how many children are in front of Vera.

HOME ACTIVITY • Show your child a set of five household objects lined up. Tell your child which object is first, and then have him or her tell you the ordinal positions of the objects that follow.

FOR MORE PRACTICE:
Florida Benchmarks Practice Book, pp. P37–P38

Chapter 2 Review/Test

Vocabulary

	same	more	fewer

Concepts

first

DIRECTIONS **1.** Draw the same number, more, and fewer counters than the set of hats at the beginning of the row. (MA.K.A.1.2) **2.** Write how many cubes are in each train. Write those numbers in order. (MA.K.A.1.2) **3.** Circle the third car. Draw a line under the fourth car. (MA.K.A.1.2)

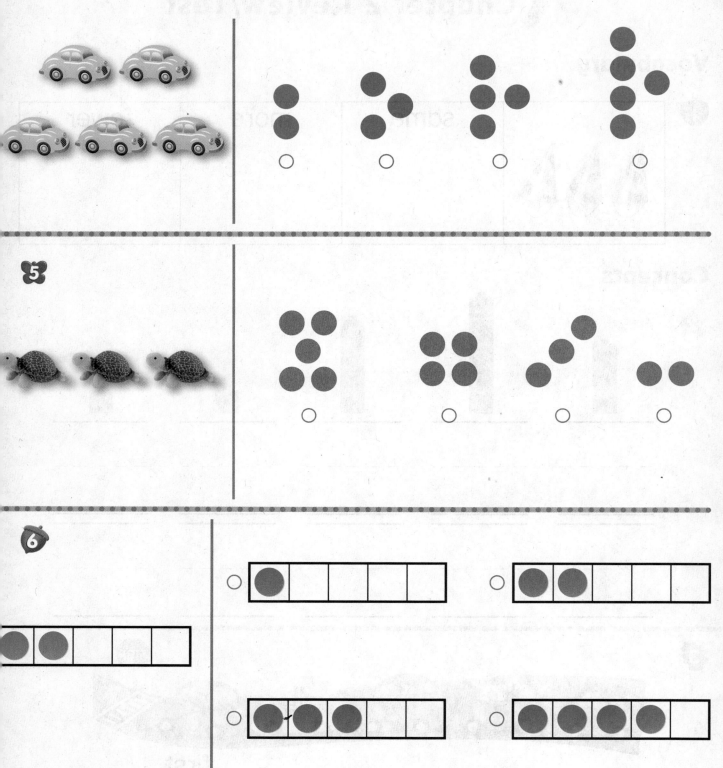

DIRECTIONS **4.** Mark under the set that has the same number of counters as the cars at the beginning of the row. (MA.K.A.1.2)   **5.** Mark under the set that has fewer counters than the turtles at the beginning of the row. (MA.K.A.1.2)   **6.** Mark beside the set that shows one more counter than the set at the beginning of the row. (MA.K.A.1.2)

Name _____

7

8

9

DIRECTIONS **7.** Mark under the set that shows one fewer counter than the set at the beginning of the row. (MA.K.A.1.2) **8.** Dennis has 3 cars. Mark under the set that has more cars than Dennis. (MA.K.A.1.2) **9.** Stephen has 4 blocks. Lauren has 5 blocks. Who has more? Mark under the picture that shows the answer. (MA.K.A.1.2)

Chapter 2

© Houghton Mifflin Harcourt

10

1 2 3 4 5   1 5 4 2 3
○   ○

1 3 4 2 3   1 3 5 4 2
○   ○

11

← | | | | | →
1 2 3 4 _

2   3   4   5
○   ○   ○   ○

12

STOP

first
○   ○   ○   ○

13

○   ○   ○   ○   **first**

DIRECTIONS **10.** Mark under the set of blocks that are numbered in order.
(MA.K.A.1.2) **11.** The numbers are in order on the number line. Mark under the
number that comes next. (MA.K.A.1.2) **12.** Mark under the truck that is fourth
in line. (MA.K.A.1.2) **13.** Mark under the third person in line. (MA.K.A.1.2)

Represent, Compare, and Order Sets of 6 to 10

Name _____

Show What You Know

Explore Numbers to 5

Compare Sets to 5

Order Numbers to 5

0

DIRECTIONS **1.** Circle all of the sets that show 3. **2.** Circle all of the sets that show 5. **3.** Write the number of cubes in each set. Circle the set with more cubes. **4.** Write the numbers 1 to 5 in order on the number line.

FAMILY NOTE: This page checks your child's understanding of important skills needed for success in Chapter 3.

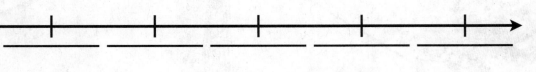

Name _____

same number

more

fewer

DIRECTIONS Circle trees to show a set with
the same number as the sheep.

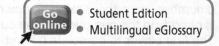

Go online
- Student Edition
- Multilingual eGlossary

Game

Number Line Up

5

5

DIRECTIONS Play with a partner. Place the 5's on the board. Shuffle the remaining cards and make a stack face down. Players take turns picking one card from the stack. They place the card to the left of the 5's to form a number line without skipping any numbers. If a player picks a card that is already in the number line, the card is returned to the bottom of the pile. The first player to complete a number line from 0 to 5 wins the game.

MATERIALS 2 sets of numeral cards 0-5

Name _____

Model 6

Essential Question How can you show 6 with objects?

MA.K.A.1.1 Represent quantities with numbers up to 20, verbally, in writing, and with manipulatives.

Listen and Draw · REAL WORLD

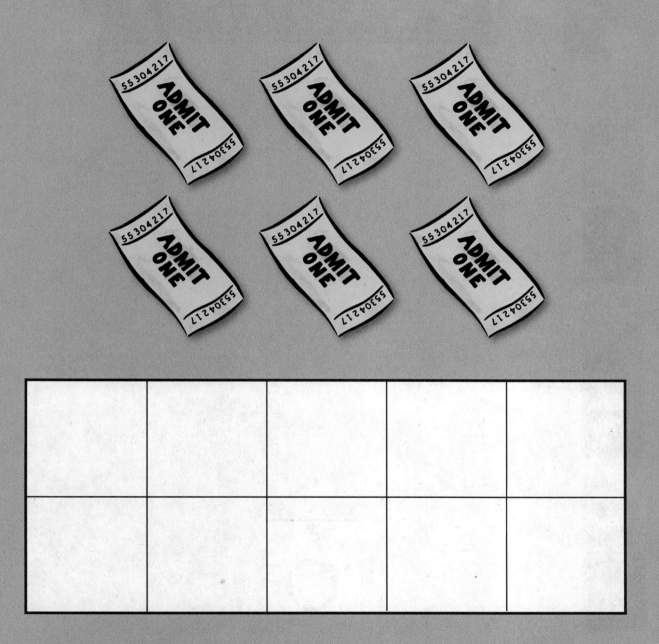

DIRECTIONS Place a counter on each ticket.
Move the counters to the ten frame. Draw the counters.

Chapter 3 · Lesson 1

seventy-seven **77**

FAIR!

DIRECTIONS I. Place a counter on each car. Move the counters to the parking lot. Draw the counters. Say the number as you trace it.

Name _____

⭐ 2 ✓

6
six

3

6
six

DIRECTIONS 2–3. Use counters to show the number.
Draw the counters. Trace the number.

Chapter 3 · Lesson 1

PROBLEM SOLVING REAL WORLD

1

2

DIRECTIONS **1.** Which sets show 6 objects? Circle those sets. **2.** Draw to show different ways to make 6. Tell about your drawing.

HOME ACTIVITY • Show 6 toys. Have your child point to each toy as he or she counts. Then have your child write the number on paper to label the toys.

80 eighty

FOR MORE PRACTICE:
Florida Benchmarks Practice Book, pp. P45–P46

Read and Write 6

Essential Question How can you show 6 with pictures, numbers, and words?

MA.K.A.1.1 Represent quantities with numbers up to 20, verbally, in writing, and with manipulatives.

Listen REAL WORLD

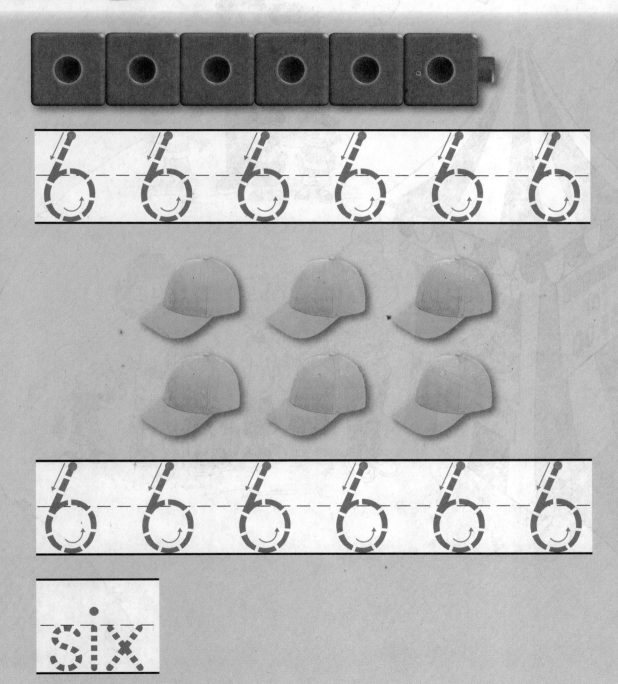

DIRECTIONS Count and tell how many cubes. Trace the numbers. Count and tell how many hats. Trace the numbers and the word.

Share and Show

DIRECTIONS 1. Look at the picture. Circle the sets of 6.

⭐ 2

6
six

6 6 6 6 6

🌟 3 ✓

_____

- - - - - - - - - - -

_____

✳ 4

_____

- - - - - - - - - - -

_____

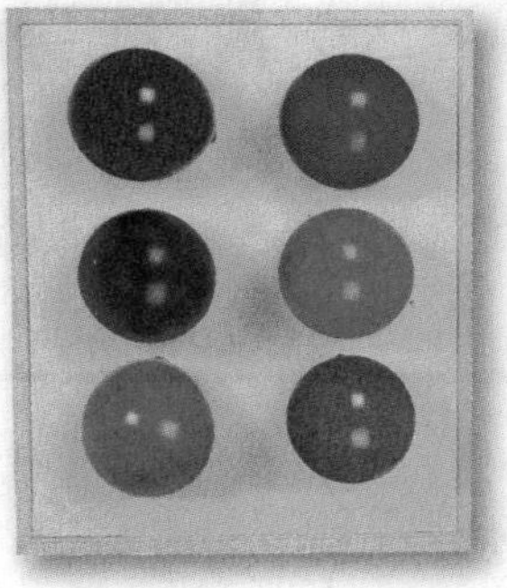

✴ 5

_____

- - - - - - - - - - -

🌰 6

_____

- - - - - - - - - - -

_____

DIRECTIONS **2.** Say the number. Trace the number.
3–6. Count and tell how many. Write the number.

PROBLEM SOLVING REAL WORLD

1

2

DIRECTIONS 1. Which set shows 2 fewer than 6 whistles? Circle that set.
2. Draw a set of objects that has one more than 5 objects. Tell about your drawing. Write how many objects.

HOME ACTIVITY • Ask your child to create a set of 6 objects. Then have your child write the number to show how many objects are in the set.

FOR MORE PRACTICE:
Florida Benchmarks Practice Book, pp. P47–P48

Name _____

Model 7

Essential Question How can you show 7 with objects?

MA.K.A.1.1 Represent quantities with numbers up to 20, verbally, in writing, and with manipulatives.

Listen and Draw REAL WORLD

DIRECTIONS Show 6 objects. Show 1 more object.
How many are there? Tell a friend how you know. Draw the objects.

Share and Show

1

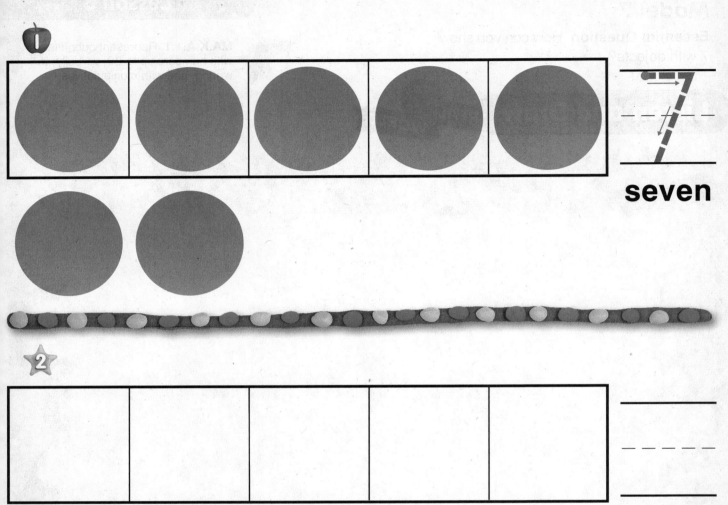

7
seven

2

3 ✓

5 and ___ more

DIRECTIONS **1.** Place counters on the ones you see. Tell how many counters. Trace the number. **2.** Use counters to show the number that is 2 more than 5. Draw the counters. Write the number. **3.** How many more than 5 is 7? Write the number.

86 eighty-six

4

●	●	●	●	●
●	●			

7

seven

5

_____
- - - - -
_____

6

_____
- - - - -

7 is ___ less than 10

DIRECTIONS **4.** Place counters on the ones in the ten frame. Tell how many counters. Trace the number. **5.** Use counters to show the number that is 3 less than 10. Draw the counters. Write the number. **6.** How many less than 10 is 7? Write the number.

PROBLEM SOLVING REAL WORLD

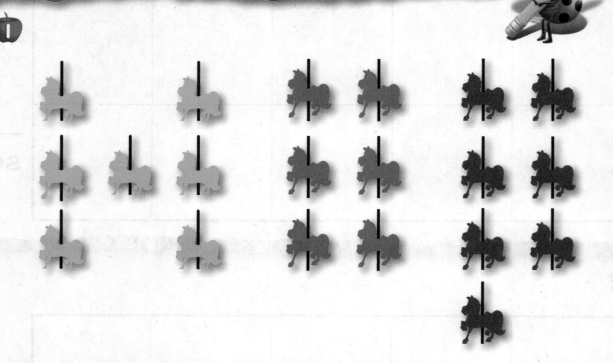

DIRECTIONS **1.** Which sets show 7 objects? Circle those sets. **2.** Draw to show different ways to make 7. Tell about your drawing.

HOME ACTIVITY • Ask your child to create a set of 7 objects. Then have your child write the number to show how many objects are in the set.

FOR MORE PRACTICE:
Florida Benchmarks Practice Book, pp. P49–P50

Name _____

Read and Write 7

Essential Question How can you show 7 with pictures, numbers, and words?

MA.K.A.1.1 Represent quantities with numbers up to 20, verbally, in writing, and with manipulatives.

Listen and Draw REAL WORLD

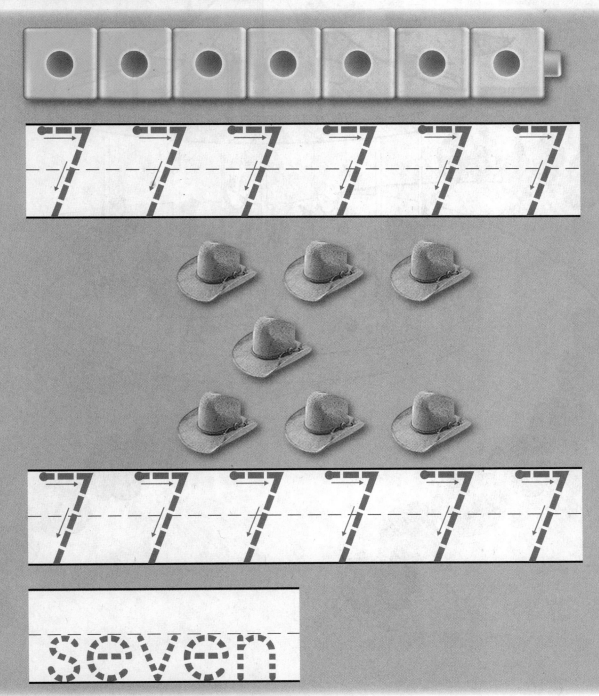

seven

DIRECTIONS Count and tell how many cubes. Trace the numbers. Count and tell how many hats. Trace the numbers and the word.

DIRECTIONS 1. Look at the picture. Circle the sets of 7 objects.

Name _____

⭐ 2

7
seven

7 7 7 7 7

🍁 3 ✓

_____

- - - - - - -

_____

❇️ 4

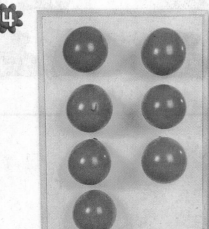

_____

- - - - - - -

_____

🦋 5

_____

- - - - - - -

_____

🌰 6

_____

- - - - - - -

_____

DIRECTIONS **2.** Say the number. Trace the number.
3–6. Count and tell how many. Write the number.

Chapter 3 • Lesson 4

1

⭐ **2**

_____

_ _ _ _ _ _

_____

DIRECTIONS **1.** Which set has 1 fewer than 7 objects? Circle that set. **2.** Draw a set of objects that has two objects more than 5. Write how many objects.

HOME ACTIVITY • Ask your child to create a set of 7 objects. Then have your child write the number to show how many objects are in the set.

FOR MORE PRACTICE:
Florida Benchmarks Practice Book, pp. P51–P52

Name _____

Model 8

Essential Question How can you show 8 with objects?

MA.K.A.1.1 Represent quantities with numbers up to 20, verbally, in writing, and with manipulatives.

Listen and Draw REAL WORLD

DIRECTIONS Show 7 objects. Show 1 more object. How many are there? Tell a friend how you know. Draw the objects.

Share and Show

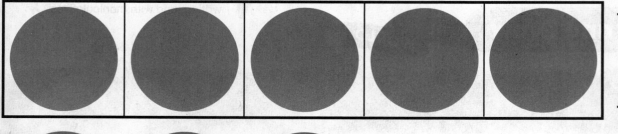

eight

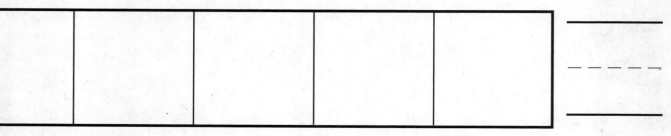

5 and _____ more

DIRECTIONS **1.** Place counters on the ones you see. Tell how many counters. Trace the number. **2.** Use counters to show the number that is 3 more than 5. Draw the counters. Write the number. **3.** How many more than 5 is 8? Write the number.

Name _____

eight

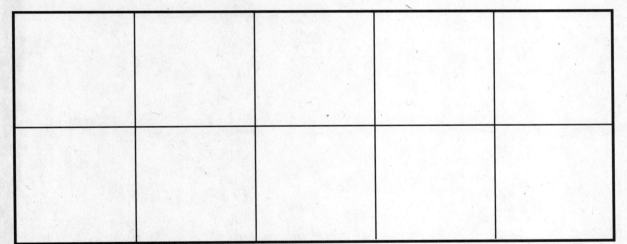

8 is ____ less than 10

DIRECTIONS 4. Place counters on the ones in the ten frame. Tell how many counters. Trace the number. 5. Use counters to show the number that is 2 less than 10. Draw the counters. Write the number. 6. How many less than 10 is 8? Write the number.

PROBLEM SOLVING REAL WORLD

1

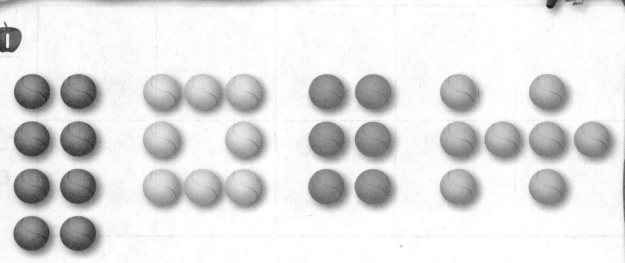

2

DIRECTIONS **1.** Which sets show 8 balls? Circle those sets. **2.** Draw to show different ways to make 8. Tell about your drawing.

HOME ACTIVITY • Ask your child to create a set of 8 objects. Then have your child write the number to show how many objects are in the set.

FOR MORE PRACTICE:
Florida Benchmarks Practice Book, pp. P53–P54

Name _____

Read and Write 8

Essential Question How can you show 8 with pictures, numbers, and words?

MA.K.A.1.1 Represent quantities with numbers up to 20, verbally, in writing, and with manipulatives.

Listen and Draw REAL WORLD

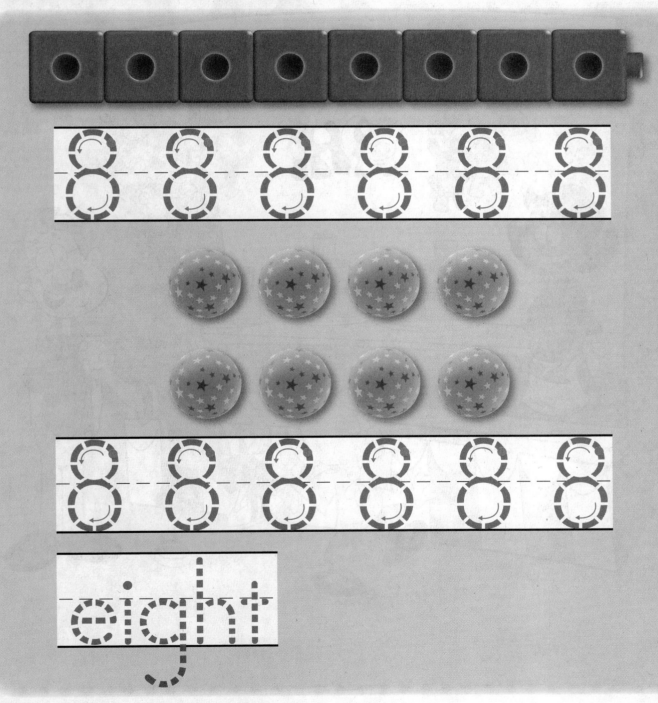

DIRECTIONS Count and tell how many cubes. Trace the numbers. Count and tell how many balls. Trace the numbers and the word.

Share and Show

DIRECTIONS 1. Look at the picture. Circle the sets of 8 objects.

Name _____

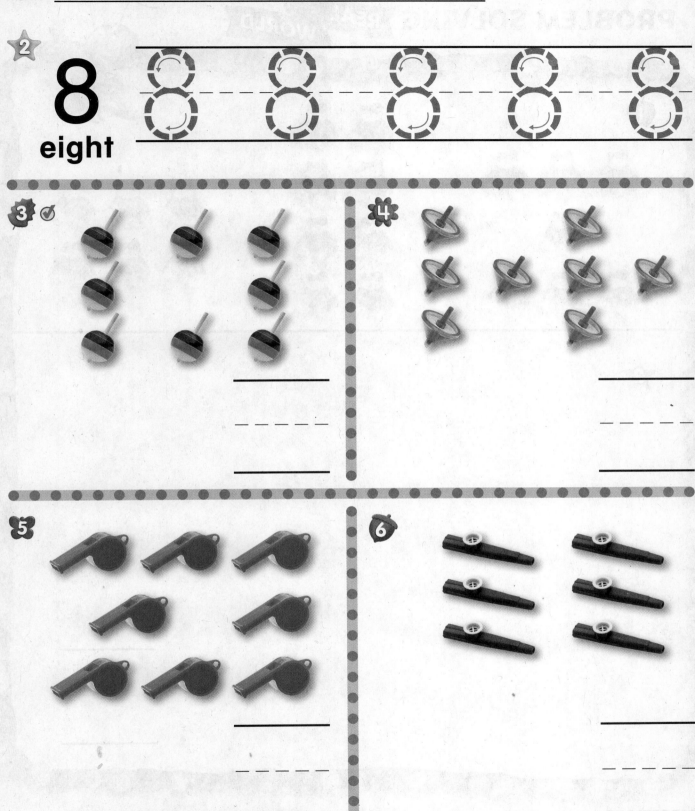

⭐ 2

8
eight

8 8 8 8 8

3 ✓

_____
- - - - - - - -
_____

4

_____
- - - - - - - -
_____

5

_____
- - - - - - - -
_____

6

_____
- - - - - - - -
_____

DIRECTIONS **2.** Say the number. Trace the number.
3–6. Count and tell how many. Write the number.

PROBLEM SOLVING REAL WORLD

1

2

_____

- - - - - - -

_____

DIRECTIONS 1. Which set has 2 more than 6? Circle that set. **2.** Robbie won 10 prizes at the fair. Marissa won 2 fewer prizes than Robbie. Draw to show Marissa's prizes. Write how many.

HOME ACTIVITY • Ask your child to create a set of 8 objects. Then have your child write the number to show how many objects are in the set.

100 one hundred

© Houghton Mifflin Harcourt

Name _____

Hands On: Model 9

Essential Question How can you show 9 with objects?

MA.K.A.I.I Represent quantities with numbers up to 20, verbally, in writing, and with manipulatives.

Listen and Draw REAL WORLD

DIRECTIONS Show 8 objects. Show I more object. How many are there? Tell a friend how you know. Draw the objects.

Chapter 3 · Lesson 7

one hundred one **101**

Share and Show

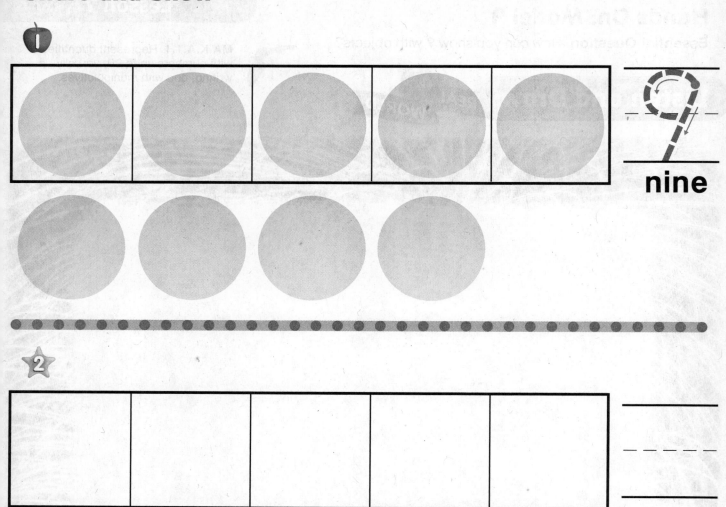

① **9**
nine

②

③ ✓ _____
       - - - - -

5 and ___ more

© Houghton Mifflin Harcourt

DIRECTIONS 1. Place counters on the ones you see. Tell how many counters. Trace the number. 2. Use counters to show the number that is 4 more than 5. Draw the counters. Write the number. 3. How many more than 5 is 9? Write the number.

Name _____

 4

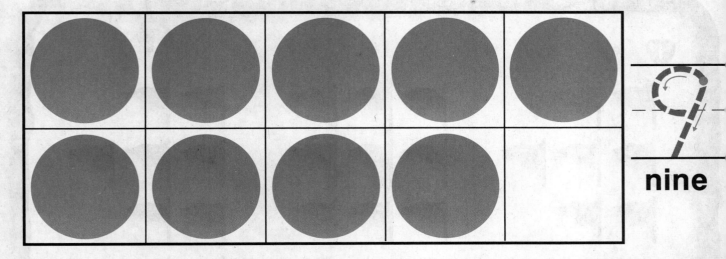

nine

5

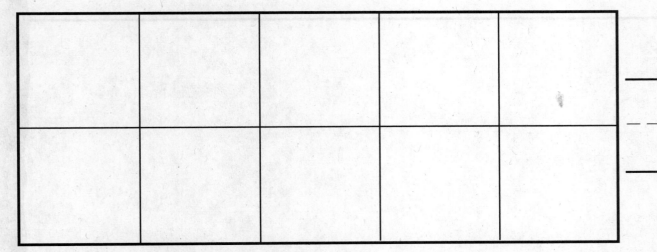

6 _____

9 is ____ less than 10

DIRECTIONS **4.** Place counters on the ones in the ten frame. Tell how many counters. Trace the number. **5.** Use counters to show the number that is 1 less than 10. Draw the counters. Write the number. **6.** How many less than 10 is 9? Write the number.

PROBLEM SOLVING REAL WORLD

❶ 🍎

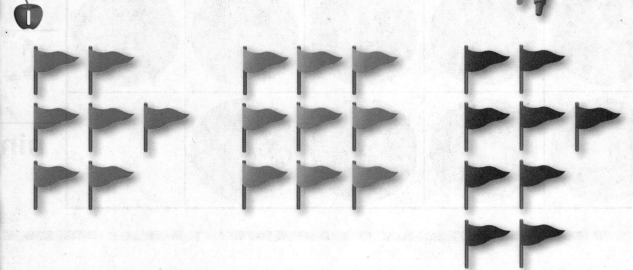

② ⭐

DIRECTIONS **I.** Which sets show 9 objects? Circle those sets. **2.** Draw to show different ways to make 9. Tell about your drawing.

HOME ACTIVITY • Ask your child to create a set of 9 objects. Then have your child write the number to show how many objects are in the set.

104 one hundred four

FOR MORE PRACTICE:
Florida Benchmarks Practice Book, pp. P57–P58

Name _____

Read and Write 9

Essential Question How can you show 9 with pictures, numbers, and words?

MA.K.A.1.1 Represent quantities with numbers up to 20, verbally, in writing, and with manipulatives.

Listen and Draw REAL WORLD

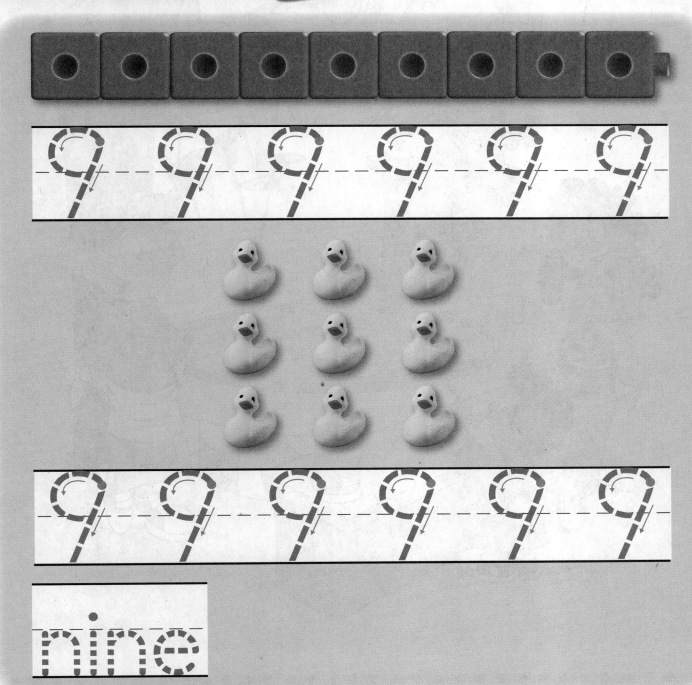

nine

DIRECTIONS Count and tell how many cubes. Trace the numbers. Count and tell how many ducks. Trace the numbers and the word.

Share and Show

DIRECTIONS 1. Look at the picture.
Circle the sets of 9 objects.

9
nine

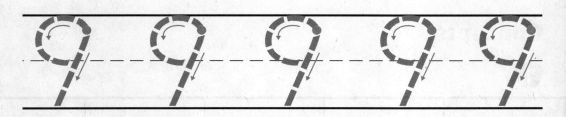

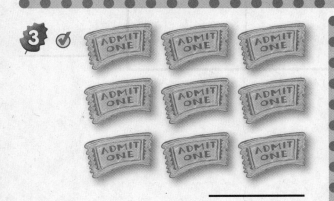

_____

- - - - - - - - - - -

_____

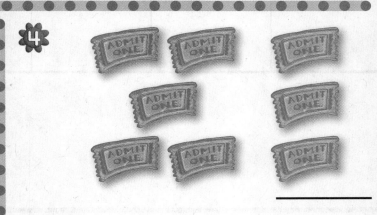

_____

- - - - - - - - - - -

_____

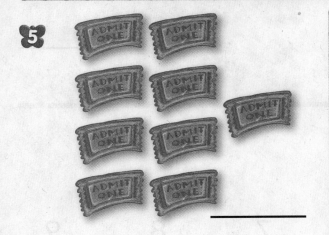

_____

- - - - - - - - - - -

_____

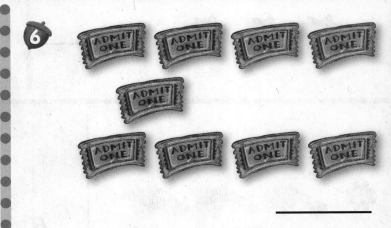

_____

- - - - - - - - - - -

_____

DIRECTIONS 2. Say the number. Trace the number. **3–6.** Count and tell how many. Write the number.

HOME ACTIVITY • Ask your child to create a set of 9 objects. Then have your child write the number to show how many objects are in the set.

Chapter 3 • Lesson 8

FOR MORE PRACTICE:
Florida Benchmarks Practice Book, pp. P59–P60

Concepts

_____

- - - - -

_____

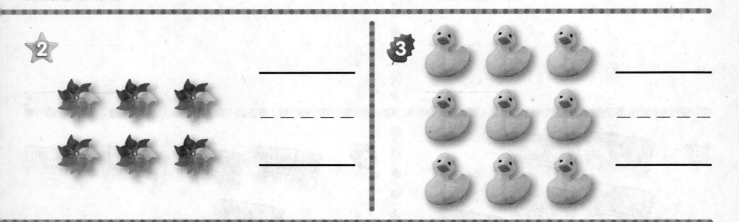

⭐ 2

_____

- - - - -

_____

❸ 3

_____

- - - - -

_____

🔷 Test Prep

❹ 4

6 ○   7 ○   8 ○   9 ○

DIRECTIONS **1.** Use counters to show the number 7. Draw the counters. Write the number. (MA.K.A.1.1) **2–3.** Count and tell how many. Write the number. (MA.K.A.1.1) **4.** Mark under the number that shows how many whistles are in the set at the beginning of the row. (MA.K.A.1.1)

Name _____

Model 10

Essential Question How can you show 10 with objects?

MA.K.A.I.I Represent quantities with numbers up to 20, verbally, in writing, and with manipulatives.

Listen and Draw

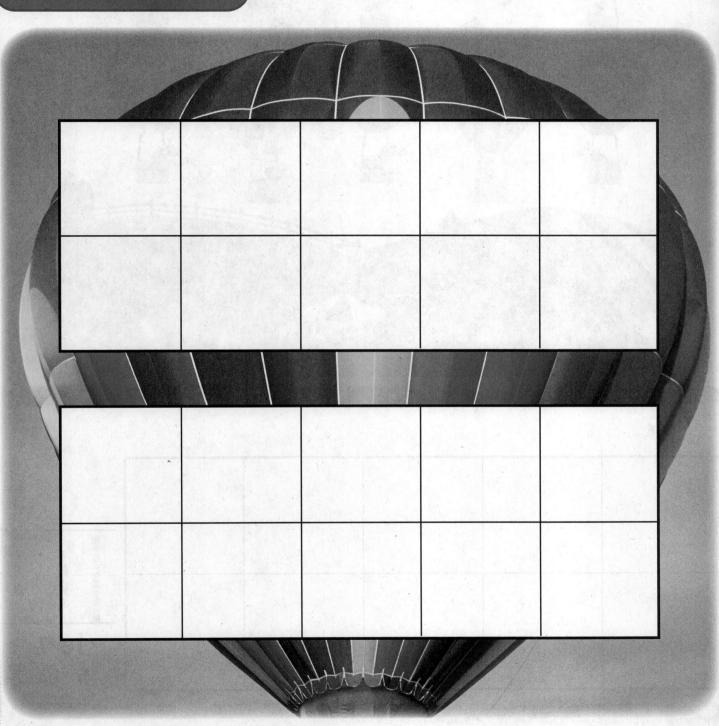

DIRECTIONS Use counters to show 9 in the top ten frame. Use counters to show 10 in the bottom ten frame. Draw the counters. Tell about the ten frames.

Chapter 3 • Lesson 9

one hundred nine **109**

Share and Show

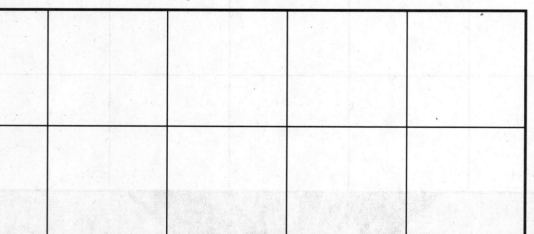

ten

DIRECTIONS **1.** Place a counter on each balloon. **2.** Move the counters to the ten frame. Draw the counters. Point to each counter as you count it. Trace the number.

3

<table>
<tr><td></td><td></td><td></td><td></td><td></td></tr>
<tr><td></td><td></td><td></td><td></td><td></td></tr>
</table>

_____   ⬤   _____   ◯
- - - -   - - - -
_____   _____

4

<table>
<tr><td></td><td></td><td></td><td></td><td></td></tr>
<tr><td></td><td></td><td></td><td></td><td></td></tr>
</table>

_____   ⬤   _____   ◯
- - - -   - - - -
_____   _____

DIRECTIONS 3–4. Spill ten two-color counters on the page. Place the counters in the ten frame by color. Draw the counters in the ten frame. Write how many of each color.

PROBLEM SOLVING REAL WORLD

 1

2

DIRECTIONS **1.** Which sets show 10 objects? Circle those sets **2.** Draw to show what you know about the number 10. Tell about your drawing.

HOME ACTIVITY • Ask your child to create a set of 10 objects. Then have your child write the number to show how many objects are in the set.

112 one hundred twelve

FOR MORE PRACTICE:
Florida Benchmarks Practice Book, pp. P61–P62

Read and Write 10

Essential Question How can you show 10 with pictures, numbers, and words?

MA.K.A.I.I Represent quantities with numbers up to 20; verbally, in writing, and with manipulatives.

Listen and Draw

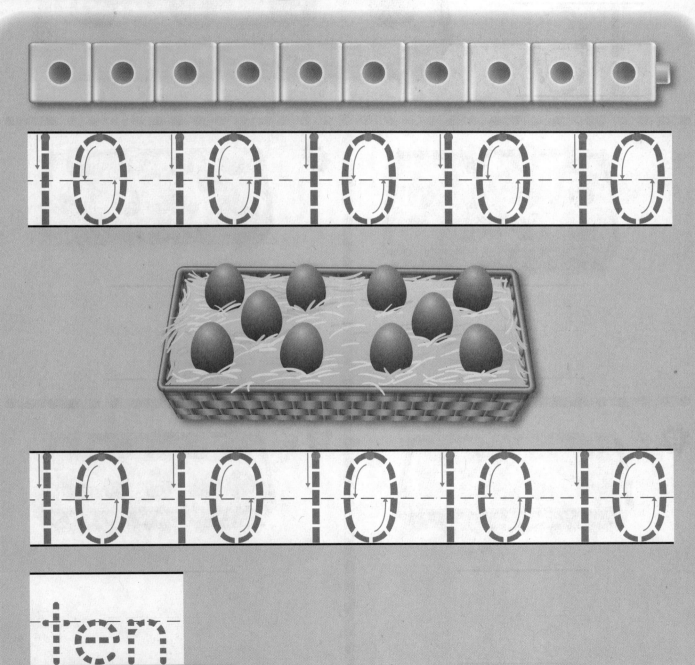

DIRECTIONS Count and tell how many cubes. Trace the numbers. Count and tell how many eggs. Trace the numbers and the word.

Share and Show

10
ten

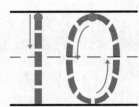

⭐ **2**

_____

\- \- \- \- \- \- \-

_____

🍁 **3**

_____

\- \- \- \- \- \- \-

_____

✿ **4** ☑

_____

\- \- \- \- \- \- \-

_____

❀ **5** ☑

_____

\- \- \- \- \- \- \-

_____

DIRECTIONS   1. Count and tell how many eggs. Trace the
number.   **2–5.** Count and tell how many eggs. Write the number.

Name _____

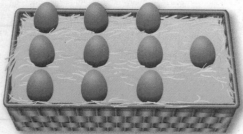

10
ten

10 10 10 10 10

7

8

9

DIRECTIONS **6.** Say the number. Trace the number.
7–9. Count and tell how many. Write the number.

© Houghton Mifflin Harcourt

PROBLEM SOLVING REAL WORLD

DIRECTIONS Draw a set of objects that has one object more than 9. Describe your drawing. Write how many objects.

HOME ACTIVITY • Ask your child to create a set of 10 objects. Then have your child write the number to show how many objects are in the set.

FOR MORE PRACTICE:
Florida Benchmarks Practice Book, pp. P63–P64

Name _____

Ways to Make 10

Essential Question How can you
show ways to make 10 with cubes?

MA.K.A.1.1 Represent quantities
with numbers up to 20, verbally, in
writing, and with manipulatives.

Listen and Draw

DIRECTIONS Use cubes of two colors to show different
ways to make 10. Color to show the ways.

Chapter 3 · Lesson 11

Share and Show

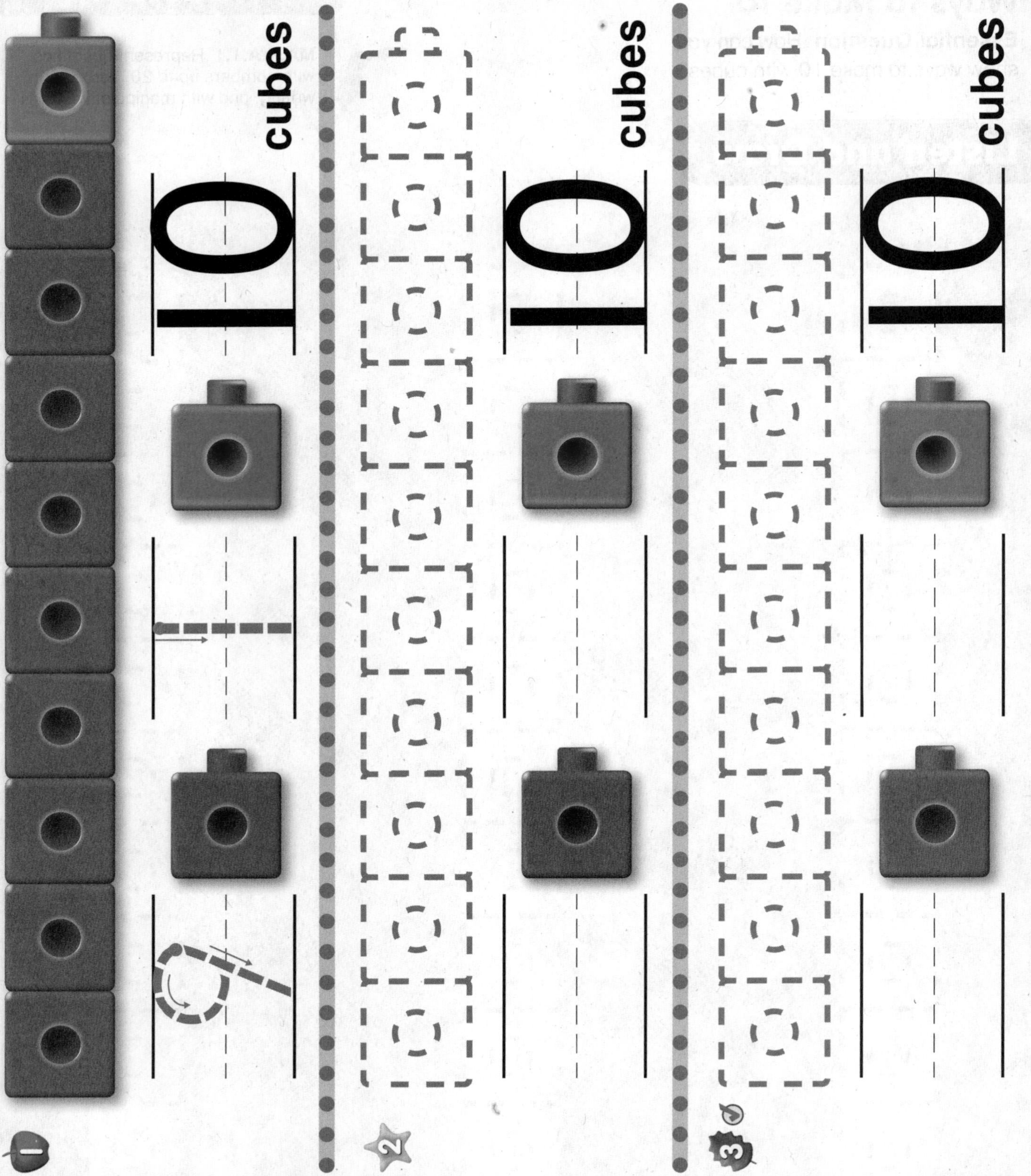

10 cubes

10 cubes

10 cubes

10 cubes

DIRECTIONS **1.** Count and tell how many cubes of each color. Trace the numbers. **2–3.** Use cubes of two colors to show different ways to make 10. Color the cubes. Write how many of each color.

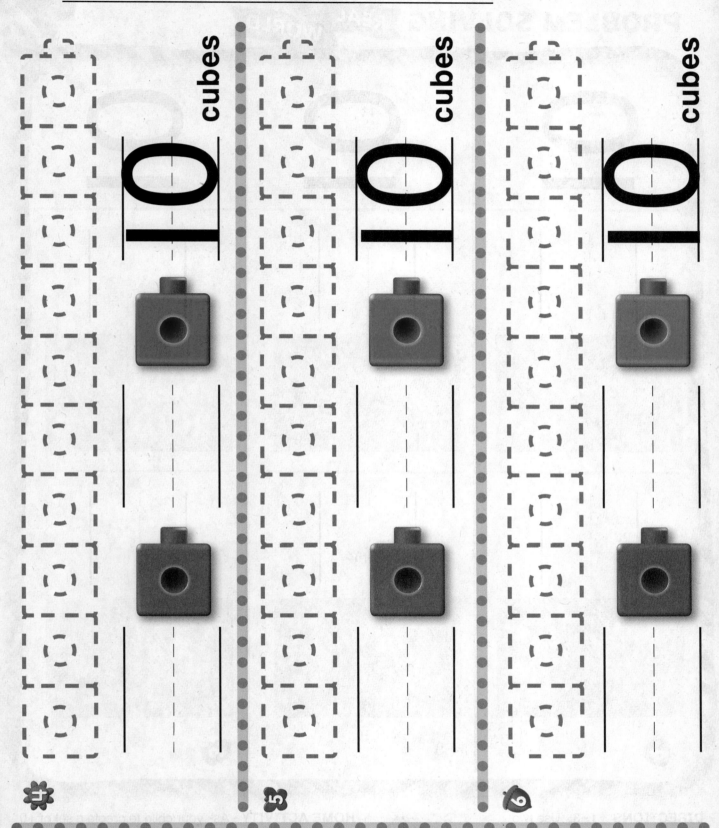

10 cubes

10 cubes

10 cubes

DIRECTIONS 4–6. Use cubes of two colors to show different ways
to make 10. Color the cubes. Write how many of each color.

Chapter 3 · Lesson 11

PROBLEM SOLVING REAL WORLD

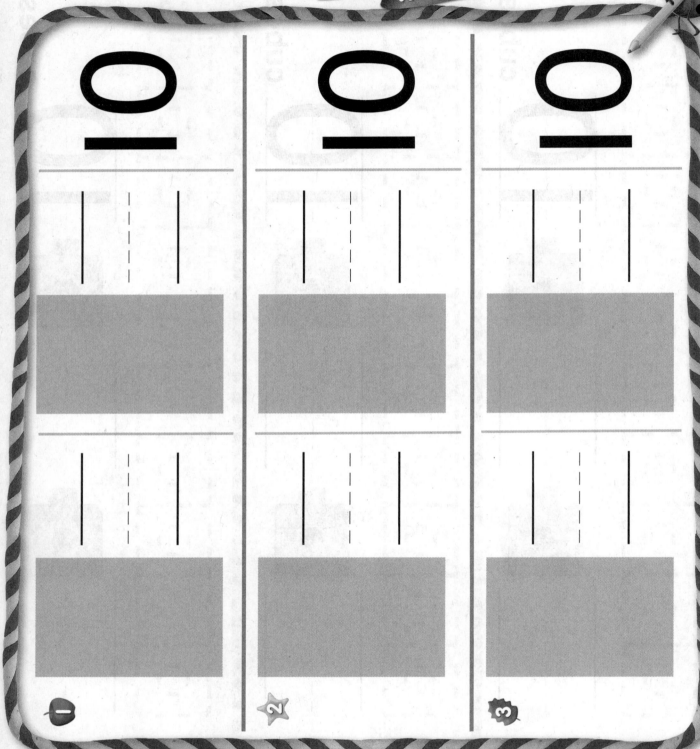

HOME ACTIVITY • Ask your child to create a set of 10 objects, using objects of the same kind that are different in one way, for example, paper clips large and small. Then have your child write the numbers that show how many of each kind are in the set and the set total.

120 one hundred twenty

FOR MORE PRACTICE:
Florida Benchmarks Practice Book, pp. P65–P66

Compare Sets to 10

Essential Question How can you solve problems by comparing sets?

MA.K.A.1.2 Solve problems including those involving sets by counting, by using cardinal and ordinal numbers, by comparing, by ordering, and by creating sets up to 20.

🔑 Unlock the Problem

DIRECTIONS Break a cube train into two parts. Place the two parts one-to-one to compare the cube trains. Tell about the cube trains. Draw the cube trains.

Share and Show

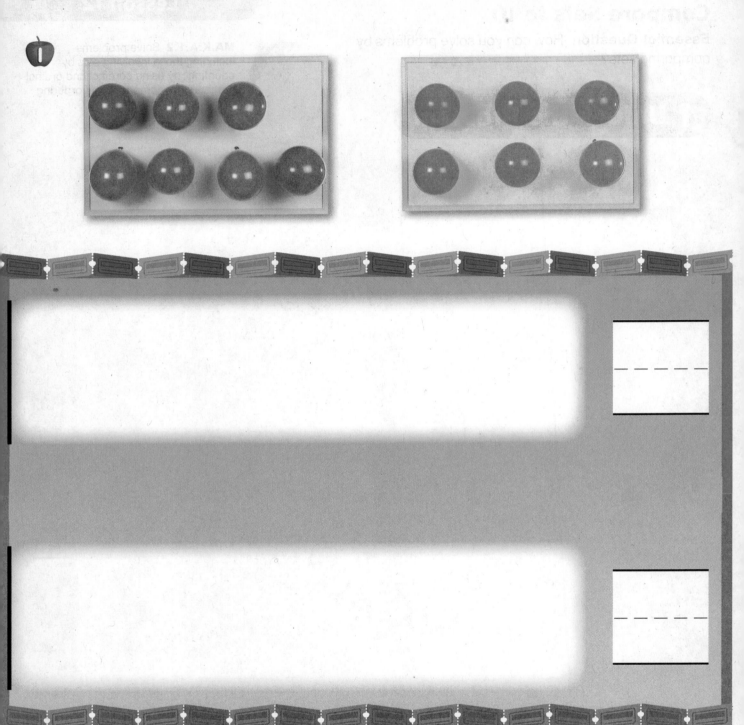

DIRECTIONS   **I.** Naomi has 6 red balloons. Malia has 7 blue balloons. Who has more balloons? Create cube trains to show the balloons. Draw and color the cube trains. Write how many cubes are in each train. Circle the greater number.

⭐ 2 ✓

_____

- - - - - - - - - - -

_____

- - - - - - - - - - -

_____

🍃 3

_____

- - - - - - - - - - -

_____

_____

- - - - - - - - - - -

_____

🌸 4

_____

- - - - - - - - - - -

_____

_____

- - - - - - - - - - -

_____

DIRECTIONS   2. Carol has 9 flowers. Annicke has 2 fewer flowers.   **3.** Jordan has 10 flowers. Jared has 1 fewer flowers.   **4.** Alison has 8 flowers. Kaci has 3 fewer flowers.   **2–4.** Draw the flowers with the fewer flowers on the bottom. Write how many flowers are in each garden. Circle the number that is less.

Chapter 3 · Lesson 12   one hundred twenty-three **123**

PROBLEM SOLVING

DIRECTIONS Look at the model. Are there more blue cubes or more red cubes? Make cube trains of each color. Draw and color the cube trains. Write how many cubes are in each train. Circle the greater number.

HOME ACTIVITY • Ask your child to create two sets of up to 10 objects each. Then have your child compare the sets and tell which set has more objects.

FOR MORE PRACTICE:
Florida Benchmarks Practice Book, pp. P67–P68

Order Numbers to 10

Essential Question How can you use a number line to order numbers to 10?

MA.K.A.1.2 Solve problems including those involving sets by counting, by using cardinal and ordinal numbers, by comparing, by ordering, and by creating sets up to 20.

Listen

DIRECTIONS Point to the numbers on the top number line and say them in order. Point to the numbers on the bottom number line and say the missing numbers.

Share and Show

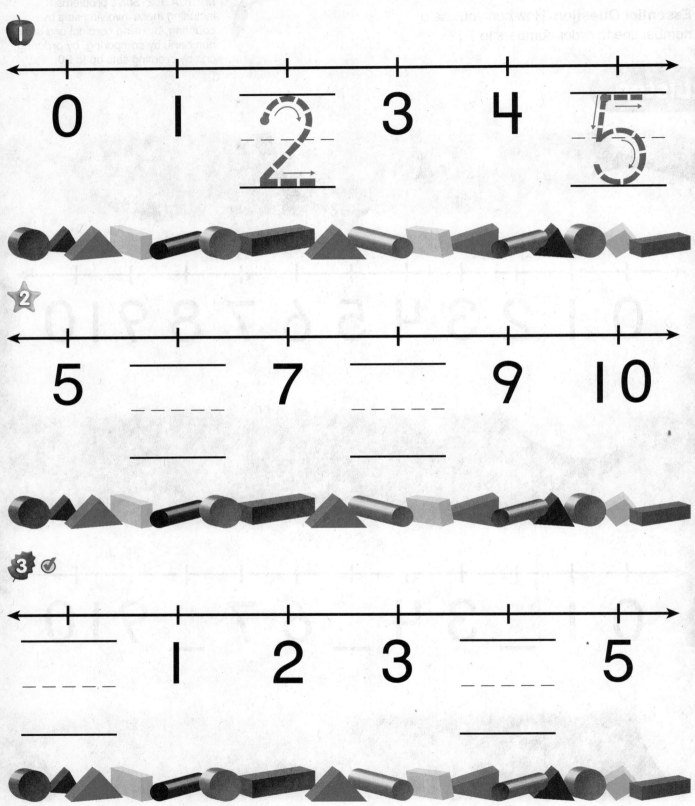

1

← 0   1   2   3   4   5 →

2

← 5 ___   7 ___   9   10 →

3 ✓

← ___   1   2   3 ___   5 →

DIRECTIONS **1.** Trace the number that is before 3. Trace the number that is after 4. **2.** Write the number that is after 5. Write the number that is before 9. **3.** Write the number that is before 1. Write the number that is after 3.

4

5   6   ___   8   9   ___

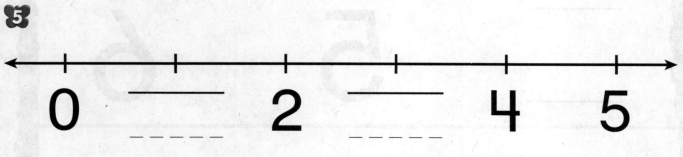

5

0   ___   2   ___   4   5

6

___   6   7   8   ___   10

DIRECTIONS **4.** Write the number that is before 8. Write the number that is after 9. **5.** Write the number that is before 2. Write the number that is after 2. **6.** Write the number that is before 6. Write the number that is after 8.

PROBLEM SOLVING REAL WORLD

1. 1 ___ 3

___ 5 6

2. 10 9 ___

7 ___ 5

DIRECTIONS 1–2. Write the missing numbers that come before or after the numbers you see.

HOME ACTIVITY • Write the numbers 0–10 on separate self-stick notes or on slips of paper. Have your child place the numbers in order from 0 to 10.

128 one hundred twenty-eight

FOR MORE PRACTICE:
Florida Benchmarks Practice Book, pp. P69–P70

Name _____

Ordinal Numbers to 10th

Essential Question How can you use ordinal numbers to tenth?

MA.K.A.1.2 Solve problems including those involving sets by counting, by using cardinal and ordinal numbers, by comparing, by ordering, and by creating sets up to 20.

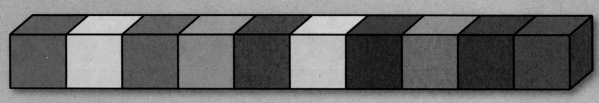

first

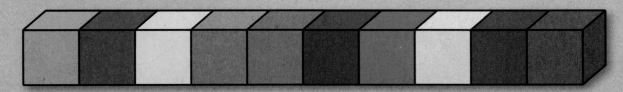

first

DIRECTIONS Use ordinal numbers to describe the positions of the blocks.

Share and Show

1

first

2

first

3 ✓

first

4 ✓

first

DIRECTIONS **1.** Trace the circle on the sixth duck. Trace the X on the tenth duck. **2.** Circle the eighth duck. Mark an X on the second duck. **3.** Circle the fifth duck. Mark an X on the ninth duck. **4.** Circle the seventh duck. Mark an X on the last duck.

5

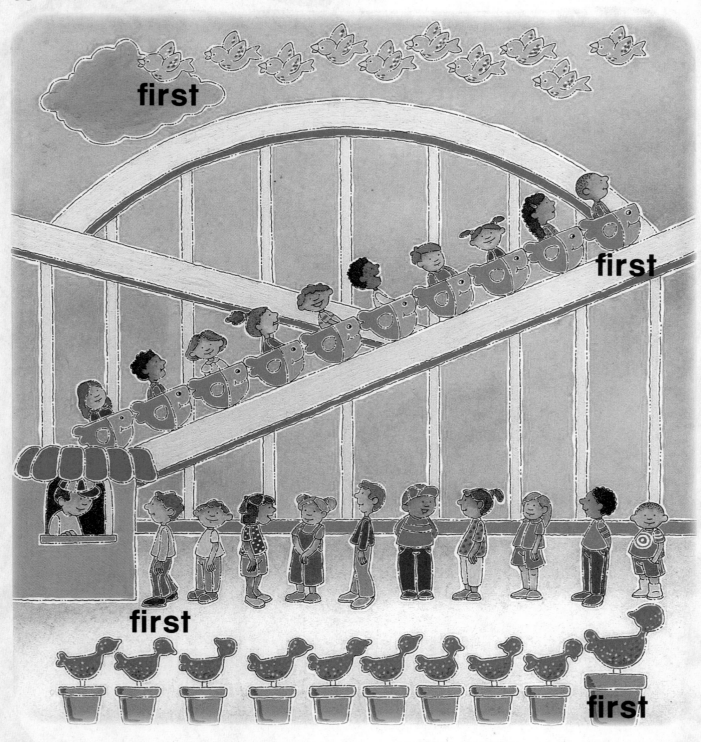

first

first

first

first

DIRECTIONS 5. Circle the fourth bird. Mark an X on the seventh bird. Circle the eighth car on the ride. Mark an X on the fifth car on the ride. Circle the third child standing in line. Mark an X on the tenth child standing in line. Circle the ninth duck. Mark an X on the sixth duck.

Chapter 3 • Lesson 14

PROBLEM SOLVING REAL WORLD

DIRECTIONS Draw 10 objects in a line. Draw a line under the first object. Circle the fifth object. Mark an X on the tenth object. Tell about your drawing.

HOME ACTIVITY • Have your child line up 10 toys and tell you the ordinal position of each toy.

132 one hundred thirty-two

FOR MORE PRACTICE:
Florida Benchmarks Practice Book, pp. P71–P72

© Houghton Mifflin Harcourt

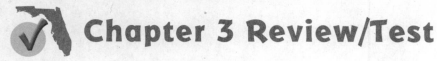 Chapter 3 Review/Test

Vocabulary

first

Concepts

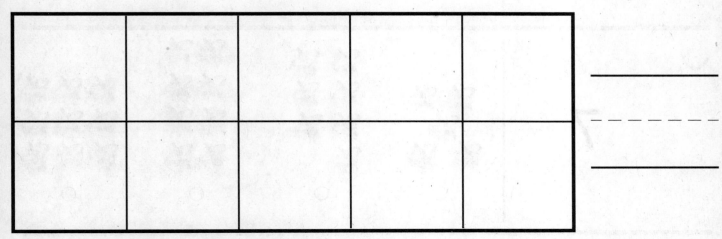

_____
- - - - - - - - - -
_____

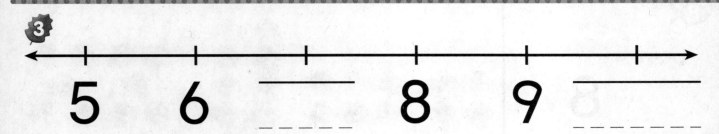

5   6   ___   8   9   ___

DIRECTIONS 1. Draw a line under the eighth duck. Circle the tenth duck. Mark an X on the sixth duck. (MA.K.A.1.2) **2.** Use cubes to show 10. Draw the cubes. Write the number. (MA.K.A.1.1) **3.** Write the number that is before 8. Write the number that is after 9. (MA.K.A.1.2)

5

2	3	5	7
○	○	○	○

6

6	8	9	10
○	○	○	○

7

7

○	○	○	○

8

8

○	○	○	○

DIRECTIONS 5–6. Mark under the number that shows how many. (MA.K.A.1.1) **7–8.** Mark under the set that shows the number at the beginning of the row. (MA.K.A.1.1)

9

○   ○   ○   ○

10

9

○   ○   ○   ○

11

○   ○   ○   ○

12

10   9   8   7

○   ○   ○   ○

DIRECTIONS **9.** Mark under the set that shows 9. (MA.K.A.1.1)
10. Mark under the set that shows the number at the beginning of the row.
(MA.K.A.1.1)   **11.** Mark under the set that shows 10. (MA.K.A.1.1)
12. Mark under the number that shows how many. (MA.K.A.1.1)

13

○

○

○

○

14

10	8	6	4
○	○	○	○

15

5   6   7   ___   9   10

6	8	9	10
○	○	○	○

16

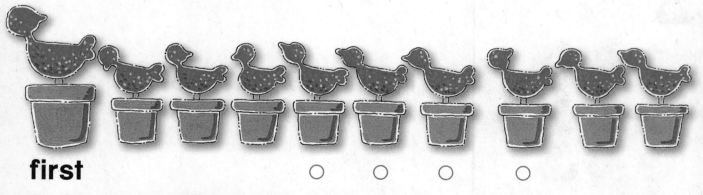

first   ○   ○   ○   ○

DIRECTIONS **13.** Mark under the cube train that shows a way to make 10.
(MA.K.A.1.1) **14.** Look at the cubes. Which color has more cubes? Mark the number
that matches that set. (MA.K.A.1.2) **15.** Mark under the number that comes after 7.
(MA.K.A.1.2) **16.** Mark under the sixth plant. (MA.K.A.1.1)

Name _____

Compare Sets to 10

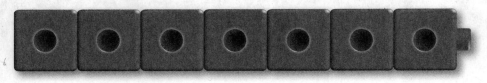

_____

- - - - - -

_____

_____

- - - - - -

_____

More and Fewer

_____

- - - - - -

_____

_____

_____

_____

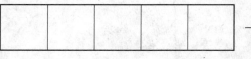

- - - - - -

_____

DIRECTIONS 1. Write the number of cubes in each set. Circle the set with fewer cubes. **2.** Count and tell how many. Draw a set with one more counter. Write how many in each set. **3.** Count and tell how many. Draw a set with one fewer counter. Write how many in each set.

FAMILY NOTE: This page checks your child's understanding of important skills needed for success in Chapter 4.

Name _____

FLORIDA BENCHMARKS
Vocabulary Power

ten

DIRECTIONS Count and tell how many are on the ground. Count and tell how many are flying. Write these numbers to show a way to write 10.

Go online • Student Edition • Multilingual eGlossary

Chapter 4

Game

Spin for More

Spin for More				
Player 1				
Player 2				

DIRECTIONS Play wih a partner. Decide who goes first. Take turns spinning to get a number from each spinner. Use cubes to model each number. Join the two sets of cubes to make a cube train to show how many in all. Compare your cube train with your partner's. Mark an X on the table for the player who has more cubes. The first player to have 5 Xs wins the game.

MATERIALS two paper clips, pencils, connecting cubes

© Houghton Mifflin Harcourt

Name _____

Joining Problems

Essential Question How can you solve joining problems?

MA.K.A.1.3 Solve word problems involving simple joining and separating situations.

🔑 Unlock the Problem

© Houghton Mifflin Harcourt

DIRECTIONS Tell a friend what is happening in this joining problem. Tell how many children in all.

Chapter 4 • Lesson 1

one hundred forty-one **141**

Share and Show

DIRECTIONS I-2. Listen to and act out the story problem. Write the number that shows how many children in all.

Name _____

_____

- - - - - - - - -

_____

_____

- - - - - - - - -

_____

DIRECTIONS Listen to and act out the story problems. **3.** Write the number that shows how many books in all. **4.** Write the number that shows how many blocks in all.

Chapter 4 • Lesson 1

On Your Own

1

2

DIRECTIONS **1.** Write the number that shows how many puppies in all. **2.** Draw to show what you know about a different joining problem. Tell about your drawing.

HOME ACTIVITY • Tell your child a short story problem about adding 2 objects to a group of 5. Have your child use toys to act out the story problem and then write the number that shows how many objects in all.

FOR MORE PRACTICE:
Florida Benchmarks Practice Book, pp. P79–P80

Name _____

Model Joining

Essential Question How can you use objects to model joining problems?

MA.K.A.1.3 Solve word problems involving simple joining and separating situations.

Listen and Draw

DIRECTIONS Place cubes on the train. Listen to the joining story problem. Model the story problem with cubes. Draw and color the cubes that are joining the group. Write how many cubes in all.

Chapter 4 · Lesson 2

one hundred forty-five **145**

Share and Show

1

2

2

3

4

8

DIRECTIONS 1–3. Listen to the joining story problem. Model the story problem with cubes. Draw and color the cubes that are joining the group. Write the number that shows how many in all.

Name _____

3

3

2

6

4

5

4

5

6

DIRECTIONS **4–6.** Listen to the joining story problem. Model the story problem with cubes. Draw and color the cubes that are joining the group. Write the number that shows how many in all.

Chapter 4 • Lesson 2

one hundred forty-seven **147**

PROBLEM SOLVING REAL WORLD

1

3   2   _____

2

DIRECTIONS **1.** Draw to show how many cubes to join. Write the number that shows how many cubes in all. **2.** Draw to show what you know about a different joining problem using objects. Tell about your drawing.

HOME ACTIVITY • Tell your child a short story problem about joining 3 objects to a group of 4. Have your child use small objects such as beans to make each group in the story problem and then write the number that shows how many objects in all.

148 one hundred forty-eight

FOR MORE PRACTICE:
Florida Benchmarks Practice Book, pp. P81–P82

Name _____

Join Groups

Essential Question How can you use pictures to solve joining problems?

MA.K.A.1.3 Solve word problems involving simple joining and separating situations.

Listen and Draw · REAL WORLD

DIRECTIONS Tell a joining story problem. Circle the two groups to join them. Write how many in all.

Share and Show

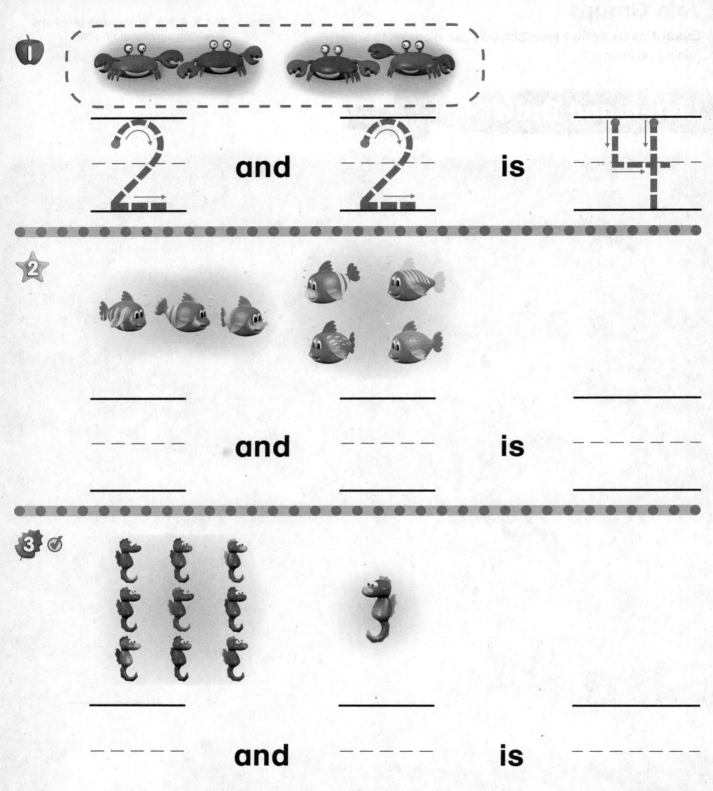

1 2 and 2 is 4

2 _____ and _____ is _____

3 ✓ _____ and _____ is _____

DIRECTIONS **1–3.** Tell a joining story problem about the groups.
Write how many in each group. Circle the two groups to join them.
Write how many in all.

4

_____   _____   _____

- - - - - -   **and**   - - - - - -   **is**   - - - - - -

_____   _____   _____

5

_____   _____   _____

- - - - - -   **and**   - - - - - -   **is**   - - - - - -

_____   _____   _____

6

_____   _____   _____

- - - - - -   **and**   - - - - - -   **is**   - - - - - -

_____   _____   _____

DIRECTIONS   4–6. Tell a joining story problem about the groups.
Write how many in each group. Circle the two groups to join them.
Write how many in all.

PROBLEM SOLVING REAL WORLD

1.

_____ _____   _____

------ and ------ is ------

_____ _____   _____

2.

DIRECTIONS **1.** Tell a joining story problem. Write how many in each group. Circle the two groups to join them. Write how many in all. **2.** Tell a different joining story problem. Draw the problem. Tell about your drawing.

HOME ACTIVITY • Have your child draw a group of 2 beach balls and a group of 7 beach balls. Have your child write how many beach balls are in each group. Then have him or her write how many beach balls in all.

152 one hundred fifty-two

FOR MORE PRACTICE:
Florida Benchmarks Practice Book, pp. P83–P84

Name _____

Introduce Symbols to Add

Essential Question How do numbers,
+, and = show joining problems?

MA.K.A.1.3 Solve word problems
involving simple joining and
separating situations.

Listen and Draw

and   is

3 plus 2 is

3 + 2 =

DIRECTIONS Tell a joining story problem. Write how
many cubes in all. Use Number and Symbol Tiles to show the
addition sentence. Circle the symbol that shows addition.

© Houghton Mifflin Harcourt

Share and Show

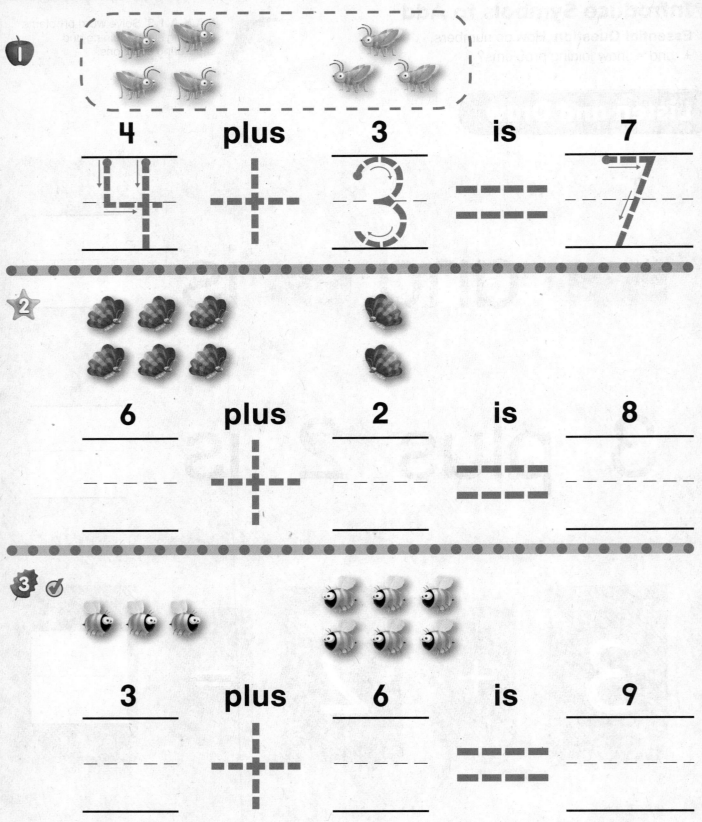

1

4 plus 3 is 7

2

6 plus 2 is 8

3 ✓

3 plus 6 is 9

DIRECTIONS   1–3. Tell a joining story problem. Write how many in each group. Circle the two groups to join them. Trace the symbols. Write how many in all.

Name _____

4

2   plus   5   is   7

5

5   plus   2   is   7

6

6   plus   4   is   10

DIRECTIONS 4–6. Tell a joining story problem. Write how many in each group. Circle the two groups to join them. Trace the symbols. Write how many in all.

© Houghton Mifflin Harcourt

Chapter 4 • Lesson 4

1

3 plus 4 is 7

2

DIRECTIONS 1. Tell a joining story problem. Circle the two groups to join them. Which Number and Symbol Tiles would you use to show the addition sentence? Write the numbers and symbols. **2.** Draw to show what you know about the plus symbol. Tell about your drawing.

HOME ACTIVITY • Have your child use small objects to model the addition sentence on this page. Then have him or her combine the groups before the = to show the same amount as the number after the =.

156 one hundred fifty-six

FOR MORE PRACTICE:
Florida Benchmarks Practice Book, pp. P85–P86

Name _____

Addition Sentences

Essential Question How can you use pictures to solve problems and complete addition sentences?

MA.K.A.1.3 Solve word problems involving simple joining and separating situations.

Listen and Draw REAL WORLD

$$4 + 1 = 5$$

DIRECTIONS Tell an addition story problem about the birds. Circle the number that shows how many in all.

Share and Show

1

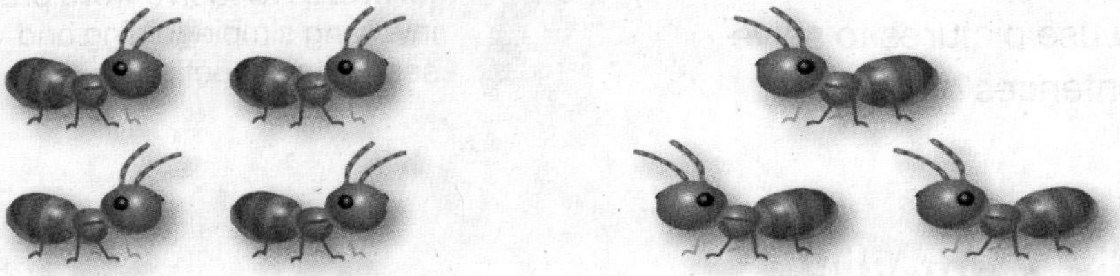

$4 + 3 = 7$

2

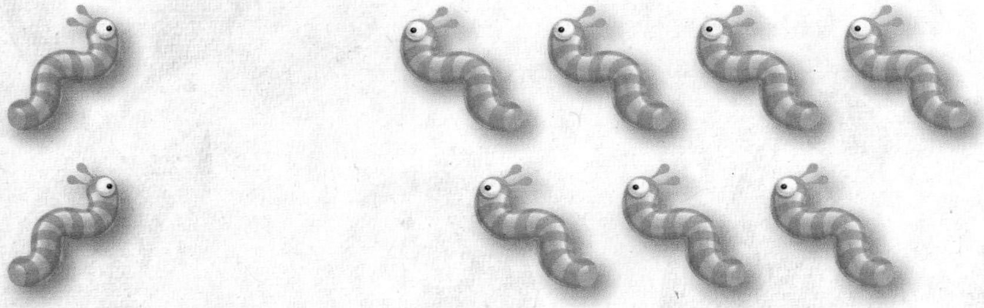

____ + ____ = ____

3 ✓

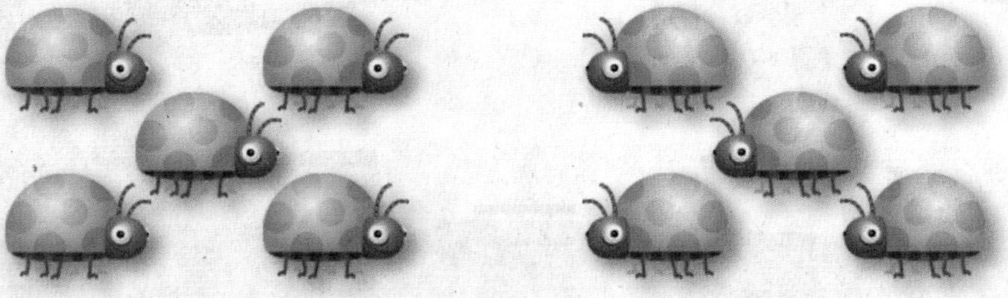

____ + ____ = ____

DIRECTIONS 1–3. Tell a joining story problem. Complete the addition sentence to show how many in all.

Name _____

4

_ _ _ _ _ _ _ _ _   **+**   _ _ _ _ _ _ _ _ _   **=**   _ _ _ _ _ _ _ _ _

5

_ _ _ _ _ _ _ _ _   **+**   _ _ _ _ _ _ _ _ _   **=**   _ _ _ _ _ _ _ _ _

6

_ _ _ _ _ _ _ _ _   **+**   _ _ _ _ _ _ _ _ _   **=**   _ _ _ _ _ _ _ _ _

DIRECTIONS 4–6. Tell a joining story problem. Complete the addition sentence to show how many in all.

Chapter 4 • Lesson 5

one hundred fifty-nine **159**

$$5 + 2 = \underline{\quad\quad}$$

DIRECTIONS 1. Complete the addition sentence. Draw to show what you know about this addition sentence. Tell about your drawing.

HOME ACTIVITY • Give your child 6 socks of one color and 4 socks of another color. Ask your child to tell a story problem about the socks. Then write this addition sentence, and have your child complete it: __ + __ = __.

FOR MORE PRACTICE:
Florida Benchmarks Practice Book, pp. P87–P88

Name _____

Create and Model Addition Problems

Essential Question How can you create and model addition problems?

MA.K.A.1.3 Solve word problems involving simple joining and separating situations.

Listen and Draw

$$6 + 4 = \underline{\quad\quad}$$

DIRECTIONS Create a joining story problem about the addition sentence. Use counters to show and solve the addition problem. Draw the counters.

Share and Show

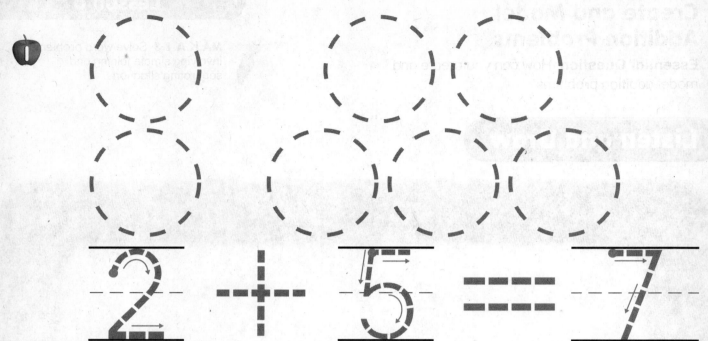

1 2 + 5 = 7

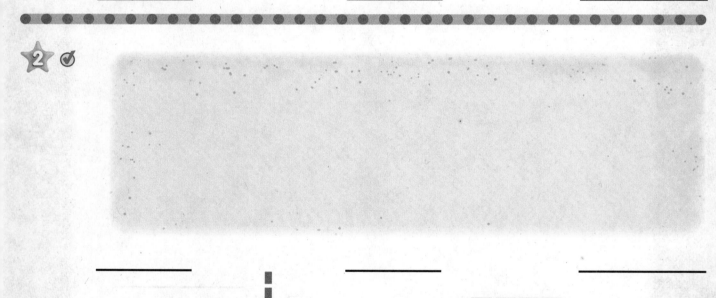

___ + ___ = ___

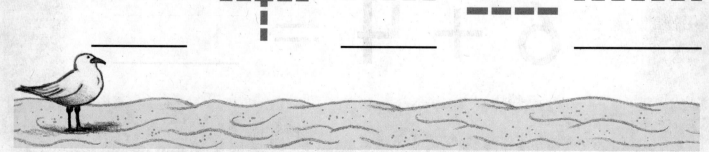

DIRECTIONS 1–2. Create an addition story problem.
Model your story with counters. Draw the counters.
Complete the addition sentence to show how many in all.

Name _____

3

_____ ＋ _____ ＝＝＝ _____

4

_____ ＋ _____ ＝＝＝ _____

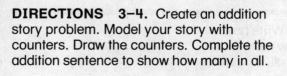

DIRECTIONS 3–4. Create an addition story problem. Model your story with counters. Draw the counters. Complete the addition sentence to show how many in all.

HOME ACTIVITY • Ask your child to choose one problem on the page. Have your child tell you the addition story and then explain how the addition sentence shows the story.

FOR MORE PRACTICE: Florida Benchmarks Practice Book, pp. P89–P90

Concepts

_____ and _____ is _____

_____ + _____ = _____

2	4	6	8
○	○	○	○

DIRECTIONS 1–2 Tell a joining story problem about the groups. Write how many are in each group. Circle the two groups to join them. Write how many in all. (MA.K.A.1.3) **3.** Mark under the number that shows how many fish in all. (MA.K.A.1.3)

Name _____

Separating Problems

Essential Question How can you solve separating problems?

MA.K.A.1.3 Solve word problems involving simple joining and separating situations.

🔑 Unlock the Problem

DIRECTIONS How many children do you need to act out this separating problem? Circle any children who leave. How many leave? How many children are left?

Share and Show

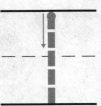

DIRECTIONS 1–2. Listen to and act out the story problem. Write
the number that shows how many children are left.

Name _____

DIRECTIONS Listen to and act out the story problems. **3.** Write the number that shows how many books are left. **4.** Write the number that shows how many cups are left.

DIRECTIONS   1. Write the number that shows how many kittens are left.   **2.** Draw to show what you know about a different separating problem. Tell about your drawing.

HOME ACTIVITY • Tell your child a short subtraction story problem. Have your child use toys to act out the story and then write the number that shows how many toys are left.

FOR MORE PRACTICE:
Florida Benchmarks Practice Book, pp. P91–P92

Name _____

Model Separating

Essential Question How can you use objects to model separating problems?

MA.K.A.I.3 Solve word problems involving simple joining and separating situations.

Listen and Draw

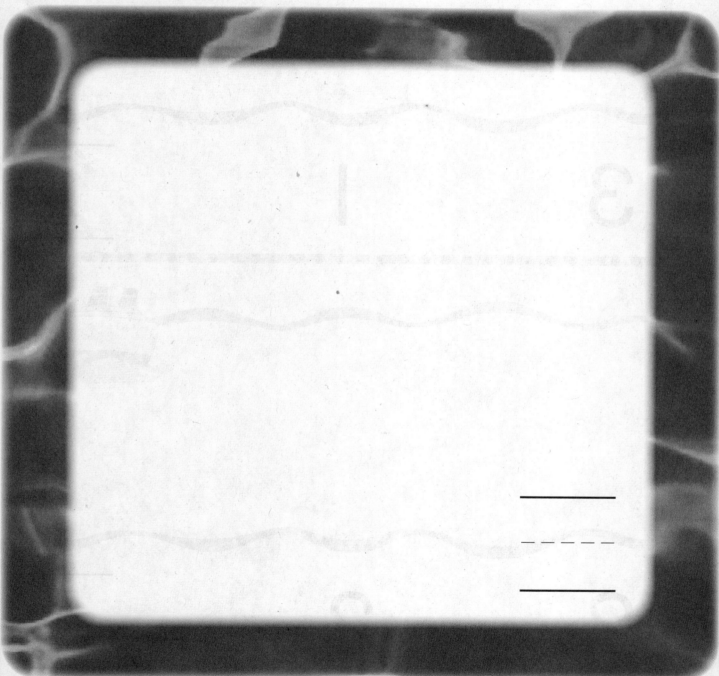

_____

- - - - - - - -

_____

DIRECTIONS Listen to the separating story problem. Model the story with a cube train. Draw the cube train. Circle the group of cubes you separated. Mark an X on that group. Write how many cubes are left.

Chapter 4 · Lesson 8

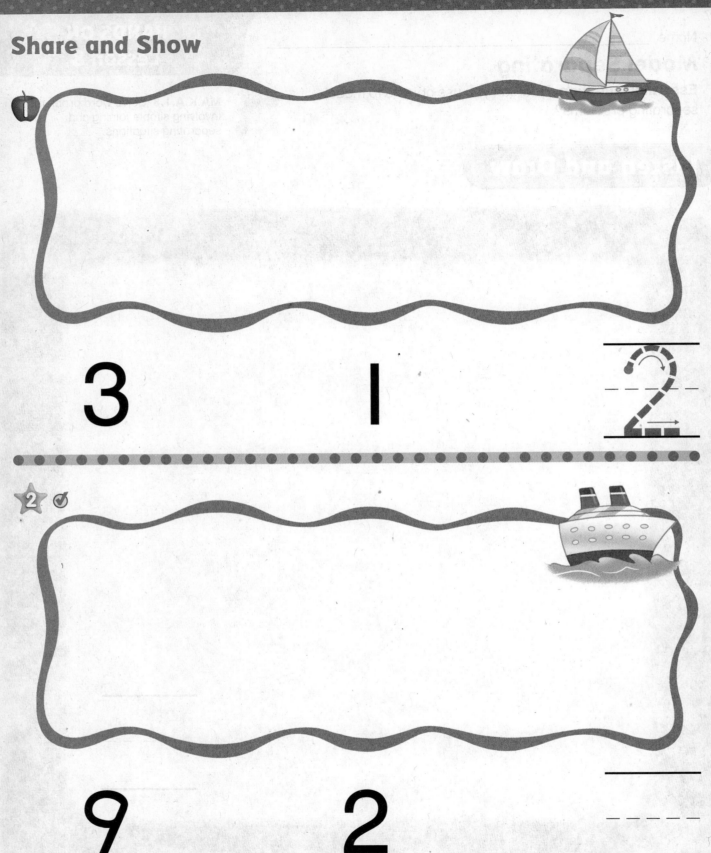

❶

3   I   2

⭐2 ✓

9   2

DIRECTIONS   I–2. Listen to the separating story problem. Model the story with cubes. Write the number that shows how many are left.

3

4   3   ___

4

7   5   ___

DIRECTIONS   3–4. Listen to the separating story problem. Model the story with cubes. Write the number that shows how many are left.

Chapter 4 · Lesson 8

PROBLEM SOLVING REAL WORLD

1

5   2   _____

2

DIRECTIONS **1.** Circle the group of cubes that are being separated. Mark an X on that group. Write how many cubes are left. **2.** Draw to show what you know about a different separating problem using objects. Tell about your drawing.

HOME ACTIVITY • Tell your child a short subtraction story problem. Have your child act out the story using objects, and tell how many objects are left.

FOR MORE PRACTICE:
Florida Benchmarks Practice Book, pp. P93–P94

Name _____

Separate Groups

Essential Question How can you use pictures to solve separating problems?

MA.K.A.1.3 Solve word problems involving simple joining and separating situations.

Listen and Draw

DIRECTIONS Tell a separating story problem about the fish. Circle and mark an X on any fish that are being separated. Write how many fish are left.

Chapter 4 • Lesson 9

one hundred seventy-three **173**

Share and Show

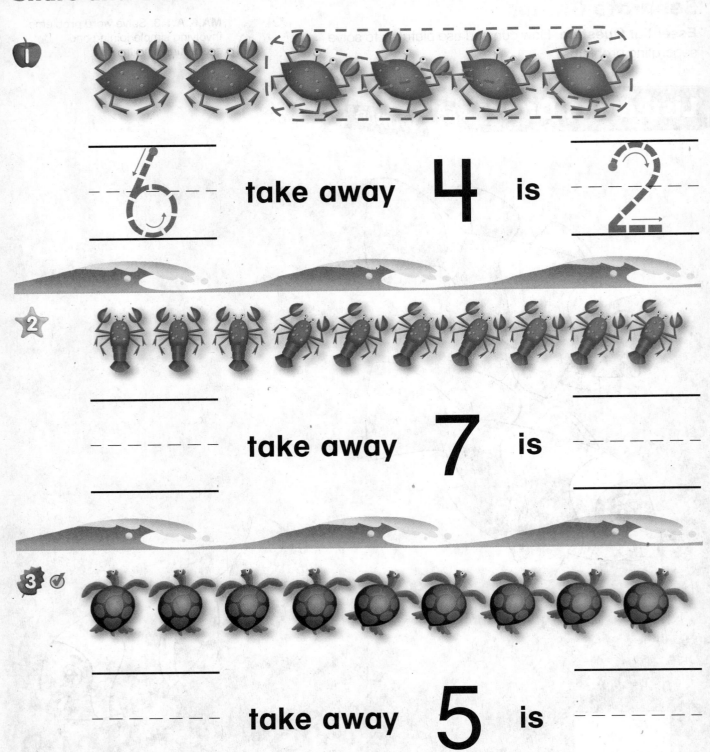

1. ___6___ take away **4** is ___2___

2. _____ take away **7** is _____

3. _____ take away **5** is _____

DIRECTIONS 1–3. Tell a separating story problem.
Write how many there are in all. Circle the group you take
away. Mark an X on that group. Write how many are left.

174 one hundred seventy-four

Name _____

_____

_ _ _ _ _ _ _ _ _ _   take away **4** is   _ _ _ _ _ _ _

_____

_____

_ _ _ _ _ _ _ _ _ _   take away **2** is   _ _ _ _ _ _ _

_____

_____

_ _ _ _ _ _ _ _ _ _   take away **7** is   _ _ _ _ _ _ _

_____

DIRECTIONS   4–6. Tell a separating story problem.
Write how many there are in all. Circle the group you take
away. Mark an X on that group. Write how many are left.

PROBLEM SOLVING REAL WORLD

1

_____

- - - - - - -   take away **3** is   - - - - - - -

_____   _____

 2

DIRECTIONS **1.** Tell a separating story problem. Write how many there are in all. Circle the group you take away. Mark an X on that group. Write how many are left. **2.** Draw to show what you know about a different separating story problem. Tell about your drawing.

HOME ACTIVITY • Have your child draw a group of ten or fewer balloons. Have him or her circle some balloons to show that they have popped, and mark an X on that group. Then have your child write the number that tells how many balloons are left.

176 one hundred seventy-six

FOR MORE PRACTICE:
Florida Benchmarks Practice Book, pp. **P95–P96**

Introduce Symbols to Subtract

Essential Question How do numbers, −, and =
show separating problems?

MA.K.A.1.3 Solve word problems
involving simple joining and
separating situations.

Listen and Draw

5 take away 2 is ☐

5 minus 2 is ☐

DIRECTIONS Tell a separating story problem. Write how many cubes are left. Use
Number and Symbol Tiles to show the subtraction sentence. Circle the symbol that
shows subtraction.

Share and Show

1

7	minus	4	is	3

2

10	minus	6	is	4

3 ✔

8	minus	2	is	6

DIRECTIONS 1–3. Tell a separating story problem. Write how many fish there are in all. Circle the group you take away. Mark an X on that group. Trace the symbols. Complete the subtraction sentence.

4

| 8 | minus | 5 | is | 3 |

_ _ _ _ _ _ _   ----   _____   ▬▬▬▬ ▬▬▬▬   _ _ _ _ _ _ _

_____   _____   _____

5

| 9 | minus | 3 | is | 6 |

_ _ _ _ _ _ _   ▬▬ ▬   _____   ▬▬▬▬ ▬▬▬▬   _ _ _ _ _ _ _
                                                  ▬▬ ▬▬ ▬▬

_____   _____   _____

6

| 10 | minus | 5 | is | 5 |

_ _ _ _ _ _ _   ▬▬ ▬   _____   ▬▬▬▬ ▬▬▬▬   _ _ _ _ _ _ _
                                                  ▬▬ ▬▬ ▬▬

_____   _____   _____

DIRECTIONS **4–6.** Tell a separating story problem. Write how many fish there are in all. Circle the group you take away. Mark an X on that group. Trace the symbols. Complete the subtraction sentence.

HOME ACTIVITY • Ask your child to explain to this sign that shows why ... They ask him or her to point to the sign that shows ... expression

7 minus 3 is 4

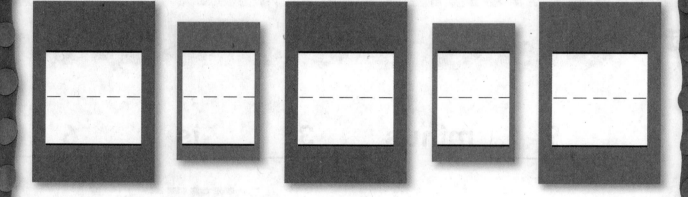

⭐ 2

DIRECTIONS **1.** Tell a separating story problem. Circle the fish you take away. Mark an X on that group. Which Number and Symbol Tiles would you use to show the subtraction sentence? Write the numbers and symbols. **2.** Draw to show what you know about the minus symbol. Tell about your drawing.

HOME ACTIVITY • Ask your child to point to the sign that shows *minus*. Then ask him or her to point to the sign that shows *is equal to*.

180 one hundred eighty

FOR MORE PRACTICE:
Florida Benchmarks Practice Book, pp. P97–P98

Name _____

Subtraction Sentences

Essential Question How can you use pictures to solve problems and complete subtraction sentences?

MA.K.A.1.3 Solve word problems involving simple joining and separating situations.

Listen and Draw REAL WORLD

$$5 - 1 = 4$$

DIRECTIONS Tell a subtraction story problem about the birds. Circle the number that shows how many are left.

Chapter 4 • Lesson 11

one hundred eighty-one **181**

Share and Show

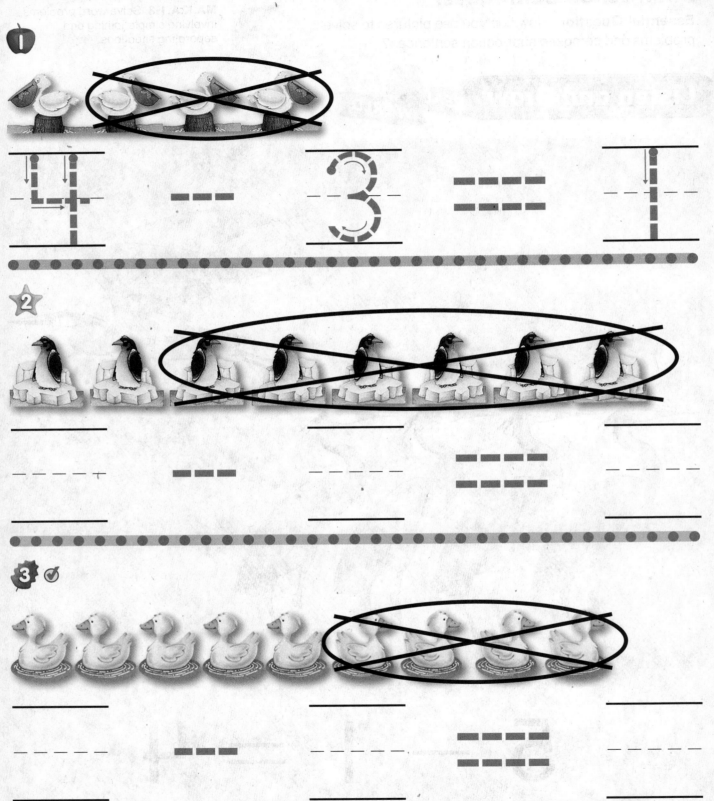

1

$$4 - 3 = 1$$

2

3 ✓

DIRECTIONS 1–3. Tell a separating story problem about the birds. Complete the subtraction sentence to show how many are left.

4

_____   _____   _____

- - -   ▪ ▪ ▪   - - -   ▪ ▪ ▪
                                           ▪ ▪ ▪   - - -

_____

5

_____   _____   _____

- - -   ▪ ▪ ▪   - - -   ▪ ▪ ▪
                                           ▪ ▪ ▪

_____

6

_____   _____   _____

- - -   ▪ ▪ ▪   - - -   ▪ ▪ ▪
                                           ▪ ▪ ▪   - - -

DIRECTIONS   4–6. Tell a separating story problem about the birds.
Complete the subtraction sentence to show how many are left.

PROBLEM SOLVING REAL WORLD

$$7 - 2 = \underline{\qquad}$$

DIRECTIONS Complete the subtraction sentence. Draw to show what you know about this subtraction sentence. Tell about your drawing.

HOME ACTIVITY · Give your child some books, and then take some away. Ask your child to tell a subtraction story problem about the books. Then write this subtraction sentence, and have your child complete it: __ − __ = __.

FOR MORE PRACTICE:
Florida Benchmarks Practice Book, pp. P99–P100

Name _____

Create and Model Subtraction Problems

Essential Question How can you use objects to create and model subtraction problems?

MA.K.A.1.3 Solve word problems involving simple joining and separating situations.

Listen and Draw

$$10 - 7 = \underline{\quad}$$

DIRECTIONS Create a separating story problem about the subtraction sentence. Use counters to show and solve the subtraction problem. Draw the counters. Circle the group you take away. Mark an X on that group. Complete the subtraction sentence to show how many are left.

© Houghton Mifflin Harcourt

Chapter 4 · Lesson 12

Share and Show

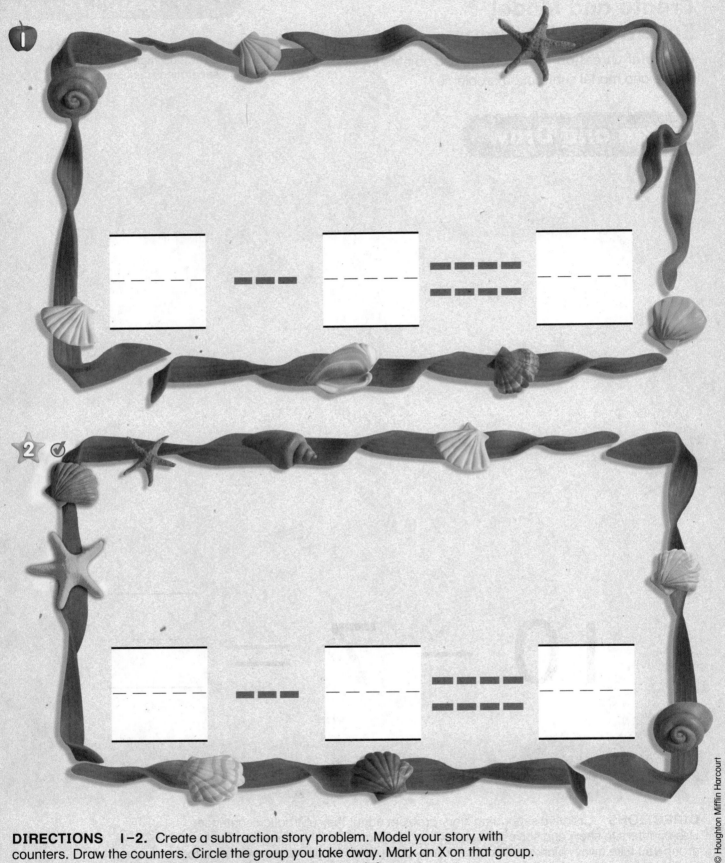

DIRECTIONS 1–2. Create a subtraction story problem. Model your story with counters. Draw the counters. Circle the group you take away. Mark an X on that group. Complete the subtraction sentence to show how many are left.

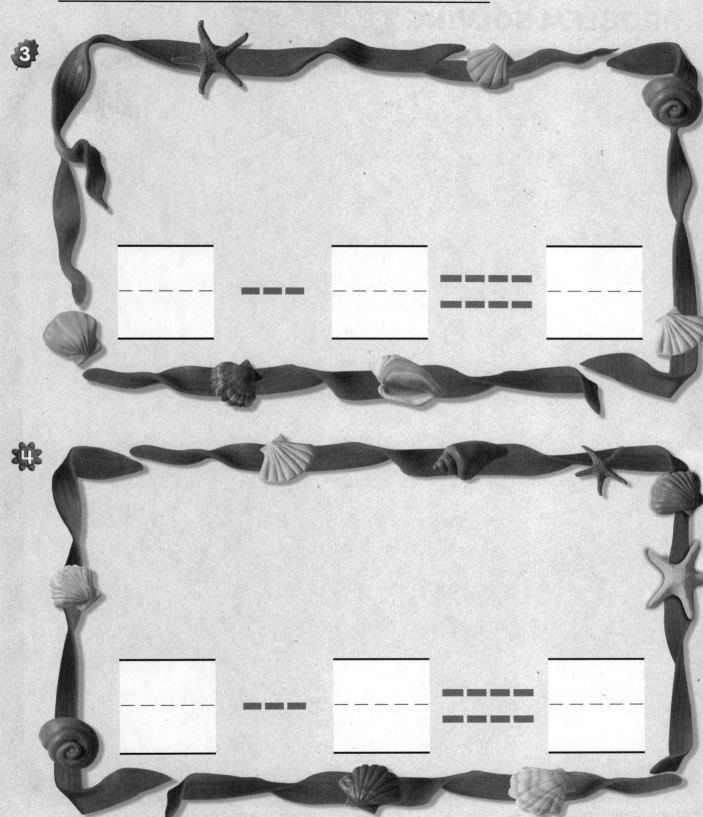

3

4

DIRECTIONS **3–4.** Create a subtraction story problem. Model your story with counters. Draw the counters. Circle the group you take away. Mark an X on that group. Complete the subtraction sentence to show how many are left.

PROBLEM SOLVING

DIRECTIONS There were nine boats at the dock. Some boats sailed away. There were two boats left at the dock. How many boats sailed away? Draw to show how you solved the problem.

HOME ACTIVITY • Ask your child to tell a subtraction story problem using objects to model the story. Then have him or her explain the subtraction sentence.

FOR MORE PRACTICE:
Florida Benchmarks Practice Book, pp. P101–P102

Addition and Subtraction

Essential Question How can you solve simple joining and separating problems?

MA.K.A.I.3 Solve word problems involving simple joining and separating situations.

Listen and Draw

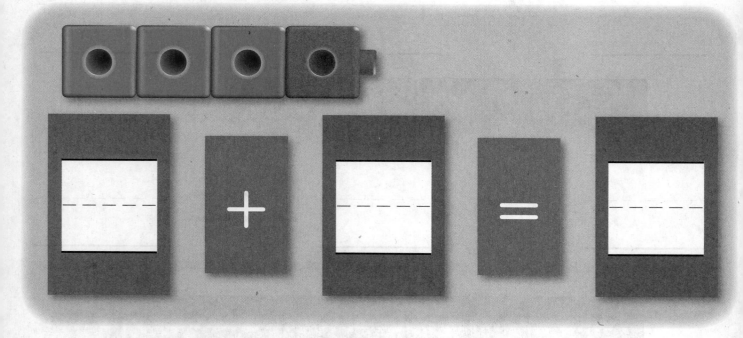

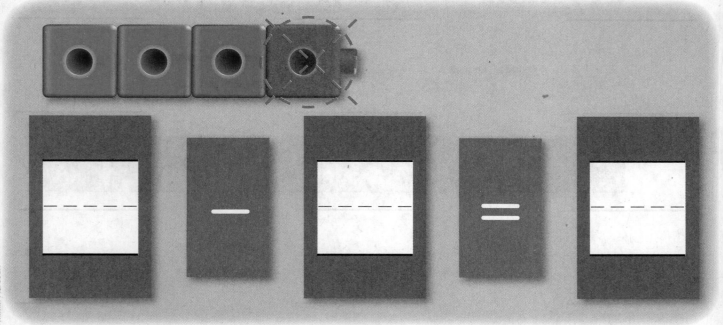

DIRECTIONS Use Number and Symbol Tiles to show the addition sentence and the subtraction sentence to match the cubes. Complete the sentences. Tell a friend about the sentences.

Share and Show

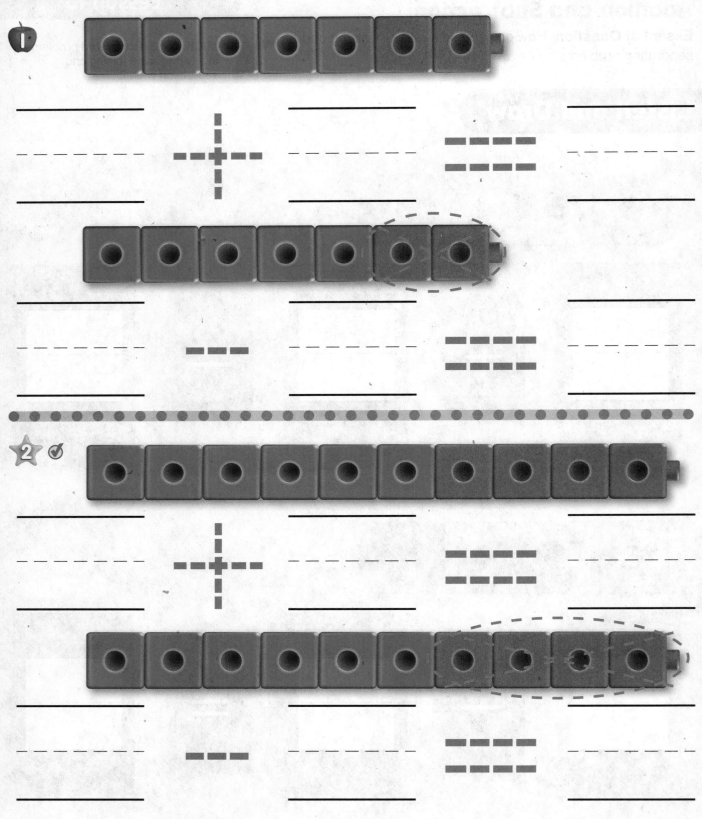

DIRECTIONS 1–2. Tell joining and separating word problems. Use cubes to add and to subtract. Complete the number sentences.

190 one hundred ninety

© Houghton Mifflin Harcourt

Name _____

3

_____

------------ $+$ ------------ = = = =

_____   = = = =

------------ - - - ------------ = = = =

_____

4

_____

------------ $+$ ------------ = = = =

_____   = = = =

------------ - - - ------------ = = = =

_____

DIRECTIONS 3–4. Tell joining and separating word problems. Use
cubes to add and subtract. Complete the number sentences.

Chapter 4 • Lesson 13   one hundred ninety-one **191**

PROBLEM SOLVING REAL WORLD

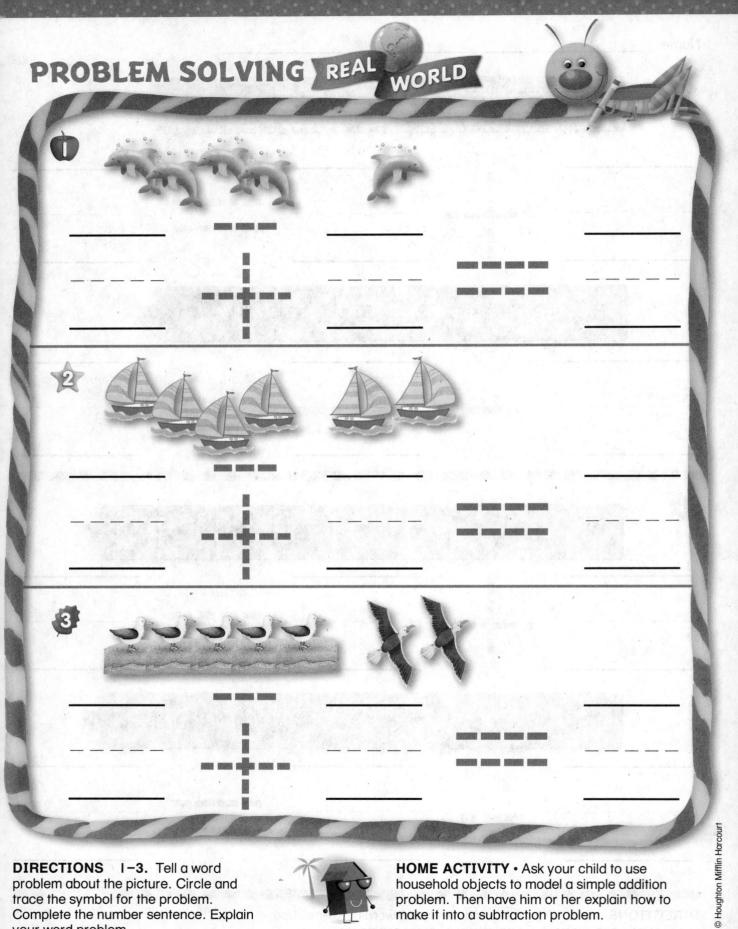

1

_____   ▀▀ ▀   _____   ▀▀▀   _ _ _ _
 |
▀ ▀ ▀   ▀▀▀ _ _ _ _
 |
_____

2

_____   ▀▀   _____   ▀▀▀
 |
_ _ _ _   ▀▀▀ _____
 |
_____

3

_____   ▀▀ ▀   _____
 |
_ _ _ _   ▀▀▀ _ _ _ _
 | ▀▀▀
_____

DIRECTIONS 1–3. Tell a word problem about the picture. Circle and trace the symbol for the problem. Complete the number sentence. Explain your word problem.

HOME ACTIVITY • Ask your child to use household objects to model a simple addition problem. Then have him or her explain how to make it into a subtraction problem.

FOR MORE PRACTICE:
Florida Benchmarks Practice Book, pp. P103–P104

✓ 🏴 Chapter 4 Review/Test

Vocabulary

 1

_____

- - - - - - -

_____

in all

2

_____

- - - - - - -

_____

are left

Concepts

 3

9   **3**

_____

- - - - - - -

_____

 4

___ ___ ___   ___

- - - ▄▄▄ ▄▄▄▄
       ▄▄▄▄

_____ _____   _____

DIRECTIONS **1.** Write how many in all. (MA.K.A.1.3) **2.** Write how many are left. (MA.K.A.1.3) **3.** Circle the group of cubes being separated. Mark an X on that group. Write how many cubes are left. (MA.K.A.1.3) **4.** Tell a separating story problem about the birds. Complete the subtraction sentence. (MA.K.A.1.3)

5

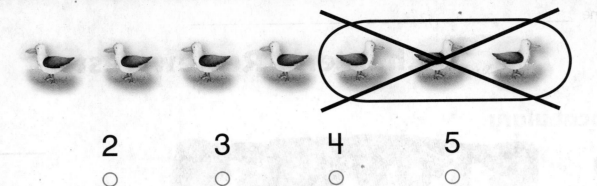

2	3	4	5
○	○	○	○

6

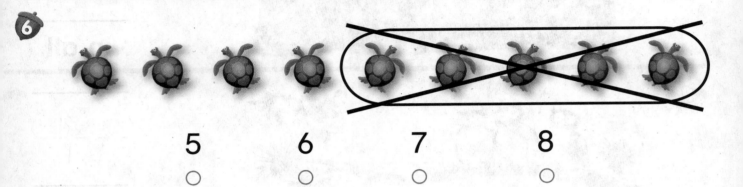

5	6	7	8
○	○	○	○

7

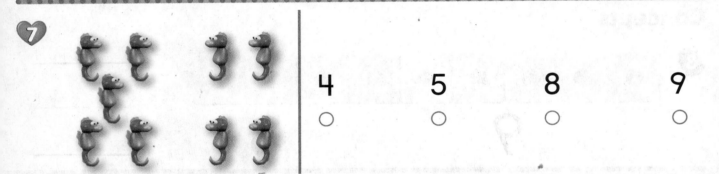

4	5	8	9
○	○	○	○

8

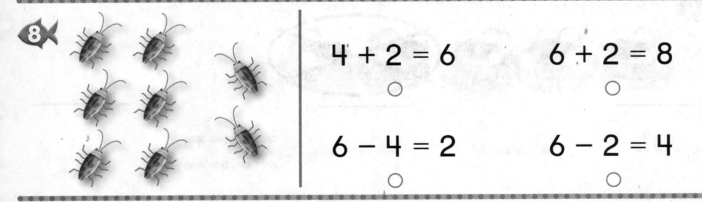

$4 + 2 = 6$ ○ $6 + 2 = 8$ ○

$6 - 4 = 2$ ○ $6 - 2 = 4$ ○

DIRECTIONS   **5.** Mark under the number that shows how many are left.
(MA.K.A.1.3)   **6.** Mark under the number that shows how many are taken away.
(MA.K.A.1.3)   **7.** Mark under the number that tells how many seahorses in all.
(MA.K.A.1.3)   **8.** Mark under the number sentence to match the picture. (MA.K.A.1.3)

I ○   5 ○   7 ○   8 ○

10

3 ○   4 ○   5 ○   6 ○

11

I ○   4 ○   5 ○   6 ○

12

7 + 2 = __

2 ○   5 ○   7 ○   9 ○

DIRECTIONS 9. Mark under the number that shows how many
cubes are left. (MA.K.A.1.3)   **10.** Mark under the number that shows
how many boats in all. (MA.K.A.1.3)   **11.** Mark under the number that
shows how many lobsters are left. (MA.K.A.1.3)   **12.** Mark under the
number that shows how many in all. (MA.K.A.1.3)

Chapter 4

$3 + 4 = \underline{\quad}$

2	5	7	9
○	○	○	○

1	2	3	4
○	○	○	○

1	4	5	6
○	○	○	○

$6 - 2 = 4$ $6 + 2 = 8$
○   ○

$8 - 2 = 6$ $8 + 2 = 10$
○   ○

DIRECTIONS **13.** Mark under the number that shows how many in all.
(MA.K.A.1.3) **14.** Mark under the number that shows how many are left. (MA.K.A.1.3)
15. Mark under the number that shows how many dragonflies in all. (MA.K.A.1.3)
16. Mark under the number sentence that matches the picture. (MA.K.A.1.3)

196 one hundred ninety-six

Name _____

Write Numbers to 10

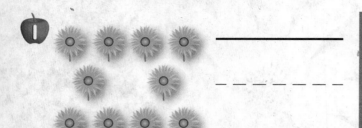

1 _____
   - - - - - - - - -
   _____

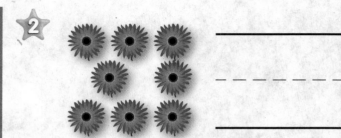

2 _____
   - - - - - - - - -
   _____

Show Amounts to 10

3

9

4

7

Count Forward to 20

5

1 2 3 4 5 6 7 8 9 10 11 12 13 14 15 16 17 18 19 20

DIRECTIONS 1–2. Count and tell how many. Write the number. 3. Draw 9 flowers. 4. Draw 7 flowers. 5. Point to the numbers and say them in order.

FAMILY NOTE: This page checks your child's understanding of important skills needed for success in Chapter 5.

198 one hundred ninety-eight

© Houghton Mifflin Harcourt

Name _____

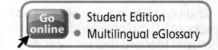

FINISH

three

four

one 1

two

2

3

4

five 5

eight 8

seven 7

six 6

nine 9

ten 10

CABBAGE
PARK
RUN

© Houghton Mifflin Harcourt

DIRECTIONS Circle the number that
shows how many cabbages.

Game

Sweet and Sour Path

START

7

9

6

10

5

2

END

DIRECTIONS Play with a partner. Place game markers on START. Take turns. Toss the number cube. Move that number of spaces. If a player lands on a lemon, the player reads the number and moves back that many spaces. If a player lands on a strawberry, the player reads the number and moves forward that many spaces. The first player to reach END wins.

MATERIALS two game markers, number cube (1–6)

© Houghton Mifflin Harcourt

Name _____

Model 11 and 12

Essential Question How can you show
11 and 12 with objects?

MA.K.A.1.1 Represent quantities
with numbers up to 20, verbally, in
writing, and with manipulatives.

Listen and Draw

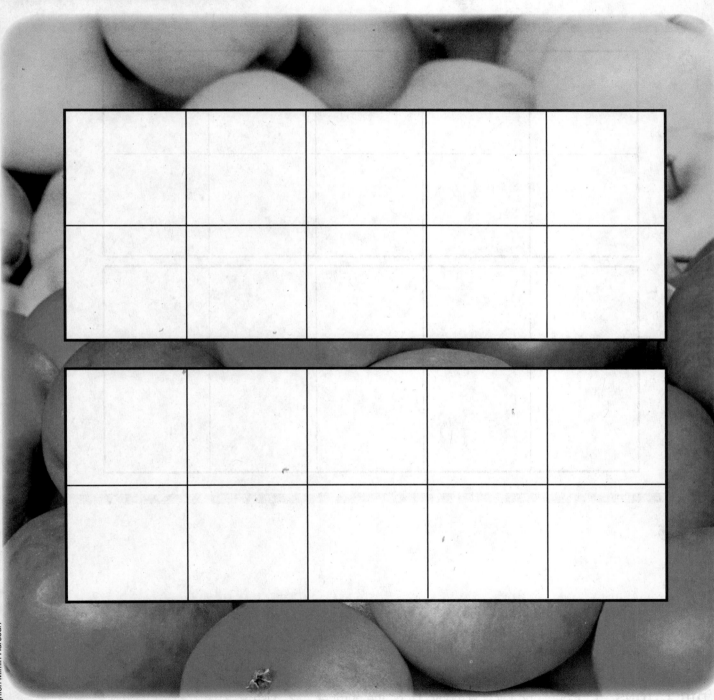

DIRECTIONS Use cubes to show the number 11. Add
more to show the number 12. Draw the cubes.

Chapter 5 • Lesson 1

Share and Show

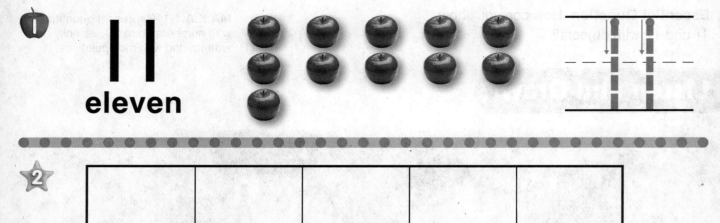

1 II
eleven

2

3 ✓

DIRECTIONS I. Count and tell how many. Trace the number. 2. Use cubes to show the number II. Draw the cubes. 3. Show the cubes as one ten-cube train and more. Draw the cubes.

202 two hundred two

© Houghton Mifflin Harcourt

Name _____

12
twelve

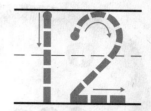

DIRECTIONS **4.** Count and tell how many. Trace the number. **5.** Use
cubes to show the number 12. Draw the cubes. **6.** Show the cubes as one
ten-cube train and more. Draw the cubes.

Chapter 5 • Lesson 1   two hundred three **203**

PROBLEM SOLVING REAL WORLD

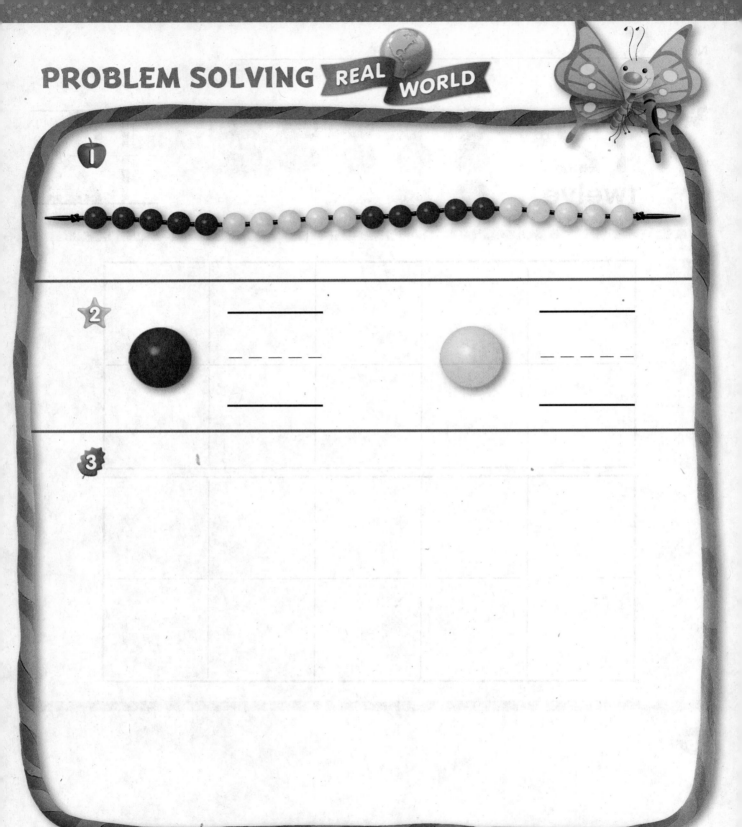

1

2

3

DIRECTIONS **1.** Start with the blue bead on the left. Circle to show 11 beads on the bead string. **2.** How many of each bead did you circle? **3.** Draw to show what you know about the number 12. Tell about your drawing.

HOME ACTIVITY • Draw two ten frames on a sheet of paper. Have your child use small objects such as buttons, pennies, or dried beans to show the numbers 11 and 12.

FOR MORE PRACTICE:
Florida Benchmarks Practice Book, pp. P111–P112

Name _____

Read and Write 11 and 12

Essential Question How can you show 11 and 12 with pictures, numbers, and words?

MA.K.A.1.1 Represent quantities with numbers up to 20, verbally, in writing, and with manipulatives.

Listen and Draw

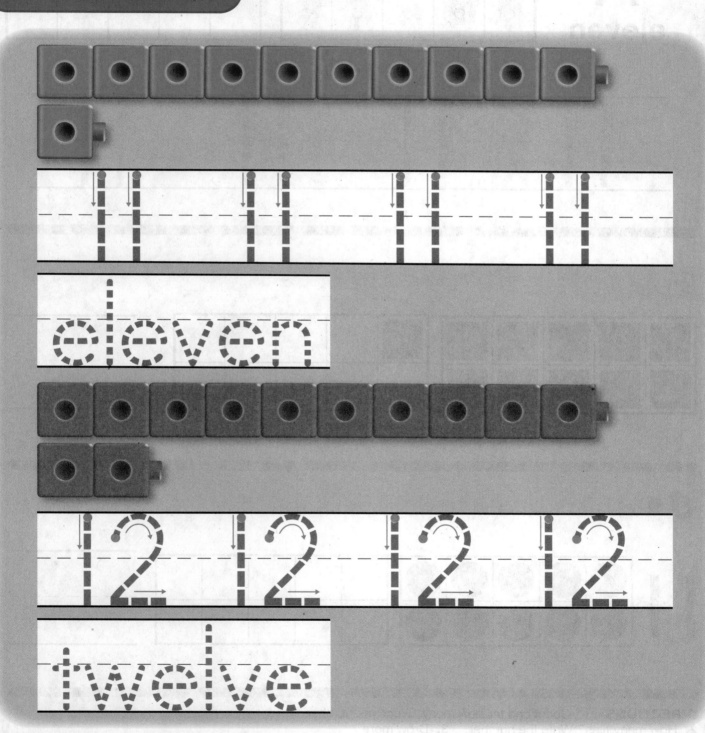

eleven

twelve

DIRECTIONS Count and tell how many. Trace the numbers and the words.

Share and Show

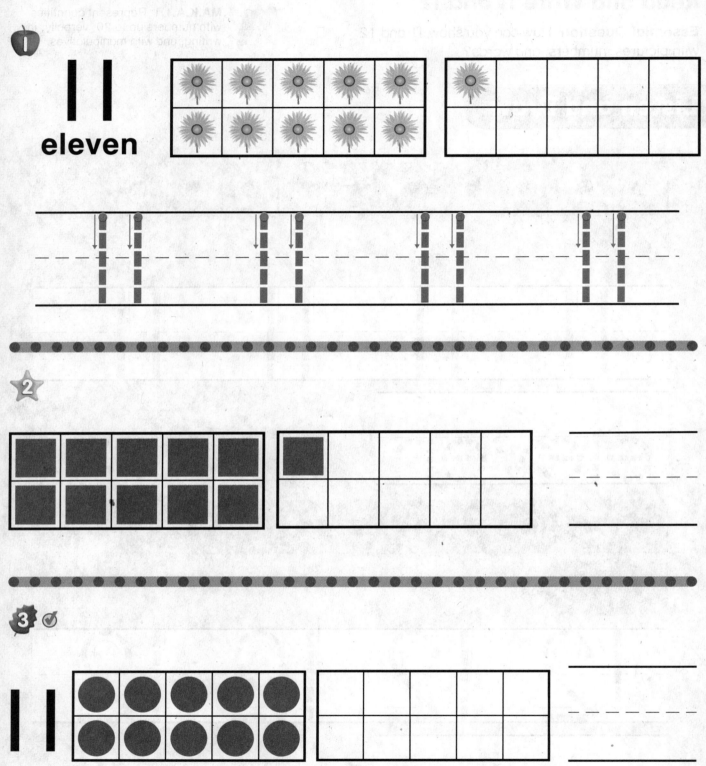

1

eleven

2

3 ☑

DIRECTIONS **1.** Count and tell how many. Trace the number.
2. How many tiles? Write the number. **3.** Draw more
counters to show the number. Write the number.

206 two hundred six

© Houghton Mifflin Harcourt

4

12
twelve

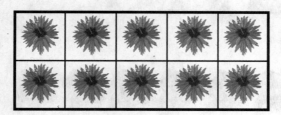

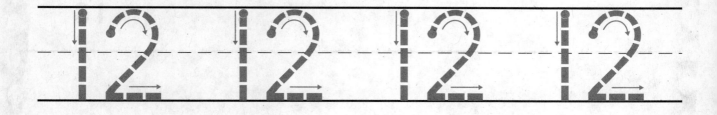

5

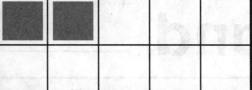

_____

6

12

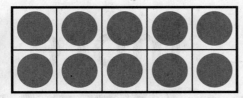

_____

DIRECTIONS **4.** Count and tell how many. Trace the number.
5. How many tiles? Write the number. **6.** Draw more
counters to show the number. Write the number.

Chapter 5 • Lesson 2

PROBLEM SOLVING REAL WORLD

1

11

12

13

2

_____
- - - - - -

10 and _____ more

3

_____
- - - - - -

10 and _____ more

DIRECTIONS 1. Circle a number. Draw more flowers to show that number. **2.** Draw 11 objects. Write how many more than 10 that is. **3.** Draw 12 objects. Write how many more than 10 that is.

HOME ACTIVITY • Ask your child to count and write the number for a set of 11 or 12 household objects, such as macaroni pieces or toothpicks.

208 two hundred eight

FOR MORE PRACTICE:
Florida Benchmarks Practice Book, pp. P113–P114

Name _____

Model 13 and 14

Essential Question How can you show 13 and 14 with objects?

MA.K.A.1.1 Represent quantities with numbers up to 20, verbally, in writing, and with manipulatives.

Listen and Draw

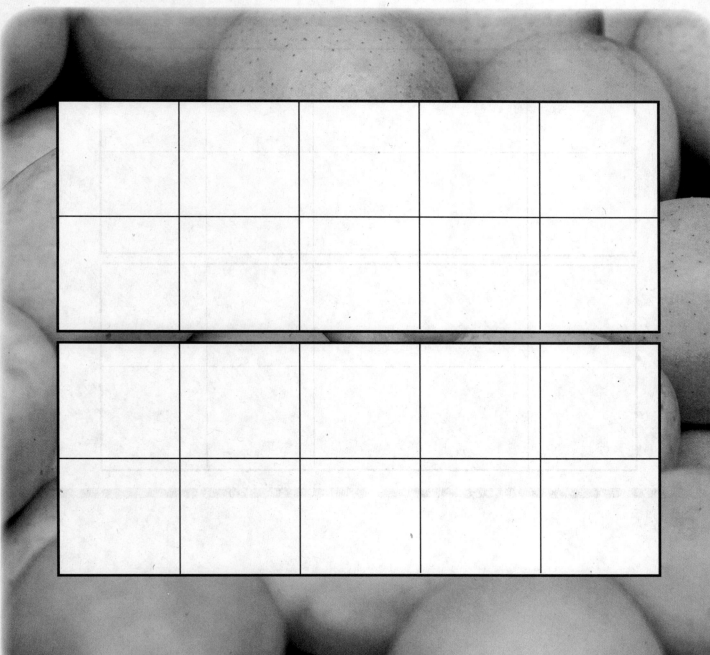

DIRECTIONS Use cubes to show the number 13. Add more to show the number 14. Draw the cubes.

Share and Show

❶ 13
thirteen

❷

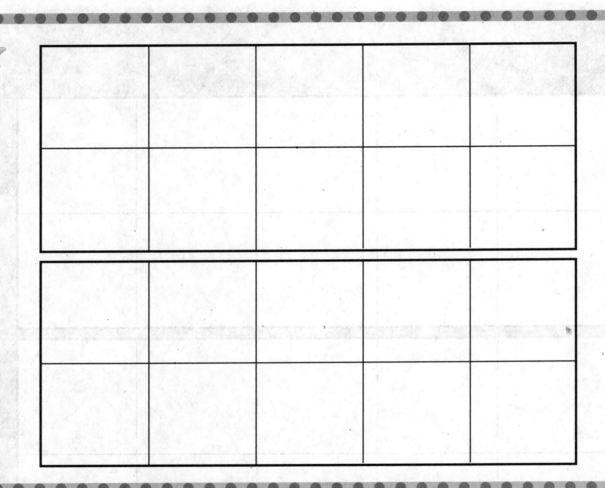

❸ ✓

DIRECTIONS **I.** Count and tell how many. Trace the number. **2.** Use cubes to show the number 13. Draw the cubes. **3.** Show the cubes as one ten-cube train and more. Draw the cubes.

4

14
fourteen

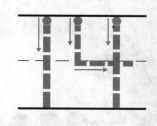

5

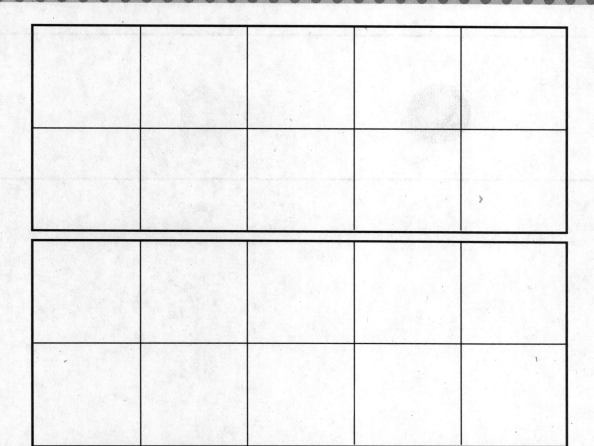

6

DIRECTIONS **4.** Count and tell how many. Trace the number. **5.** Use cubes to show the number 14. Draw the cubes. **6.** Show the cubes as one ten-cube train and more. Draw the cubes.

Chapter 5 · Lesson 3

two hundred eleven **211**

PROBLEM SOLVING REAL WORLD

1

2

3

DIRECTIONS **1.** Start with the blue bead on the left. Circle to show 13 beads on the bead string. **2.** Are there more blue beads or more yellow beads in those 13 beads? Circle the color bead that has more. **3.** Draw to show what you know about the number 14. Tell about your drawing.

HOME ACTIVITY • Draw two ten frames on a sheet of paper. Have your child use small objects such as buttons, pennies, or dried beans to show the numbers 13 and 14.

212 two hundred twelve

Name _____

Read and Write 13 and 14

Essential Question How can you show 13 and 14 with pictures, numbers, and words?

MA.K.A.1.1 Represent quantities with numbers up to 20, verbally, in writing, and with manipulatives.

Listen and Draw

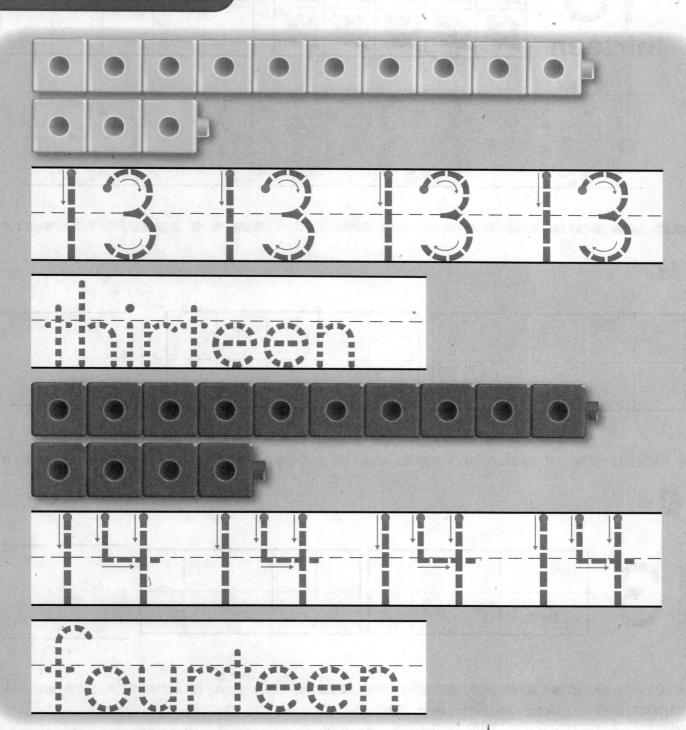

DIRECTIONS Count and tell how many. Trace the numbers and the words.

Share and Show

1

13
thirteen

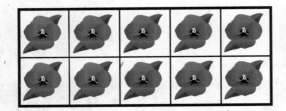 

13 13 13 13

 2

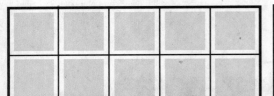 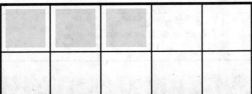

3 ✓

13

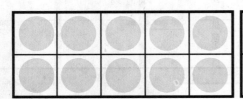 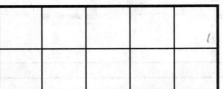

DIRECTIONS 1. Count and tell how many. Trace the number. **2.** How many tiles? Write the number. **3.** Draw more counters to show the number. Write the number.

Name _____

14
fourteen

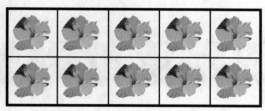

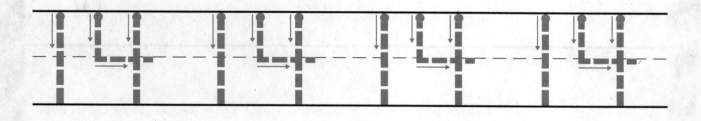

5

_____

6

14

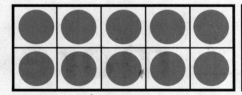

_____

DIRECTIONS   4. Count and tell how many. Trace the
number. **5.** How many tiles? Write the number.   **6.** Draw
more counters to show the number. Write the number.

Chapter 5 • Lesson 4

PROBLEM SOLVING REAL WORLD

1

12

13

14

2

_____

- - - - - - -

10 and _____ more

3

_____

- - - - - - -

10 and _____ more

DIRECTIONS **1.** Circle a number. Draw more flowers to show that number. **2.** Draw 13 objects. Write how many more than 10 that is. **3.** Draw 14 objects. Write how many more than 10 that is.

HOME ACTIVITY • Ask your child to count and write the number for a set of 13 or 14 household objects, such as macaroni pieces or toothpicks.

FOR MORE PRACTICE:
Florida Benchmarks Practice Book, pp. P117–P118

Name _____

Understand 15

Essential Question How can you solve problems by using 15 objects?

MA.K.A.1.1 Represent quantities with numbers up to 20, verbally, in writing, and with manipulatives.

🔑 Unlock the Problem

_____

_ _ _ _ _ _ **chairs**

DIRECTIONS There are 14 children sitting on chairs. There is one chair with no child on it. How many chairs are there? Draw to show how you solved the problem.

Chapter 5 • Lesson 5

two hundred seventeen **217**

Share and Show

1 **15**

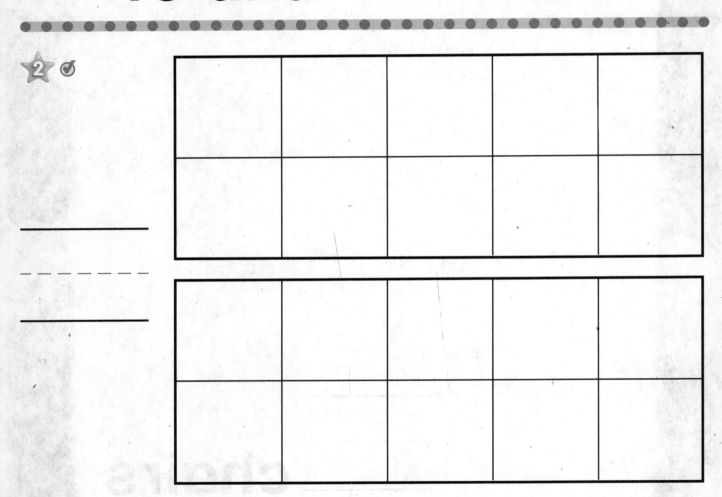

_____

------

10 and _____ more

2 ✓

_____

_____

DIRECTIONS **1.** How many more cubes do you need to show the number? Draw to solve the problem. Write how many more than 10 that is. **2.** One ten frame is filled with cubes and the other ten frame has 5 cubes. How many cubes are there? Draw to solve the problem.

218 two hundred eighteen

Name _____

_____
_ _ _ _
_____ **boys**

DIRECTIONS **3.** There are 15 children in Mrs. Joiner's class. They sit in rows of 5. There are 3 boys and 2 girls in each row. How many boys are in the class? Draw to solve the problem.

HOME ACTIVITY • Draw two ten frames on a sheet of paper. Have your child use small objects such as buttons, pennies, or dried beans to show the number 15.

Chapter 5 • Lesson 5

FOR MORE PRACTICE:
Florida Benchmarks Practice Book, pp. P119–P120

two hundred nineteen **219**

Concepts

1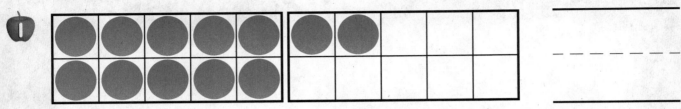

_____

- - - - - - - - - -

2

_____
- - - - - -

10 and _____ more

3 _____
- - - - - - -

_____

4 _____
- - - - - - -

_____

5

12 ○   13 ○   14 ○   15 ○

DIRECTIONS 1. How many counters? Write the number. (MA.K.A.1.1)
2. Draw 14 objects. Write how many more than 10. (MA.K.A.1.1)
3–4. Count and tell how many. Write the number. (MA.K.A.1.1)
5. Mark under the number that shows how many flowers. (MA.K.A.1.1)

Name _____

Model 16 and 17

Essential Question How can you show 16 and 17 with objects?

MA.K.A.1.1 Represent quantities with numbers up to 20, verbally, in writing, and with manipulatives.

Listen and Draw

DIRECTIONS Use cubes to show the number 16. Add more to show the number 17. Draw the cubes.

Share and Show

 16
sixteen

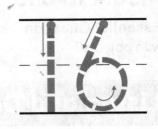

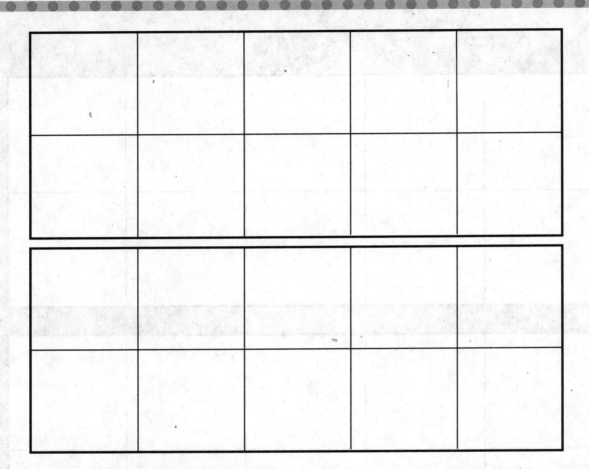

DIRECTIONS   **1.** Count and tell how many. Trace the number.   **2.** Use cubes to show the number 16. Draw the cubes.   **3.** Show the cubes as one ten-cube train and more. Draw the cubes.

222   two hundred twenty-two

© Houghton Mifflin Harcourt

Name _____

 4 # 17
seventeen

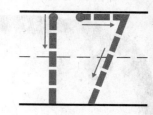

5

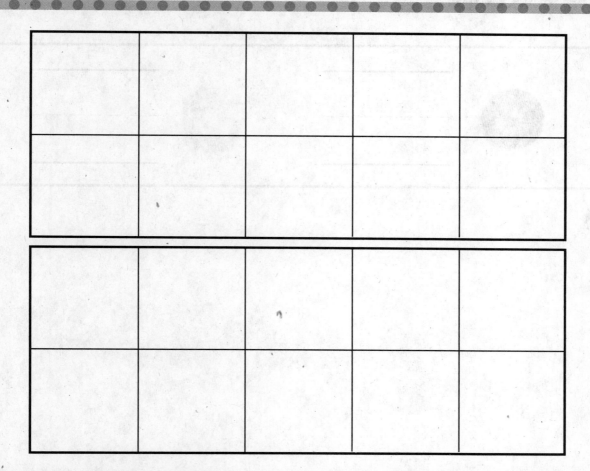

6

DIRECTIONS **4.** Count and tell how many. Trace the number. **5.** Use cubes to show the number 17. Draw the cubes. **6.** Show the cubes as one ten-cube train and more. Draw the cubes.

Chapter 5 · Lesson 6

PROBLEM SOLVING **REAL WORLD**

①

②

_____   _____

- - - - - - - - - - - - - - - -   - - - - - - - - - - - - - - - -

_____   _____

③

DIRECTIONS 1. Start with the blue bead on the left. Circle to show 16 beads on the bead string. **2.** How many of each bead did you circle? **3.** Draw to show what you know about the number 17. Tell about your drawing.

HOME ACTIVITY • Draw two ten frames on a sheet of paper. Have your child use small objects such as buttons, pennies, or dried beans to show the numbers 16 and 17.

FOR MORE PRACTICE: Florida Benchmarks Practice Book, pp. P121–P122

Name _____

Read and Write 16 and 17

Essential Question How can you show 16 and 17 with pictures, numbers, and words?

MA.K.A.1.1 Represent quantities with numbers up to 20, verbally, in writing, and with manipulatives.

Listen and Draw

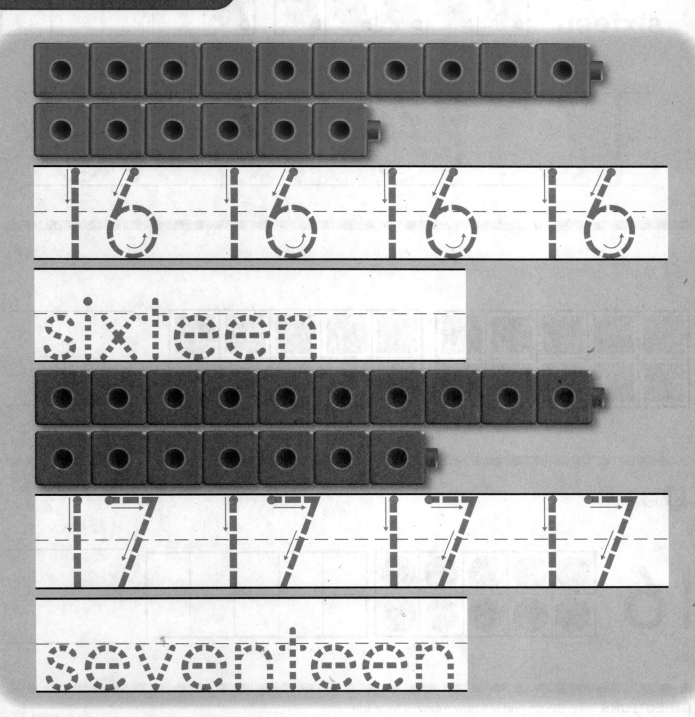

16 16 16 16 16

sixteen

17 17 17 17 17

seventeen

DIRECTIONS Count and tell how many. Trace the numbers and the words.

Chapter 5 • Lesson 7

two hundred twenty-five **225**

Share and Show

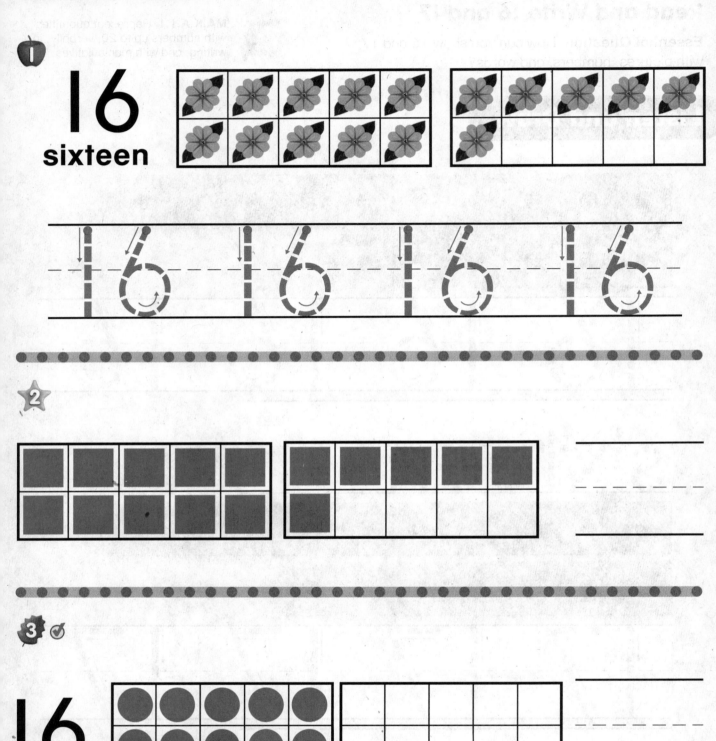

1

16
sixteen

2

3

16

DIRECTIONS **1.** Count and tell how many. Trace the number. **2.** How many tiles? Write the number. **3.** Draw more counters to show the number. Write the number.

226 two hundred twenty-six

© Houghton Mifflin Harcourt

17
seventeen

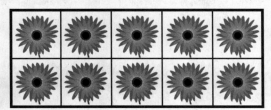

17 17 17 17 17

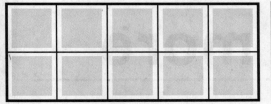  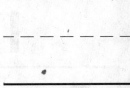

17

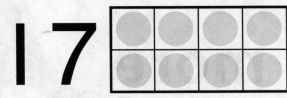 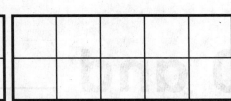

DIRECTIONS **4.** Count and tell how many. Trace the number. **5.** How many tiles? Write the number. **6.** Draw more counters to show the number. Write the number.

PROBLEM SOLVING  REAL WORLD

 1

🌻 🌻 🌻 🌻 🌻 🌻 🌻 🌻 🌻 🌻

17

18

19

 2

_____

10 and ___ more

 3

_____

10 and ___ more

DIRECTIONS   1. Circle a number. Draw more flowers to show that number.   **2.** Draw 16 objects. Write how many more than 10 that is.   **3.** Draw 17 objects. Write how many more than 10 that is.

HOME ACTIVITY • Ask your child to count and write the number for a set of 16 or 17 household objects, such as macaroni pieces or toothpicks.

FOR MORE PRACTICE:
Florida Benchmarks Practice Book, pp. P123–P124

Name _____

Model 18 and 19

Essential Question How can you show 18 and 19 with objects?

MA.K.A.1.1 Represent quantities with numbers up to 20, verbally, in writing, and with manipulatives.

Listen and Draw

DIRECTIONS Use cubes to show the number 18. Add more to show the number 19. Draw the cubes.

Share and Show

 1

18
eighteen

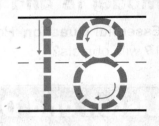

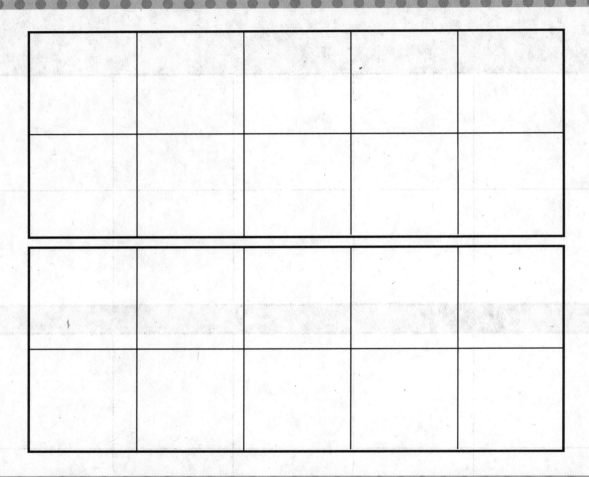

 3 ✅

DIRECTIONS **1.** Count and tell how many. Trace the number. **2.** Use cubes to show the number 18. Draw the cubes. **3.** Show the cubes as one ten-cube train and more. Draw the cubes.

19
nineteen

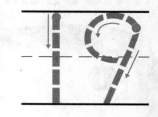

DIRECTIONS **4.** Count and tell how many. Trace the number.
5. Use cubes to show the number 19. Draw the cubes. **6.** Show the cubes as one ten-cube train and more. Draw the cubes.

Chapter 5 • Lesson 8

PROBLEM SOLVING REAL WORLD

❶

★❷

🍂❸

DIRECTIONS **1.** Start with the blue bead on the left. Circle to show 18 beads on the bead string. **2.** Are there more blue beads or more yellow beads in those 18 beads? Circle the color bead that has more. **3.** Draw to show what you know about the number 19. Tell about your drawing.

HOME ACTIVITY • Draw two ten frames on a sheet of paper. Have your child use small objects such as buttons, pennies, or dried beans to model the numbers 18 and 19.

FOR MORE PRACTICE:
Florida Benchmarks Practice Book, pp. P125–P126

Read and Write 18 and 19

Essential Question How can you show 18 and 19 with pictures, numbers, and words?

MA.K.A.1.1 Represent quantities with numbers up to 20, verbally, in writing, and with manipulatives.

Listen and Draw

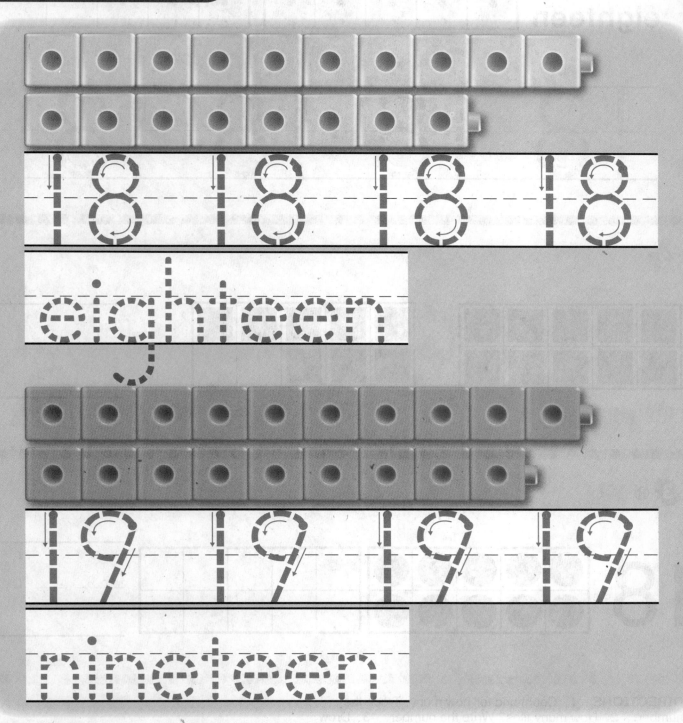

18 18 18 18

eighteen

19 19 19 19

nineteen

DIRECTIONS Count and tell how many. Trace the numbers and the words.

Chapter 5 • Lesson 9

Share and Show

1

18
eighteen

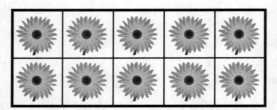 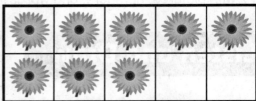

18 18 18 18

 2

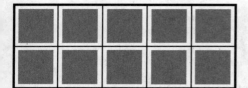 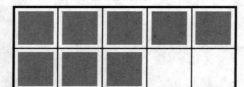

_____
- - - - - - - - - - -
_____

3 ✓

18

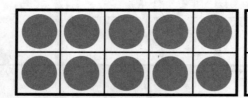

_____
- - - - - - - - - - -
_____

DIRECTIONS **1.** Count and tell how many. Trace the
number.   **2.** How many tiles? Write the number.   **3.** Draw
more counters to show the number. Write the number.

Name _____

19
nineteen

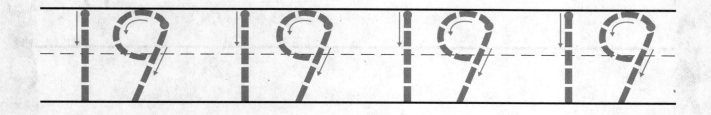

5

_____

6

19

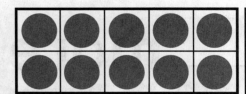

_____

_____

DIRECTIONS **4.** Count and tell how many. Trace the number. **5.** How many tiles? Write the number. **6.** Draw more counters to show the number. Write the number.

Chapter 5 • Lesson 9

PROBLEM SOLVING REAL WORLD

1

17

18

19

2

_____
- - - - - - -
10 and _____ more

3

_____
- - - - - - -
10 and _____ more

DIRECTIONS **1.** Circle a number. Draw more flowers to show that number. **2.** Draw 18 objects. Write how many more than 10 that is. **3.** Draw 19 objects. Write how many more than 10 that is.

HOME ACTIVITY • Ask your child to count and write the number for a set of 18 or 19 household objects, such as macaroni pieces or toothpicks.

FOR MORE PRACTICE:
Florida Benchmarks Practice Book, pp. P127–P128

Chapter 5 Review/Test

Vocabulary

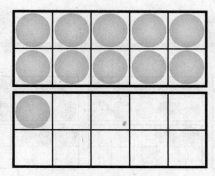   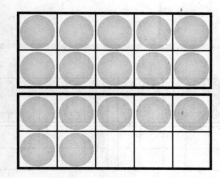   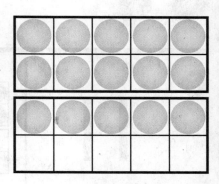

fifteen   eleven   seventeen

Concepts

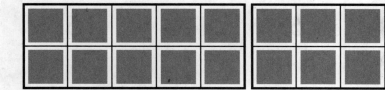

_____

 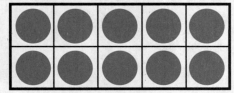   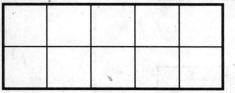

_____

DIRECTIONS **1.** Draw lines to match the counters in the ten frames to the number word. (MA.K.A.1.1) **2.** Count and tell how many. Write the number. (MA.K.A.1.1) **3.** Draw more counters to show the number. Write the number. (MA.K.A.1.1) **4.** Circle to show 14 beads on the bead string. (MA.K.A.1.1)

5

12   13   14   15
○   ○   ○   ○

6

11

○   ○   ○   ○

7

16   17   18   19
○   ○   ○   ○

8

14   15   16   17
○   ○   ○   ○

DIRECTIONS **5.** Mark under the number that shows how many. (MA.K.A.1.1)   **6.** Mark under the set that shows the number at the beginning of the row. (MA.K.A.1.1)   **7–8.** Mark under the number that shows how many. (MA.K.A.1.1)

9

13   15   17   18
○   ○   ○   ○

10

13   16   17   18
○   ○   ○   ○

11

13   14   15   16
○   ○   ○   ○

12

17

○   ○   ○   ○

DIRECTIONS 9–11. Mark under the number that shows how many. (MA.K.A.1.1) 12. Mark under the set that shows the number at the beginning of the row. (MA.K.A.1.1)

13

14

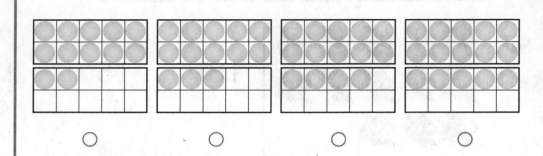

○   ○   ○   ○

12   13   17   18

○   ○   ○   ○

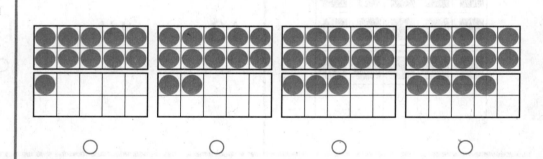

12

○   ○   ○   ○

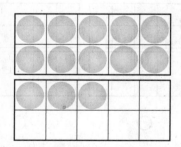

13   14   15   16

○   ○   ○   ○

DIRECTIONS **13.** Mark under the set that shows the number at the beginning of the row. (MA.K.A.1.1) **14.** Mark under the number that shows how many. (MA.K.A.1.1) **15.** Mark under the set that shows the number at the beginning of the row. (MA.K.A.1.1) **16.** Mark under the number that shows how many. (MA.K.A.1.1)

240 two hundred forty

Chapter 6
Represent, Compare, and Order Sets to 20

Persian Limes

Key Limes

Name _____

Show What You Know

Explore Numbers to 10

Order Numbers to 10

3 _____ _____ 6 _____ 8

Compare Sets to 10

 _____

 _____

_____

DIRECTIONS **1.** Circle all of the sets that show 9. **2.** Circle all of the sets that show 8. **3.** Write the missing numbers on the number line. **4.** Count and tell how many. Write the number. Circle the set with fewer fruit.

FAMILY NOTE: This page checks your child's understanding of important skills needed for success in Chapter 6.

Name _____

three

two

one

five

four

six

seven

eight

nine

ten

eleven

twelve

thirteen

fourteen

fifteen

sixteen

seventeen

eighteen

DIRECTIONS Point to each otter as you count. How many are wearing glasses? Write the number.

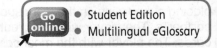

Game

Who Has More?

Player 1

Player 2

DIRECTIONS Play with a partner. Each player shuffles a set of numeral cards and places them facedown in a stack. Both players turn over the top card on their stack to display the number. Model the number by placing cube trains on the work space. Compare your cube train with your partner's. The player with the greater number keeps both of the numeral cards. The player with the most cards at the end of the game wins.

MATERIALS two sets of numeral cards 11–20; cubes

Name _____

Model 20

Essential Question How can you show 20
with objects?

MA.K.A.1.1 Represent quantities
with numbers up to 20, verbally, in
writing, and with manipulatives.

Listen and Draw

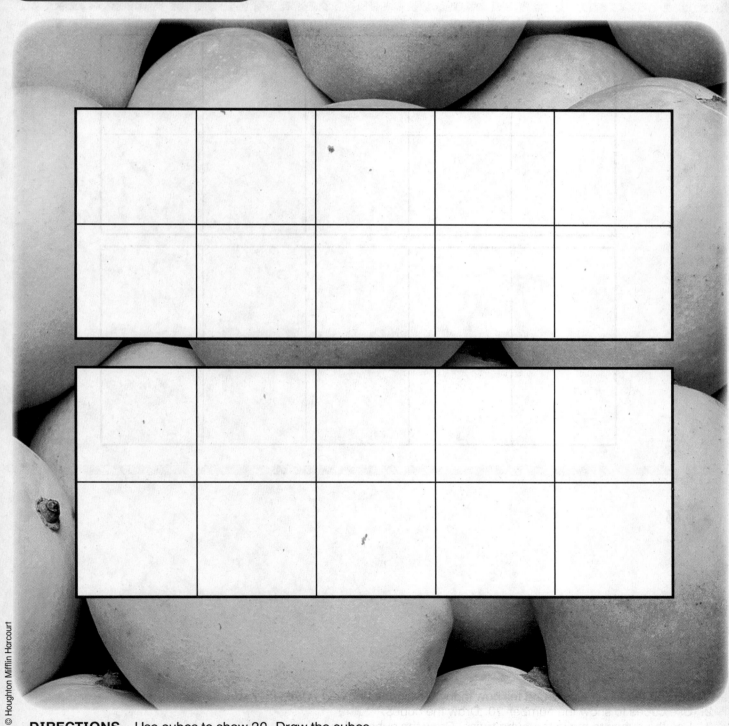

DIRECTIONS Use cubes to show 20. Draw the cubes.

Chapter 6 · Lesson 1

two hundred forty-five **245**

Share and Show

 **20**
twenty

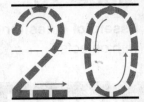

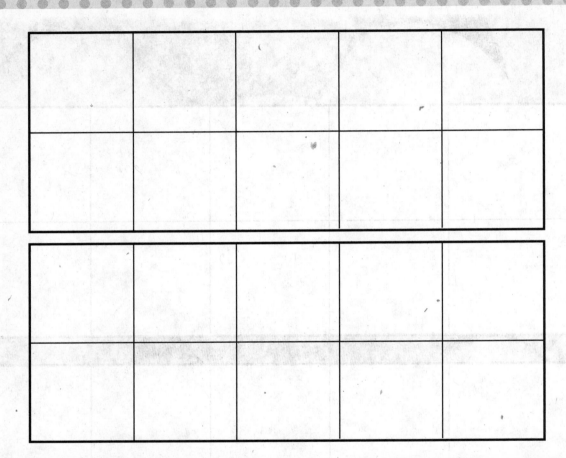

DIRECTIONS 1. Count and tell how many. Trace the number.
2. Use cubes to show the number 20. Draw the cubes.
3. Use the cubes to make ten-cube trains. Draw the cube trains.

4

5

DIRECTIONS 4. Use cubes to show the number 20. Draw the cubes. 5. Use those cubes to make ten-cube trains. Draw and color the cube trains.

PROBLEM SOLVING REAL WORLD

1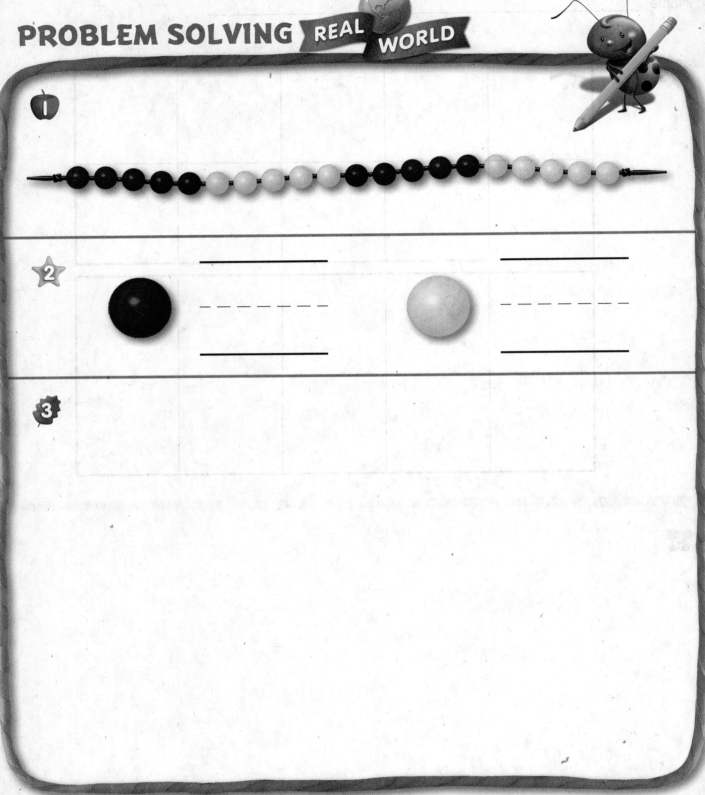

2

_____   _____
- - - - - - - - -   - - - - - - - - -
⚫   🟡
_____   _____

3

HOME ACTIVITY • Draw two ten frames on a sheet of paper. Have your child show the number 20 using small objects such as buttons, pennies, or dried beans.

FOR MORE PRACTICE:
Florida Benchmarks Practice Book, pp. P135–P136

Read and Write 20

Essential Question How can you show 20 with pictures, numbers, and words?

MA.K.A.1.1 Represent quantities with numbers up to 20, verbally, in writing, and with manipulatives.

Listen and Draw

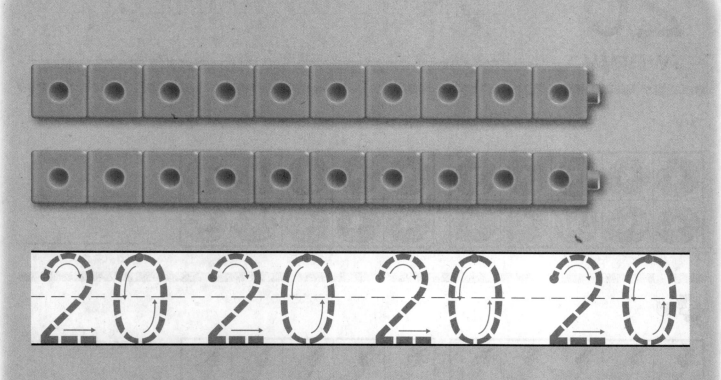

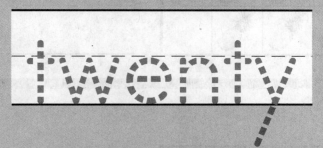

DIRECTIONS Count and tell how many. Trace the numbers and the word.

Chapter 6 · Lesson 2

two hundred forty-nine **249**

Share and Show

❶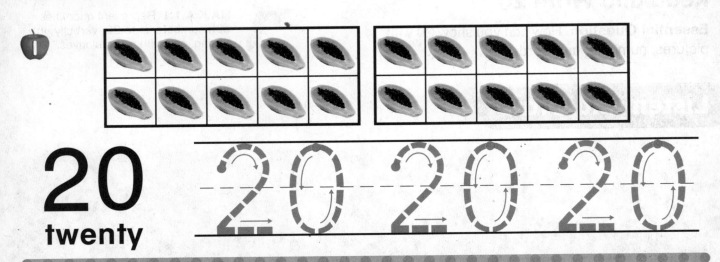

20
twenty

⭐2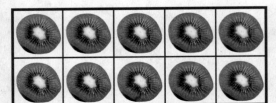

3 ✓

4 ✓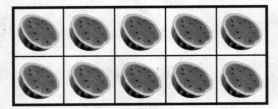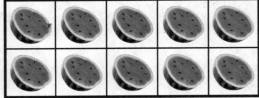

DIRECTIONS I. Trace the number as you say it.
2-4. Count and tell how many pieces of fruit. Write the number.

250 two hundred fifty

5

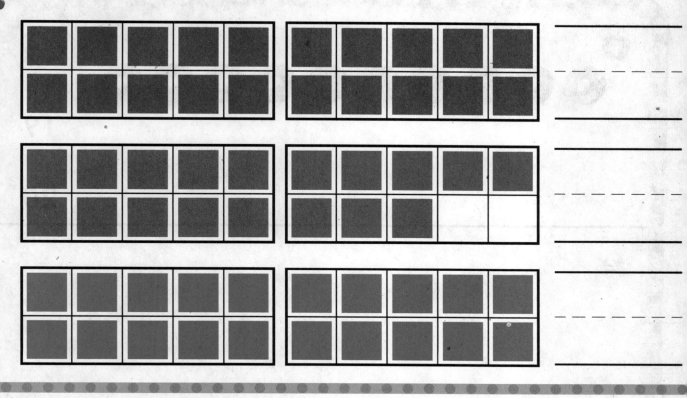

6

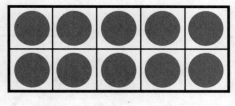

20

19

20

DIRECTIONS 5. Count and tell how many tiles. Write the numbers.
6. Draw more counters to show the numbers. Write the numbers.

1

18

19

20

2

DIRECTIONS   1. Circle a number. Draw more fruit to show that number.   **2.** Draw a set of objects that has two objects more than 18. Write how many objects are in the set. Tell about your drawing.

HOME ACTIVITY • Have your child use small objects such as pebbles or pasta pieces to model the number 20.

252 two hundred fifty-two

FOR MORE PRACTICE:
Florida Benchmarks Practice Book, pp. P137–P138

Name _____

Create Sets to 20

Essential Question How can you use objects to create sets to 20?

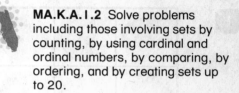

MA.K.A.1.2 Solve problems including those involving sets by counting, by using cardinal and ordinal numbers, by comparing, by ordering, and by creating sets up to 20.

Listen and Draw

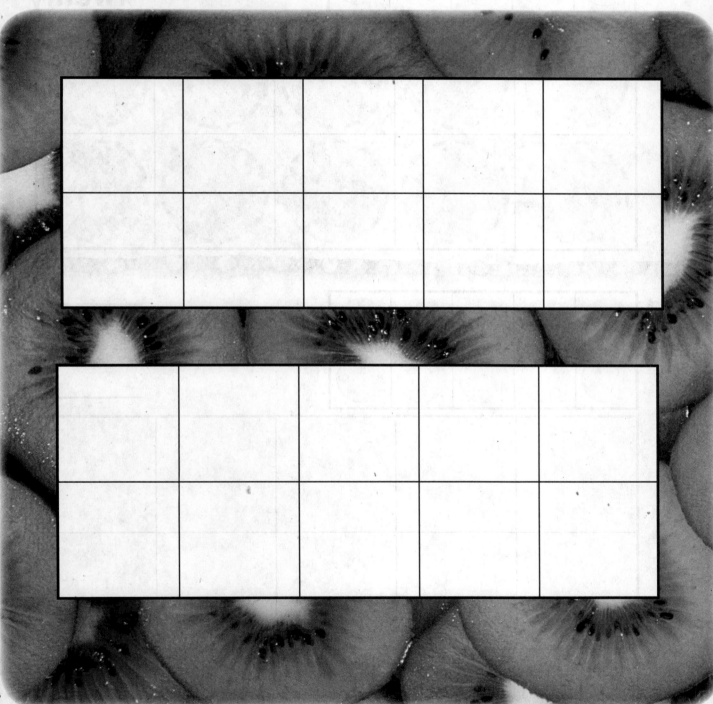

DIRECTIONS Use counters to create a set that has 11 to 20 objects.

Chapter 6 • Lesson 3

two hundred fifty-three **253**

© Houghton Mifflin Harcourt

Share and Show

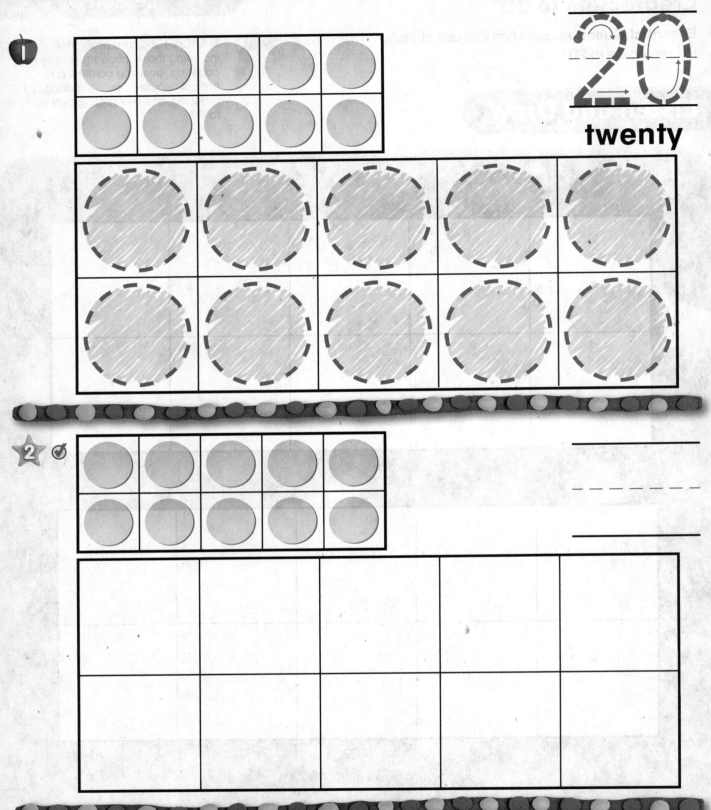

1.

20

twenty

2.

DIRECTIONS **1.** Place more counters in the ten frame to model 20. Say the number. Trace the number. Trace the counters. **2.** Use more counters to model the number that is 2 less than 20. Write that number. Draw and color the counters.

254 two hundred fifty-four

© Houghton Mifflin Harcourt

Name _____

3

_____

- - - - - - - - - - -

_____

4

_____

- - - - - - - - - - -

_____

DIRECTIONS   3. Use more counters to model the number that is 2 greater than 18. Write that number. Draw and color the counters.   **4.** Use more counters to model the number that is 3 less than 20. Write that number. Draw and color the counters.

PROBLEM SOLVING REAL WORLD

DIRECTIONS Create a set with up to 20 objects. Draw the objects. Write how many. Tell about your drawing.

HOME ACTIVITY • Ask your child to model 20 with objects. Then have your child model 2 fewer than 20 with objects. Ask your child to tell how many objects that will be.

FOR MORE PRACTICE:
Florida Benchmarks Practice Book, pp. P139–P140

Name _____

Compare Sets to 20

Essential Question How can you solve problems by comparing sets of objects?

MA.K.A.I.2 Solve problems including those involving sets by counting, by using cardinal and ordinal numbers, by comparing, by ordering, and by creating sets up to 20.

Unlock the Problem

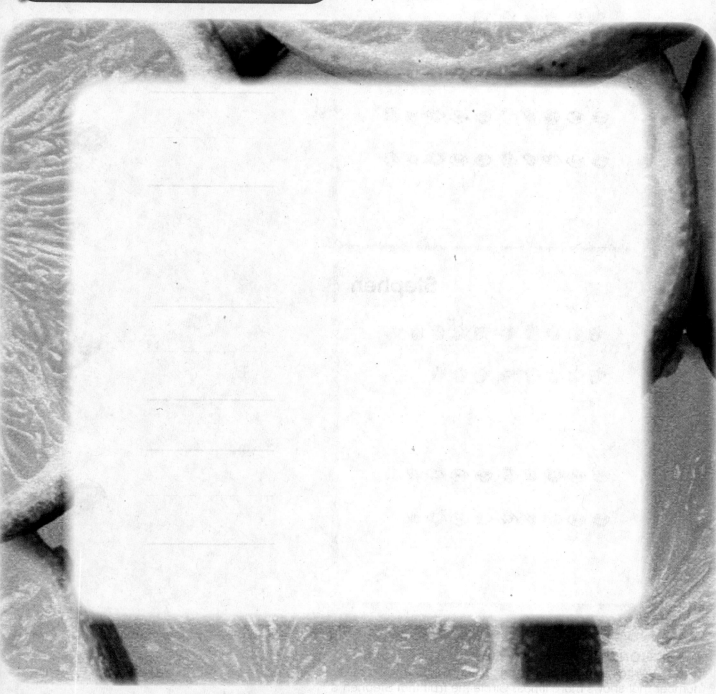

DIRECTIONS Ali has 1 more than 15 yellow cubes. Josh has 1 fewer than 17 green cubes. Show the cubes. Compare the sets of cubes. Draw the cubes. Tell about your drawing.

Share and Show

Amy

Stephen

DIRECTIONS I. Write how many apples are in each picture. Write how many limes are in each picture. Circle the number that shows more limes. Circle the fruit that Stephen's picture shows 2 more of than Amy's picture shows.

Name _____

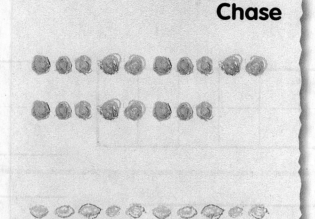

Chase

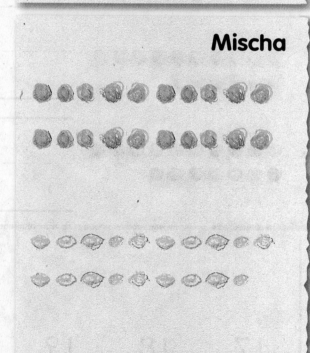

Mischa

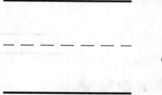

DIRECTIONS 2. Write how many oranges are in each picture. Write how many lemons are in each picture. Circle the number that shows fewer lemons. Circle the fruit that Chase's picture shows 2 fewer of than Mischa's picture shows.

HOME ACTIVITY • Have your child count objects in your home, such as spoons and forks, and write how many are in each group. Then have your child circle the greater number. Repeat with different numbers of objects.

Chapter 6 • Lesson 4

FOR MORE PRACTICE: Florida Benchmarks Practice Book, pp. P141–P142

Concepts

1 20

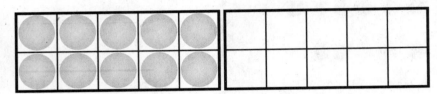

_____

2

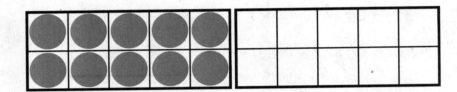

_____

3

_____

_____

_____

_____

_____

✿ Test Prep

4

17 ○   18 ○   19 ○   20 ○

DIRECTIONS **1.** Draw more counters to show the number. Write the number. (MA.K.A.1.1) **2.** Draw more counters on the ten frame to model the number that is 4 less than 20. Write the number. (MA.K.A.1.2) **3.** Write how many apricots are in each picture. Write how many red plums are in each picture. Circle the number that shows fewer red plums. (MA.K.A.1.2) **4.** Mark under the number that shows how many kiwis. (MA.K.A.1.1)

Name _____

Count and Order Sets to 20

Essential Question How can you solve problems by counting and ordering sets to 20?

MA.K.A.1.2 Solve problems including those involving sets by counting, by using cardinal and ordinal numbers, by comparing, by ordering, and by creating sets up to 20.

Listen and Draw REAL WORLD

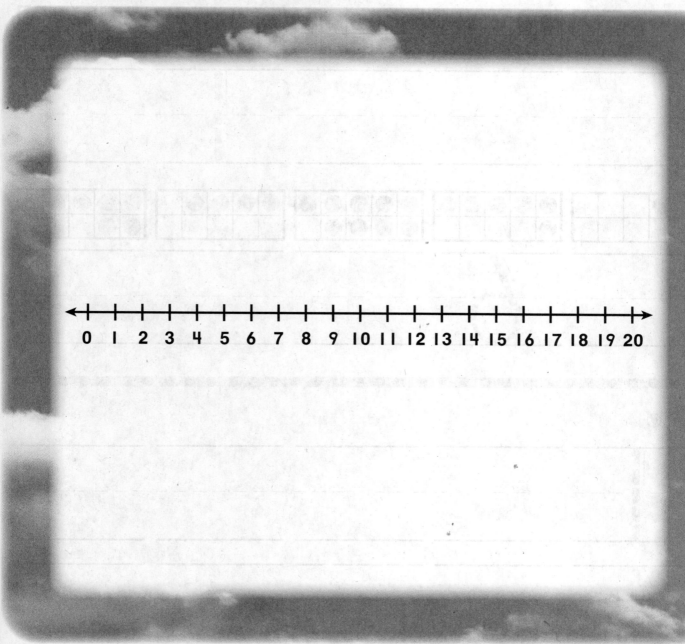

0 1 2 3 4 5 6 7 8 9 10 11 12 13 14 15 16 17 18 19 20

DIRECTIONS Point to the numbers on the number line and say them in order. Use the terms *greater than* and *less than* to compare and describe the order of numbers. Circle a number that is less than 10. Create a set of cubes for that number. Draw the cubes. Mark an X on a number that is greater than 10. Create a set of cubes for that number. Draw the cubes.

Share and Show

<-------|---|---|---|---|---|---|---|---|---|---|---|---|---|---|---|---|---|---|---|---|------->
0 1 2 3 4 5 6 7 8 9 10 11 12 13 14 15 16 17 18 19 20

🍎

2 ✓

DIRECTIONS **1.** Count the dots in each ten frame. Write the number. **2.** Write those numbers in order.

262 two hundred sixty-two

© Houghton Mifflin Harcourt

3

4

DIRECTIONS **3.** Count the dots in the ten frames.
Write the number. **4.** Write those numbers in order.

PROBLEM SOLVING REAL WORLD

DIRECTIONS Draw dots in the blank ten frames so the frames will be in order. Write the numbers in order.

HOME ACTIVITY • Give your child a set of 11 objects, a set of 12 objects, and a set of 13 objects. Have your child count the objects in each set and place the sets in numerical order.

FOR MORE PRACTICE:
Florida Benchmarks Practice Book, pp. P143–P144

Order Numbers Forward and Backward

Essential Question How can you solve problems by ordering numbers to 20?

MA.K.A.1.2 Solve problems including those involving sets by counting, by using cardinal and ordinal numbers, by comparing, by ordering, and by creating sets up to 20.

Listen and Draw

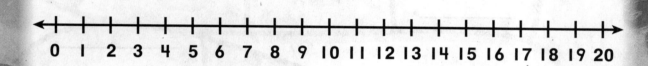

9 _____ 11

_____

14 _____ 16

DIRECTIONS Point to the numbers on the number line and say them in order. What number comes right before 11? What number comes right after 14? Write the numbers.

Share and Show

START

1

2

___

___

___

6

5

___

9

10

11

___

___

16

15

14

___

18

19

20

DIRECTIONS 1. Count forward. Write the missing numbers.

266 two hundred sixty-six

© Houghton Mifflin Harcourt

②

START
20 19 18
17
14 15 16
13
12 11 10
___
___
6 7
___
___
3 2 ___

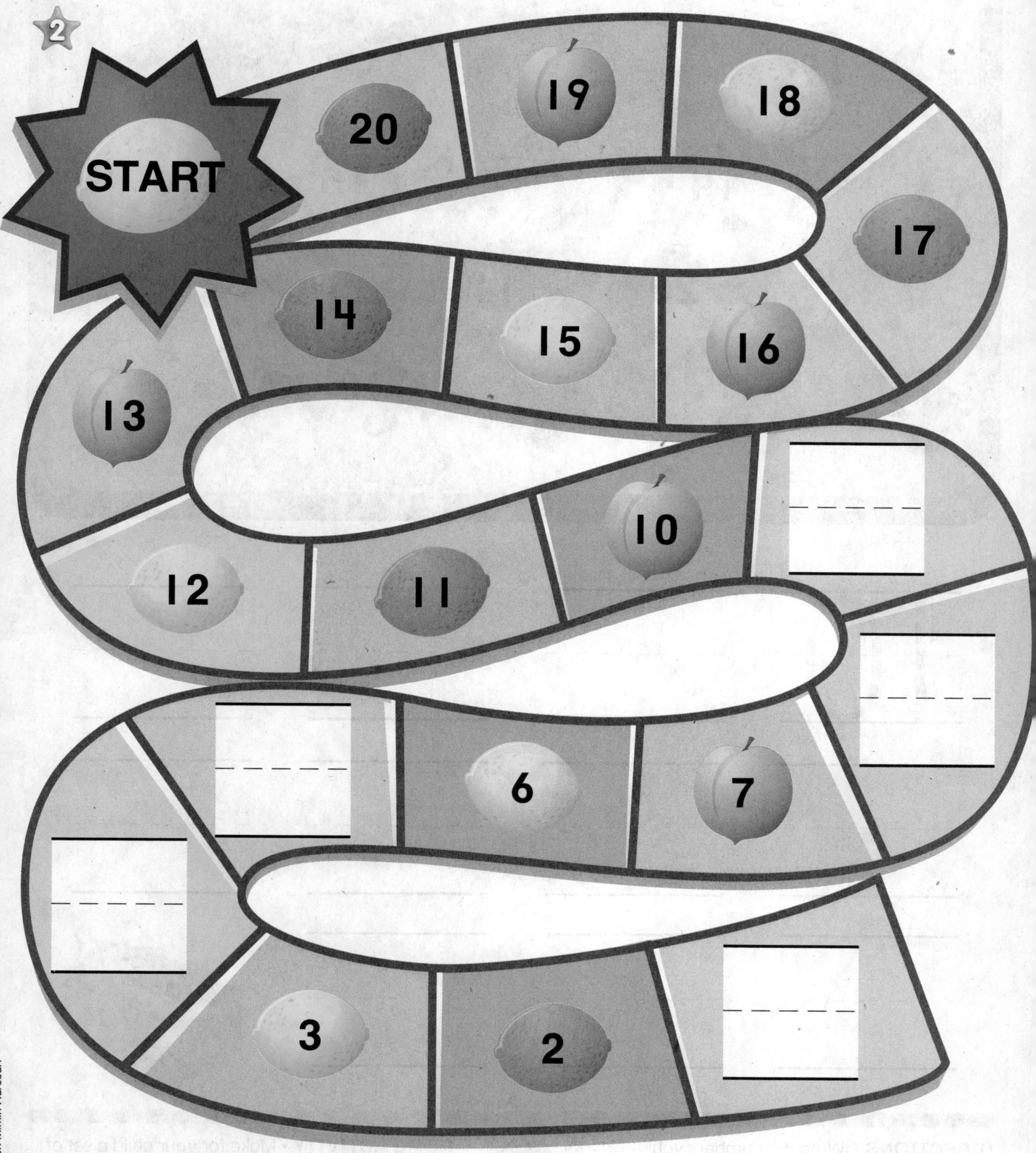

DIRECTIONS 2. Count backward. Write the missing numbers.

PROBLEM SOLVING

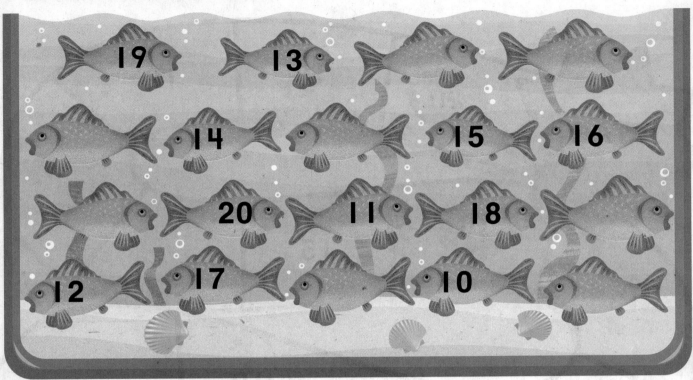

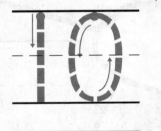

268 two hundred sixty-eight

Ordinal Numbers to 20th

Essential Question How can you solve problems using ordinal numbers to twentieth?

MA.K.A.I.2 Solve problems including those involving sets by counting, by using cardinal and ordinal numbers, by comparing, by ordering, and by creating sets up to 20.

Name _____

Listen and Draw REAL WORLD

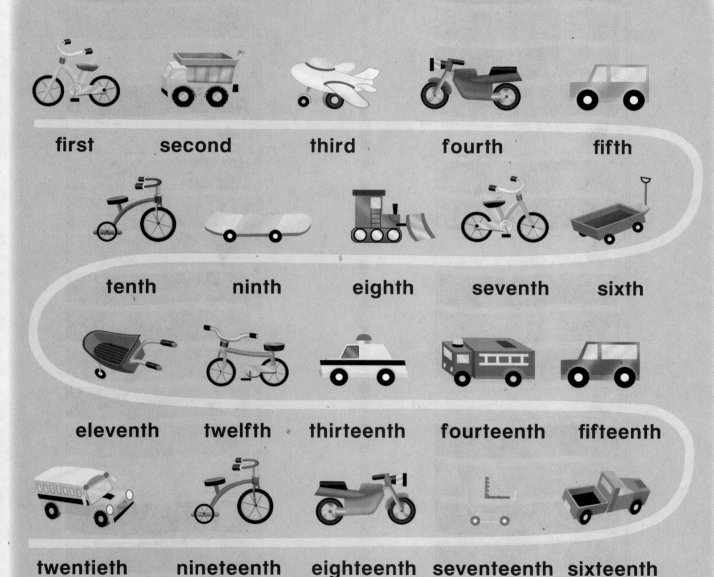

first   second   third   fourth   fifth

tenth   ninth   eighth   seventh   sixth

eleventh   twelfth   thirteenth   fourteenth   fifteenth

twentieth   nineteenth   eighteenth   seventeenth   sixteenth

DIRECTIONS Point to each object as you say the ordinal numbers. Circle the first object. Mark an X on the tenth object.

Share and Show

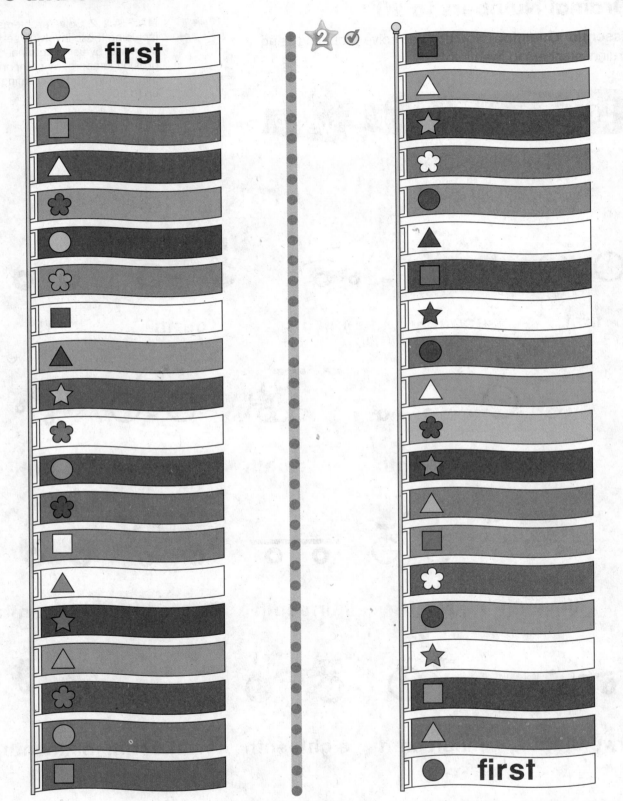

1 ★ **first**

2 ✓

DIRECTIONS 1–2. Circle the tenth flag. Mark an X on the thirteenth flag. Color the fifteenth flag.

3

first

4

first

5

first

DIRECTIONS **3.** Mark an X on the eleventh bead. Circle the twentieth bead. **4.** Mark an X on the fourteenth bead. Circle the eighteenth bead. **5.** Mark an X on the twelfth bead. Circle the ninth bead.

PROBLEM SOLVING REAL WORLD

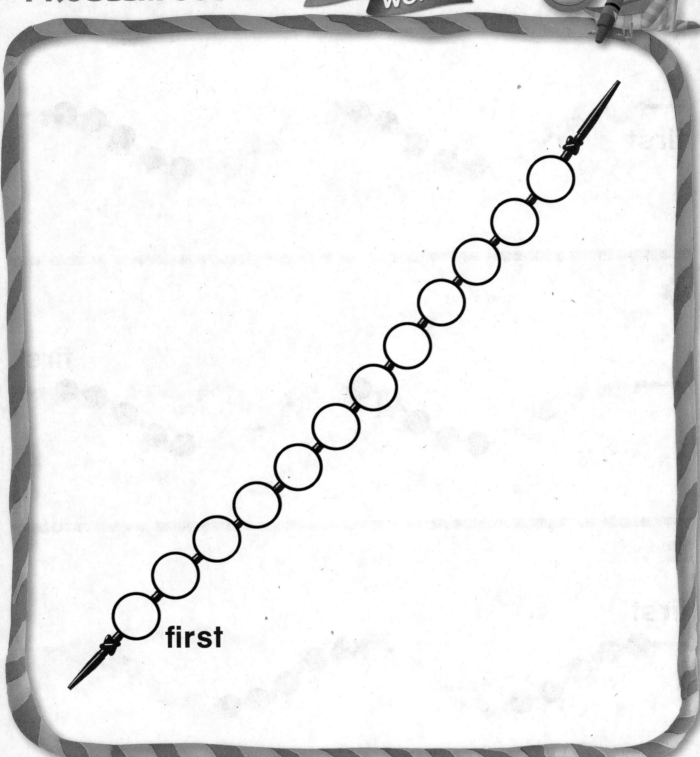

first

DIRECTIONS 1. There are 12 beads on a string. The first bead is red. After every red bead there are 2 blue beads. What color is the 12th bead? Draw to solve the problem.

HOME ACTIVITY • Have your child line up 20 household objects and point to each one as he or she says its ordinal number.

FOR MORE PRACTICE:
Florida Benchmarks Practice Book, pp. P147–P148

Chapter 6 Review Test

Vocabulary

first   thirteenth   nineteenth

Concepts

15 ___ ___ ___ 20

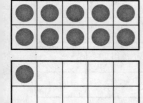  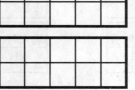  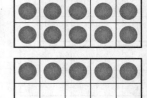

 first

DIRECTIONS   I. Draw a line from the word thirteenth to the thirteenth bead.
Draw a line from the word nineteenth to the nineteenth bead. (MA.K.A.1.2)
2. Count forward. Write the missing numbers. (MA.K.A.1.2)   **3.** Draw the dots
on the blank ten frames to order them. Write the numbers in order. (MA.K.A.1.2)
4. Mark an X on the tenth bead. Circle the twentieth bead. (MA.K.A.1.2)

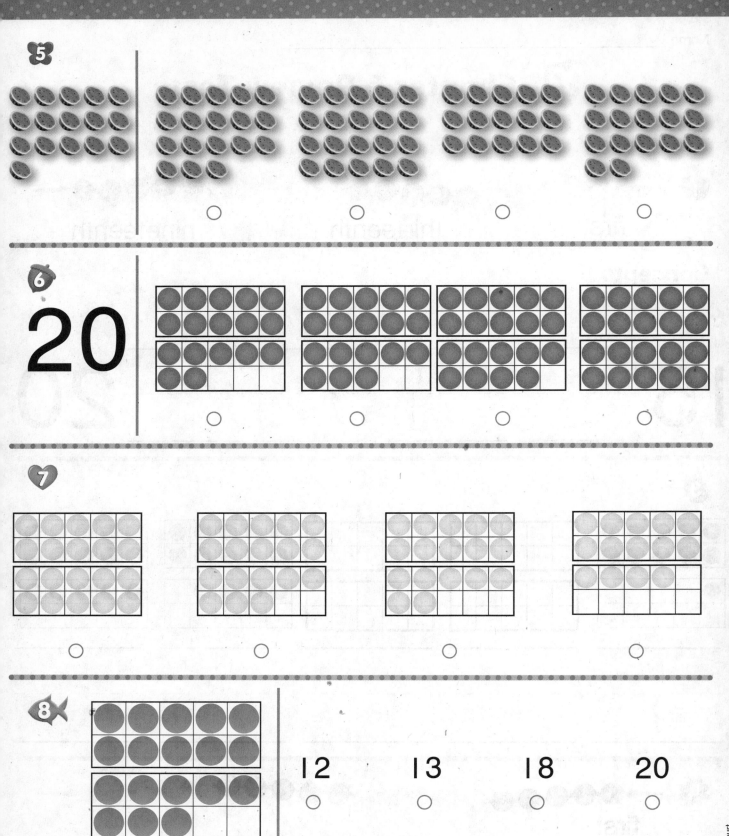

DIRECTIONS 5. Mark under the set that has fewer watermelons than the set at the beginning of the row. (MA.K.A.1.2) 6. Mark under the set that shows the number at the beginning of the row. (MA.K.A.1.1) 7. Mark under the set that has 3 more than 17. (MA.K.A.1.2) 8. Mark under the number that shows how many. (MA.K.A.1.1)

Name _____

9

Chandra	Sam	Meg	Jamal
○	○	○	○

10

←|——|——|——|→   ←|——|——|——|→   ←|——|——|——|→   ←|——|——|——|→

11 12 10   13 17 15   14 15 16   15 14 19

○   ○   ○   ○

11

15   16   17   18

○   ○   ○   ○

12

○   ○   ○   ○

DIRECTIONS 9. Mark under the drawing that has the most oranges. (MA.K.A.1.2)
10. Mark under the number line that shows the numbers in order. (MA.K.A.1.2)
11. Mark under the number that shows how many. (MA.K.A.1.1) **12.** Mark under
the group that shows 1 less than 20. (MA.K.A.1.2)

Chapter 6   two hundred seventy-five **275**

© Houghton Mifflin Harcourt

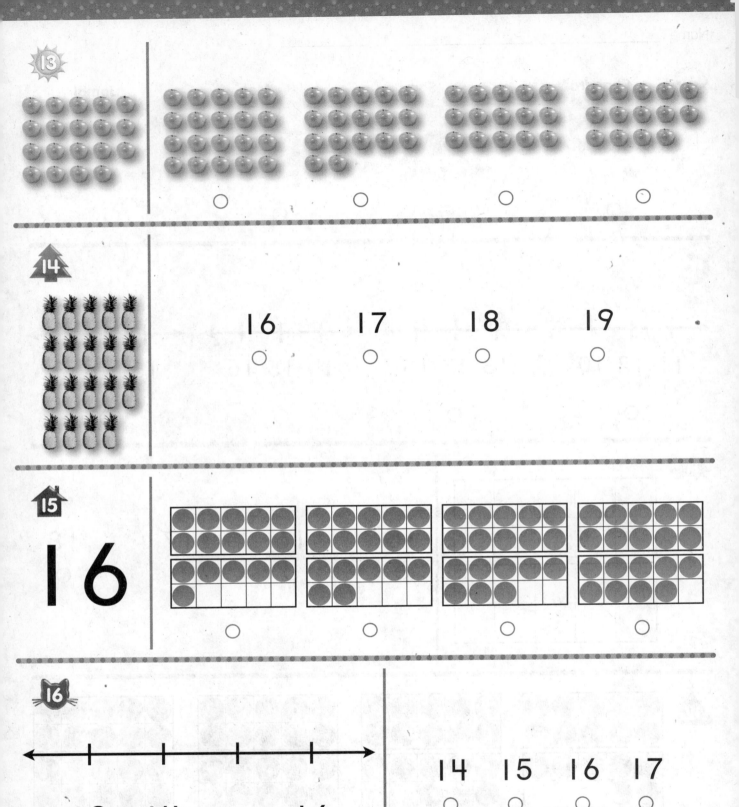

16

17

18

19

16

14   15   16   17

13   14   ___   16

DIRECTIONS **13.** Mark under the set that has more apples than the set at the beginning of the row. (MA.K.A.1.2) **14.** Mark under the number that shows how many. (MA.K.A.1.1) **15.** Mark under the set that shows the number at the beginning of the row. (MA.K.A.1.1) **16.** Mark under the missing number. (MA.K.A.1.2)

276 two hundred seventy-six

Back to School Fun

written by Ann Dickson

BIG
IDEA

Describe
shapes and space.

A

Here is my classroom, come on in.

Learning time is about to begin.

B

Why do we have rules?

These are the book bags

we hang by our names.

Circle the ones that look the same.

Social Studies

Why do we need to take turns?

c

Here are the books. We read them all!

Which books are big?

Which books are small?

Social Studies

Why do we help others?

Here are markers of every kind.

Name all the colors you can find.

Social Studies

Why do we put things away?

E

Our blocks and toys are over there.

Which shapes are round?

Which shapes are square?

Social
Studies

Why do we share?

Write About the Story

Vocabulary Review

alike

different

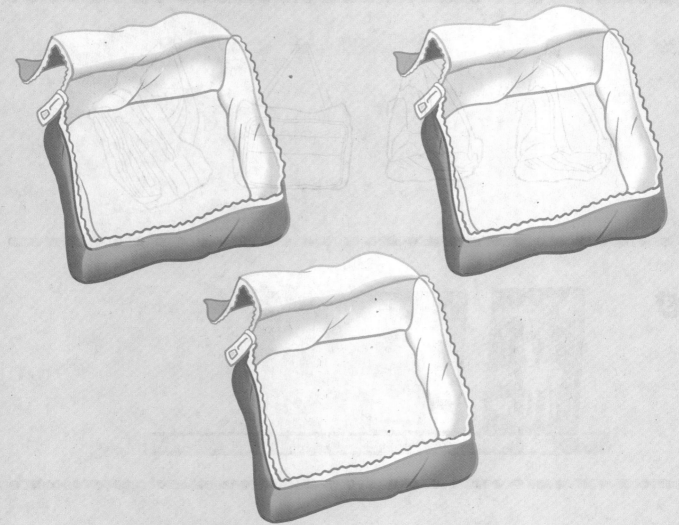

DIRECTIONS These lunch boxes are alike. Draw in one lunch box something that you like to eat. Now circle the lunch box that is different.

G

Alike and Different

DIRECTIONS **1.** Color the markers so they match the color of the cup.
2. Color the book bags that are alike by shape.
3. This classroom needs some books. Draw a book that is a different size.

Name _____

Sort by Color

 1

 2

Order Numbers to 10

3

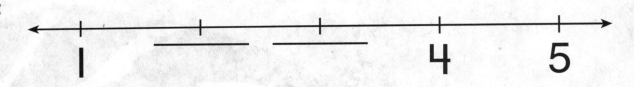

1 ___ ___ 4 5

4

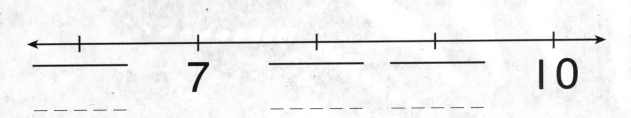

___ 7 ___ ___ 10

DIRECTIONS **1.** Circle the fruits that are red.
2. Circle the shapes that are blue. **3–4.** Write
the missing numbers on the number line.

FAMILY NOTE: This page checks your
child's understanding of important skills
needed for success in Chapter 7.

© Houghton Mifflin Harcourt

278 two hundred seventy-eight

FLORIDA BENCHMARKS
Vocabulary Power

different

alike

DIRECTIONS The ladybugs are alike. Three of the ladybugs have something that make them different. Circle those ladybugs and tell why they are different. Talk about how the butterflies are different.

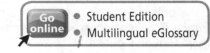

Go online • Student Edition
• Multilingual eGlossary

Game At the Farm

© Houghton Mifflin Harcourt

DIRECTIONS Use the picture to play I Spy with a partner. Decide who will go first. Player 1 looks at the picture, selects an object, and tells Player 2 the color of the object. Player 2 must guess what Player 1 sees. Once Player 2 guesses correctly, it is his or her turn to choose an object and have Player 1 guess.

Name _____

Above, Below, Over, and Under

Essential Question How can you describe objects using the positional words *above*, *below*, *over*, and *under*?

MA.K.G.2.1 Describe, sort and re-sort objects using a variety of attributes such as shape, size, and position.

Listen and Draw REAL WORLD

DIRECTIONS Place a red cube above the fence and a blue cube below the fence. Draw and color the cubes. Mark an X over the fence and draw a circle under the fence.

Chapter 7 • Lesson 1

two hundred eighty-one **281**

Share and Show

DIRECTIONS   1. Place a red cube below the water. Place a red cube under the ladder. Use red to draw these cubes. Place a blue cube over the window. Place a blue cube above the horses. Use blue to draw these cubes.

DIRECTIONS **2.** Place a red cube above the pond. Place a blue cube below the table. Draw and color the cubes. **3.** Place a blue cube under the tree. Place a red cube over the house. Draw and color the cubes.

1

2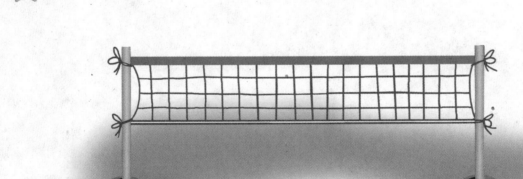

DIRECTIONS **1.** Circle the ball that is above the net. Mark an X on the water bottle that is below the net. **2.** Draw to show things that might be over and under the net. Tell about your drawing.

HOME ACTIVITY • Tell your child you are thinking of something in the room that is above, below, over, or under another object. Have your child tell you what the object is.

FOR MORE PRACTICE:
Florida Benchmarks Practice Book, pp. P157–P158

Name _____

Beside, Next To, and Between

Essential Question How can you describe objects using the positional words *beside*, *next to*, and *between*?

MA.K.G.2.1 Describe, sort and re-sort objects using a variety of attributes such as shape, size, and position.

Listen and Draw REAL WORLD

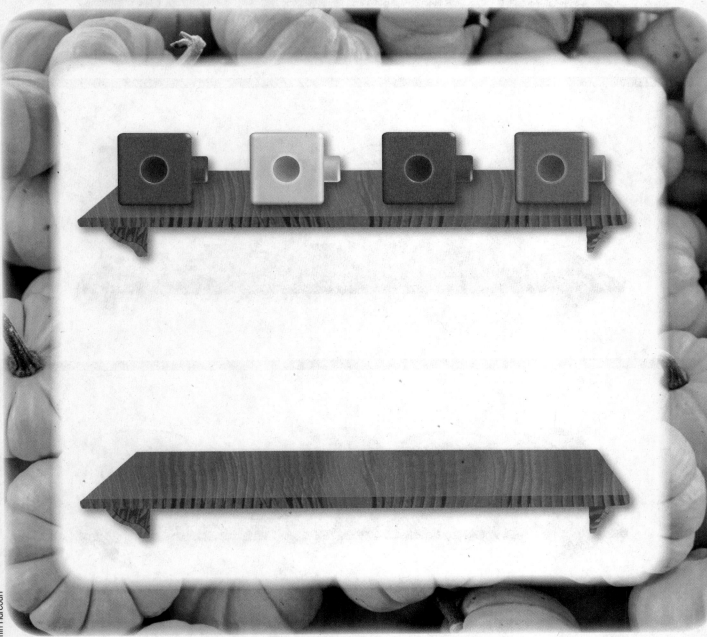

DIRECTIONS Which color cube is between the blue cubes? Which color cube is next to the green cube? Which color cube is beside the yellow cube? On the other shelf, place a red cube beside a blue cube. Now place a yellow cube between the red cube and the blue cube. Draw and color the cubes.

Chapter 7 • Lesson 2

two hundred eighty-five **285**

Share and Show

1

2

3 ✓

DIRECTIONS **I.** Place a cube on the football that is next to the basket. Mark an X on that football. **2.** Place a cube on the pumpkin that is between two paint cans. Mark an X on that pumpkin. **3.** Place a cube on the ball that is beside a cap. Mark an X on that ball.

286 two hundred eighty-six

DIRECTIONS 4. Place a cube on the pumpkin that is between two other pumpkins. Mark an X on that pumpkin. Place a cube on the pumpkin next to the hay. Circle that pumpkin. Place a cube next to the tree. Draw the cube.

Chapter 7 • Lesson 2

⭐ 2

DIRECTIONS **1.** Circle the watering can that is between the pumpkins. Mark an X on the pumpkin that is next to the hay. **2.** Draw to show objects that are beside, next to, and between other objects. Tell about your drawing.

HOME ACTIVITY • Use language such as *beside*, *next to*, and *between* to describe the position of one object in relation to another.

288 two hundred eighty-eight

© Houghton Mifflin Harcourt

Name _____

Inside and Outside

Essential Question How can you describe objects using the positional words *inside* and *outside*?

MA.K.G.2.1 Describe, sort and re-sort objects using a variety of attributes such as shape, size, and position.

DIRECTIONS Place a red counter inside the fence. Place a yellow counter outside the fence. Draw and color the counters.

Chapter 7 • Lesson 3

Share and Show

1

2

3 ✓

4 ✓

DIRECTIONS 1. Place a counter on the child who is outside the house. Circle that child. **2.** Place a counter on the bird that is inside the nest. Circle that bird. **3.** Place a counter on the squirrel that is inside the tree. Circle that squirrel. **4.** Place a counter on the dog that is outside the dog house. Circle that dog.

290 two hundred ninety

5

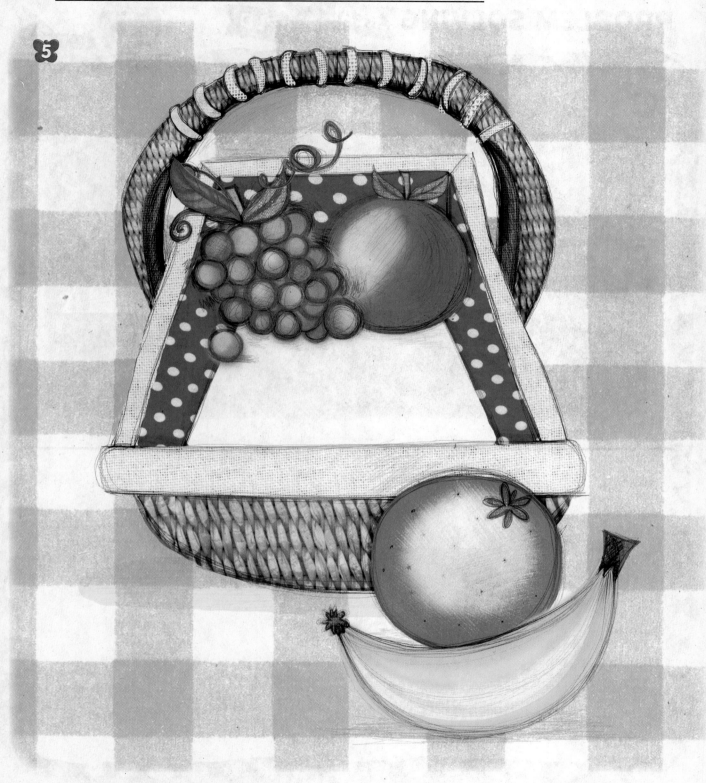

DIRECTIONS 5. Place a red counter inside the basket.
Use red to draw the counter. Place a yellow counter outside
the basket. Use yellow to draw the counter.

1.

2. ☆

DIRECTIONS 1. Mark an X on the bucket that is inside the sandbox. Circle the shovel that is outside the sandbox. **2.** Draw to show what you know about objects that are inside and outside other objects. Tell about your drawing.

HOME ACTIVITY • Give your child a block and a dish that is large enough to hold the block. Ask your child to place the block inside the dish. Then ask your child to place the block outside the dish.

FOR MORE PRACTICE:
Florida Benchmarks Practice Book, pp. P161–P162

Name _____

Describe Positions

Essential Question How can you describe positions using the words *left* and *right*?

MA.K.G.2.1 Describe, sort and re-sort objects using a variety of attributes such as shape, size, and position.

Listen and Draw

 Left

Right

DIRECTIONS Trace your left hand on the left side of the mat. Trace your right hand on the right side of the mat.

Share and Show

Left

Right

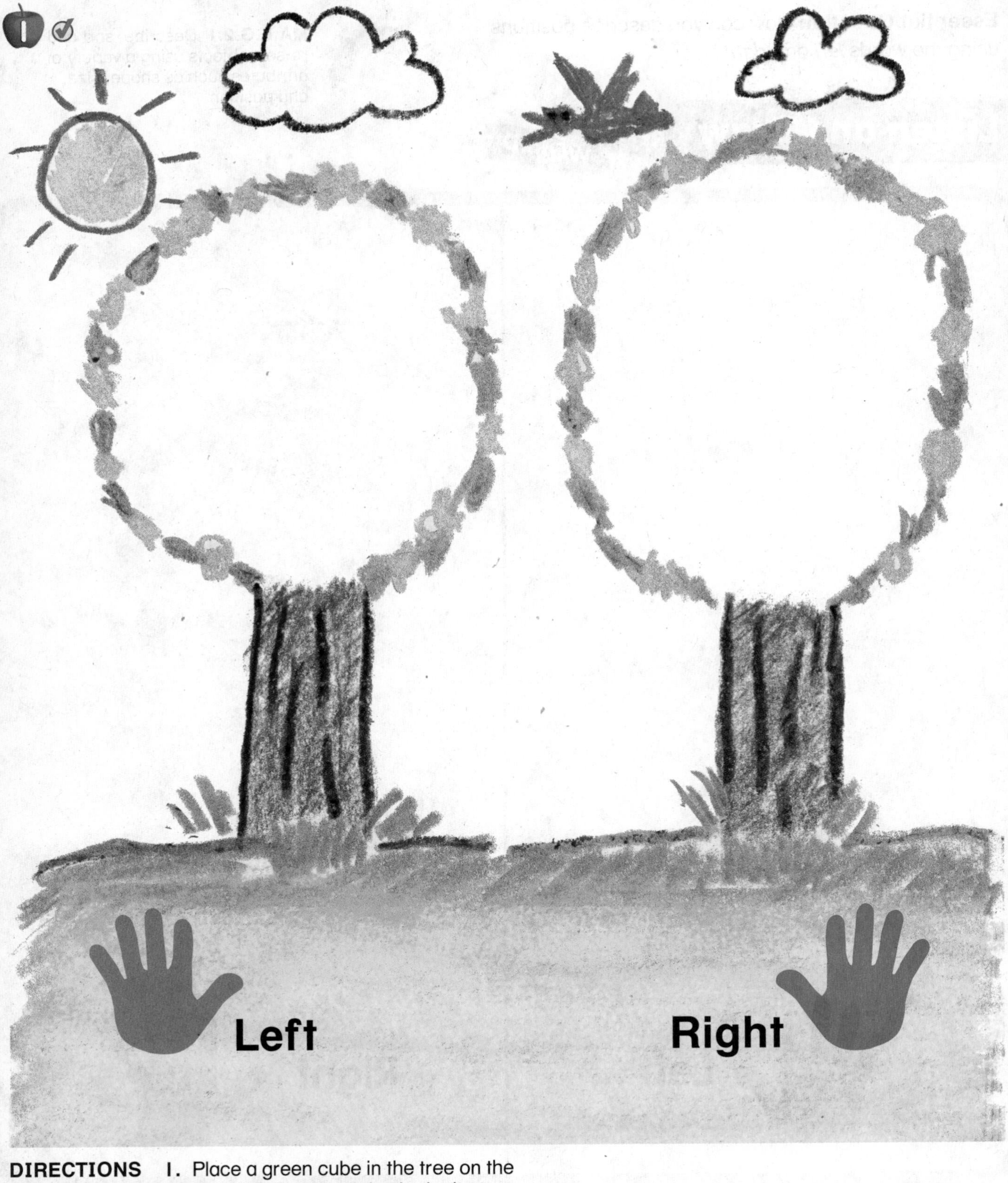

DIRECTIONS 1. Place a green cube in the tree on the left. Draw and color the cube. Place a red cube in the tree on the right. Draw and color the cube.

Name _____

Left

Right

DIRECTIONS 2. Place a counter on START. Move forward two steps. Turn right and move forward two steps. Use red to color that stepping stone. Place the counter back on START. Move forward four steps. Turn left and move forward one step. Use green to color that stepping stone.

FOR MORE PRACTICE: Florida Benchmarks Practice Book, pp. P163–P164

Mid-Chapter Checkpoint

Concepts

Test Prep

○   ○   ○   ○

DIRECTIONS 1. Draw an apple in the tree on the right. Draw a bird in the tree on the left. MA.K.G.2.1 **2.** Circle the pumpkin beside the flowers. Mark an X on the pumpkin next to the door. MA.K.G.2.1 **3.** Circle the dog that is outside the dog house. Mark an X on the dog that is inside the dog house. MA.K.G.2.1 **4.** Mark under the picture that shows the butterfly above the bird. MA.K.G.2.1

Name _____

Sort and Describe by Shape

Essential Question How can you sort and describe objects by shape?

MA.K.G.2.1 Describe, sort and re-sort objects using a variety of attributes such as shape, size, and position.

Listen and Draw

© Houghton Mifflin Harcourt

DIRECTIONS Choose a shape. Sort a handful of shapes by that shape and not that shape. Draw and color the shapes.

Share and Show

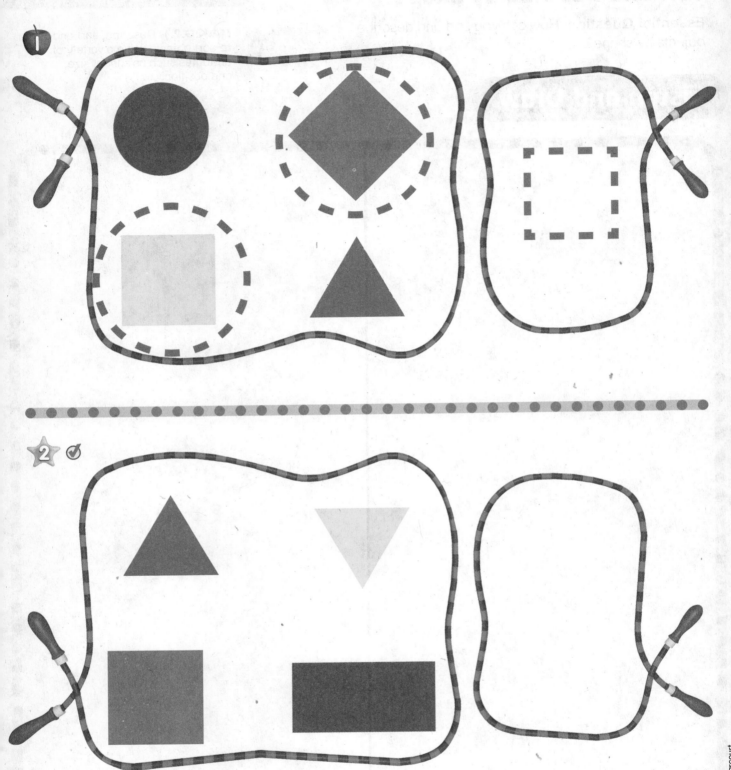

DIRECTIONS 1–2. Use shapes to match each shape.
Circle the two shapes that are alike. Draw that shape in
the workspace. Tell what you know about that shape.

298 two hundred ninety-eight

Name _____

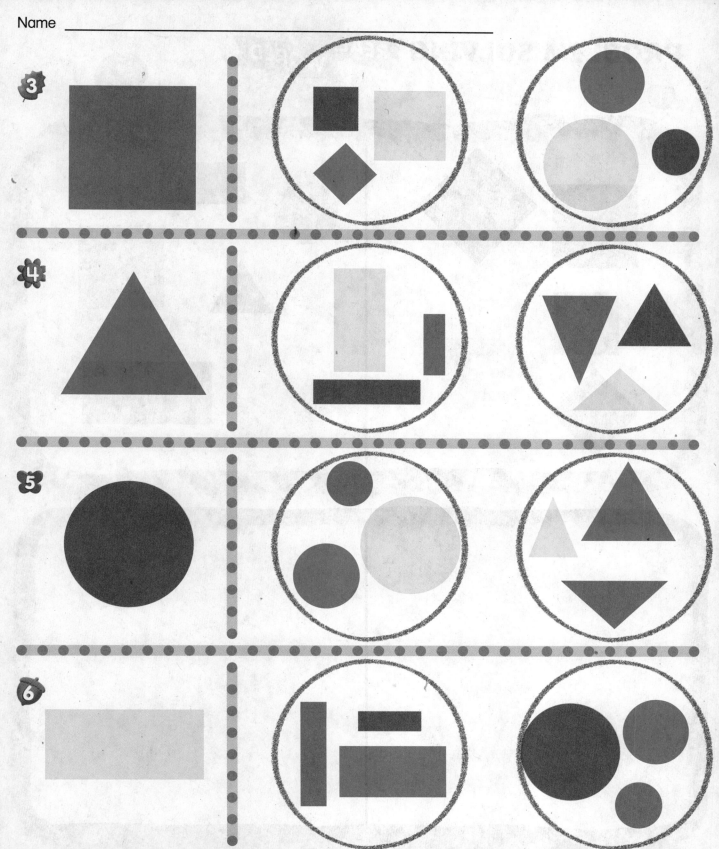

DIRECTIONS 3–6. Look at the shape at the beginning of the row. Tell what you know about the shape. Mark an X on the group in which the shape belongs.

Chapter 7 • Lesson 5   two hundred ninety-nine **299**

PROBLEM SOLVING REAL WORLD

DIRECTIONS **1.** Which group is sorted by shape? Mark an X on that group. **2.** Draw to show what you know about sorting by shape.

HOME ACTIVITY • Help your child find a household object to match each of the following shapes: a square, a triangle, a rectangle, and a circle.

300 three hundred

FOR MORE PRACTICE:
Florida Benchmarks Practice Book, pp. P165–P166

Name _____

Sort and Describe by Size

Essential Question How can you sort and describe objects by size?

MA.K.G.2.I Describe, sort and re-sort objects using a variety of attributes such as shape, size, and position.

Listen and Draw

DIRECTIONS Sort shapes by size. Draw and color the shapes.

Share and Show

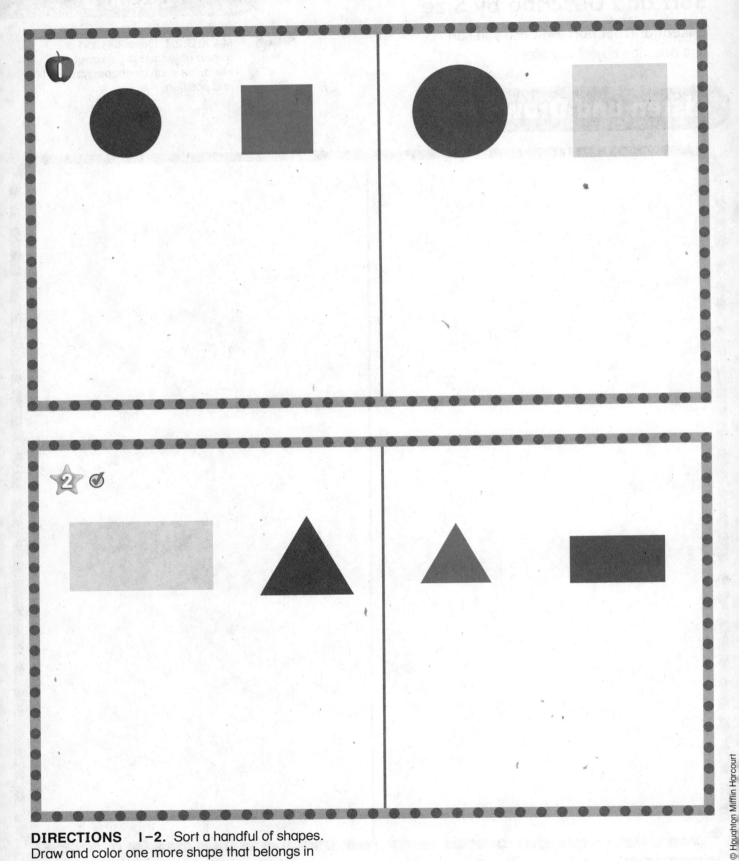

DIRECTIONS 1–2. Sort a handful of shapes.
Draw and color one more shape that belongs in
each group. Tell how the shapes are alike.

302 three hundred two

© Houghton Mifflin Harcourt

3

4

5

6

DIRECTIONS **3–6.** Mark an X on the object that does not belong.

Chapter 7 • Lesson 6

three hundred three **303**

PROBLEM SOLVING REAL WORLD

DIRECTIONS **1.** How are these groups sorted? Draw one more shape in each group. **2.** Draw to show what you know about sorting by size.

HOME ACTIVITY • Provide your child with big and small versions of the same objects, such as spoons, shoes, shirts, or stuffed animals. Ask your child to tell which objects are big and which are small.

FOR MORE PRACTICE:
Florida Benchmarks Practice Book, pp. P167–P168

Name _____

Sort and Describe by Position

Essential Question How can you sort and describe objects by position?

MA.K.G.2.1 Describe, sort and re-sort objects using a variety of attributes such as shape, size, and position.

Listen and Draw

DIRECTIONS Use position words such as *above*, *below*, *over*, *under*, *beside*, *next to*, *between*, *left* and *right* to describe the position of a cube. Mark an X on the red cube that is above the green cube. Circle the blue cube that is below the yellow cube.

Share and Show

DIRECTIONS 1. Place green cubes on the ones on the shelf. Place a red cube above each green cube. Place a blue cube below each green cube. Place a yellow cube beside each set of cubes. Color the cubes. Describe the position of the cubes.

306 three hundred six

Name _____

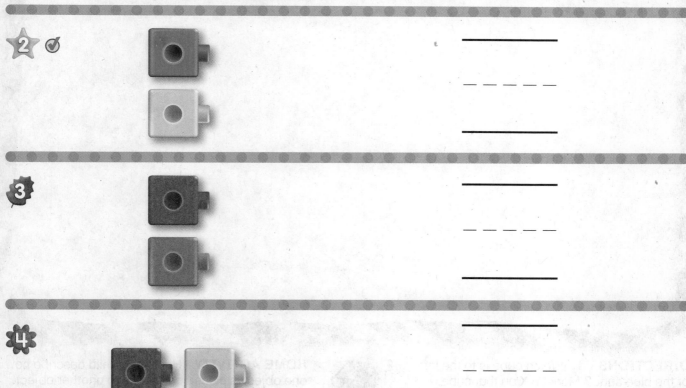

⭐ **2** ☑

3

4

DIRECTIONS **2.** How many red cubes are above the yellow cubes? **3.** How many green cubes are below the blue cube? **4.** How many yellow cubes are to the right of the blue cube?

Chapter 7 • Lesson 7

three hundred seven **307**

PROBLEM SOLVING REAL WORLD

1

2

DIRECTIONS   1. Which cube is to the left of the blue cube? Mark an X on that cube. Which cube is between two other cubes? Circle that cube. Which cube is to the right of the blue cube? Draw a line under that cube.   **2.** Draw to show 6 cubes in 3 rows. Each row has a different number of cubes. The top row has the fewest cubes. Describe the position of each cube.

HOME ACTIVITY • Have your child describe how one object is placed compared to another object.

308   three hundred eight

FOR MORE PRACTICE:
Florida Benchmarks Practice Book, pp. P169–P170

Sort in Different Ways

Essential Question How can you sort the same objects in different ways?

MA.K.G.2.1 Describe, sort and re-sort objects using a variety of attributes such as shape, size, and position.

Listen and Draw

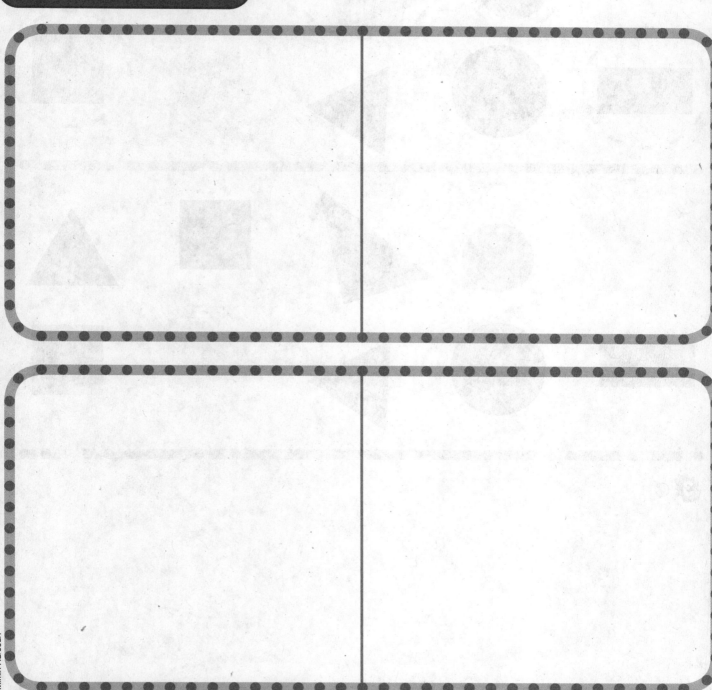

DIRECTIONS Use shapes to sort. Draw the shapes. Then use those same shapes to sort in a different way. Draw the shapes. Tell how you sorted the shapes.

Share and Show

1.

2.

3. ✓

© Houghton Mifflin Harcourt

DIRECTIONS **1.** Circle all the red shapes. **2.** Circle all the triangles. **3.** Mark an X on the shape that is circled in both Exercise 1 and Exercise 2. Draw and color the shape.

310 three hundred ten

Name _____

4.

5.

6.

DIRECTIONS **4.** Circle all the green shapes. **5.** Circle all
the squares. **6.** Mark an X on the shape that is circled in both
Exercise 4 and Exercise 5. Draw and color the shape.

Chapter 7 • Lesson 8

PROBLEM SOLVING REAL WORLD

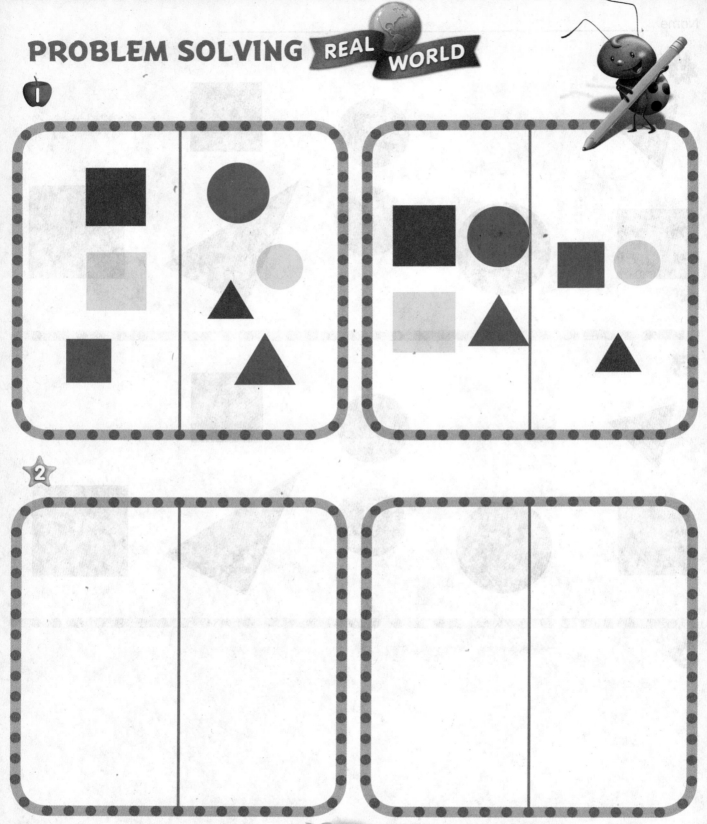

DIRECTIONS **1.** How are these sets of objects alike? Which mat shows the set sorted by shape? Mark an X on that mat. Which mat shows the set sorted by size? Circle that mat. **2.** Draw to show what you know about sorting the same objects in different ways.

HOME ACTIVITY • Have your child sort a handful of toys in one way, such as by size, color, or shape. Then have him or her re-sort those same toys in a different way.

FOR MORE PRACTICE:
Florida Benchmarks Practice Book, pp. P171–P172

Name _____

Sort by Two Attributes

Essential Question How can you solve problems by sorting?

MA.K.G.2.1 Describe, sort and re-sort objects using a variety of attributes such as shape, size, and position.

🔑 Unlock the Problem

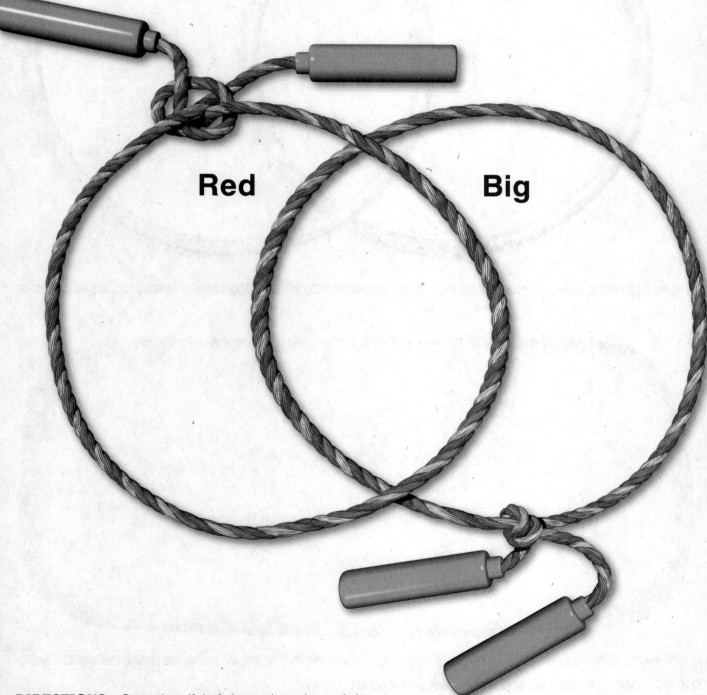

Red

Big

DIRECTIONS Sort a handful of shapes by color and size. Draw the shapes. Where does a big red shape belong?

Share and Show

1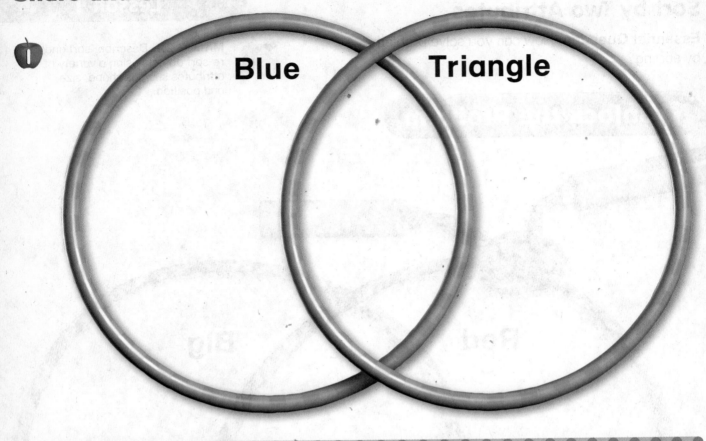

Blue   Triangle

2 ✓

DIRECTIONS **1.** Sort the shapes by color and shape. Draw the shapes. **2.** What shape is in both sorting rings? Draw and color that shape.

3

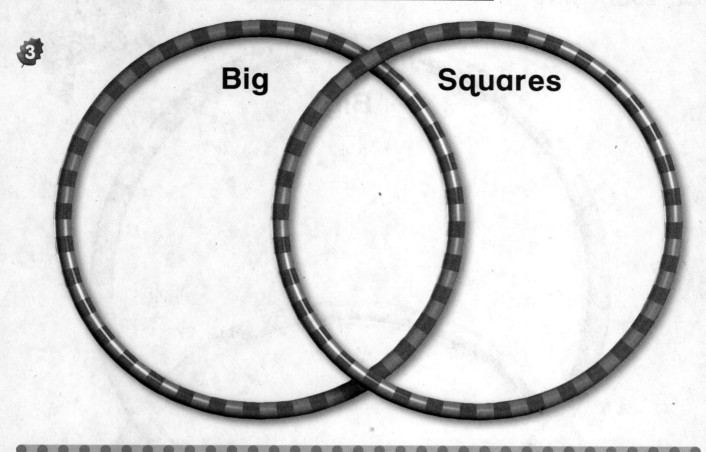

Big   **Squares**

4

DIRECTIONS **3.** Sort the shapes by size and shape. Draw the shapes. **4.** What shape is in both sorting rings? Draw and color that shape.

Chapter 7 • Lesson 9   three hundred fifteen **315**

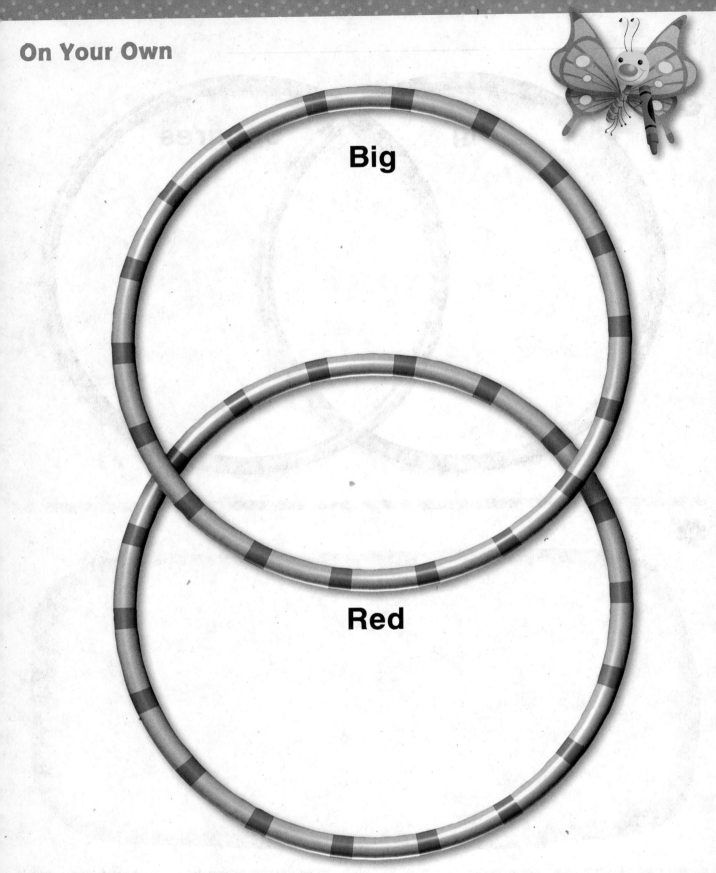

Big

Red

DIRECTIONS What shapes could be in the sorting rings? Draw the shapes.

HOME ACTIVITY • Have your child sort a group of household objects in two ways. Have him or her tell which objects could be in both groups.

FOR MORE PRACTICE:
Florida Benchmarks Practice Book, pp. P173–P174

Sort by Own Rule

Essential Question How can you sort objects?

MA.K.G.2.1 Describe, sort and re-sort objects using a variety of attributes such as shape, size, and position.

Listen and Draw

DIRECTIONS Use blocks to sort. Draw and color the blocks. Tell how you sorted the blocks.

Share and Show

PURPLE · YELLOW · RED · BLUE · BLACK · BROWN · GREEN

PINK

ORANGE

ORANGE

PINK

GREEN · BROWN · BLACK · BLUE · RED · YELLOW · PURPLE

DIRECTIONS 1. Place a handful of crayons on the workspace. Sort the crayons on the workmat by your own rule. Draw and color the crayons.

Name _____

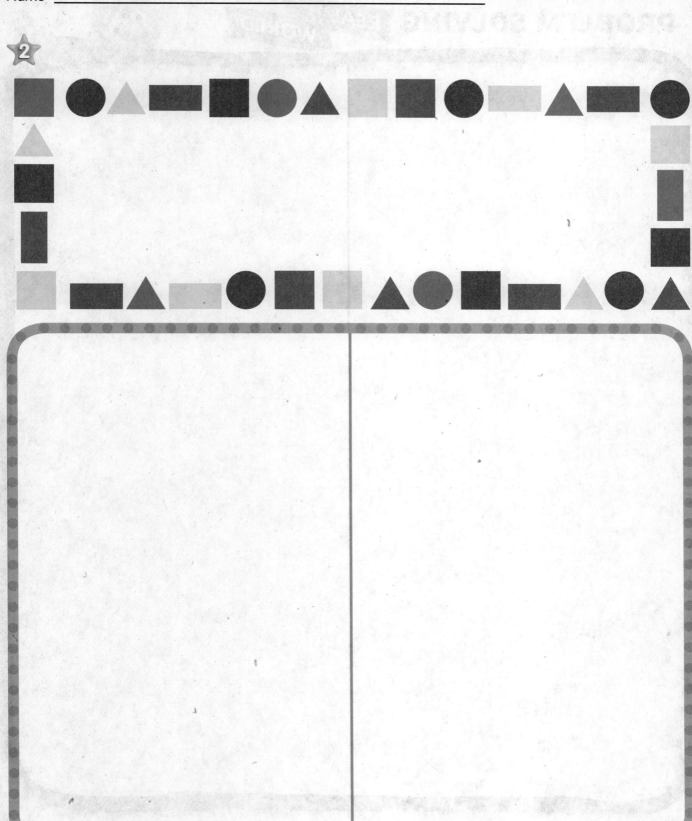

DIRECTIONS 2. Place a handful of shapes on the workspace.
Sort the shapes on the workmat by your own rule. Draw and color the shapes.

PROBLEM SOLVING REAL WORLD

DIRECTIONS Place a handful of objects on the workspace. Sort the objects by your own rule. Draw and color the objects.

HOME ACTIVITY • Have your child sort a mixed group of household objects, such as forks and spoons or coins, into two groups and describe how he or she sorted the objects.

FOR MORE PRACTICE:
Florida Benchmarks Practice Book, pp. P175–P176

Chapter 7 Review/Test

Vocabulary

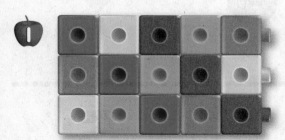

over

under

between

Concepts

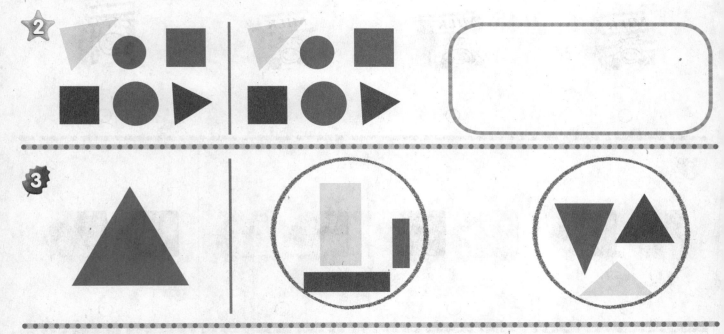

DIRECTIONS 1. Draw a line from the orange cube under the blue cube to the word *under*. Draw a line from the yellow cube over the red cube to the word *over*. Draw a line from the green cube that is between the red and blue cubes to the word *between*. (MA.K.G.2.1) 2. Circle all the green shapes on the left. Circle all the squares on the right. Mark an X on the shape that is circled in both sets. Draw and color the shape. (MA.K.G.2.1) 3. Look at the shape at the beginning of the row. Mark an X on the group of shapes in which it belongs. (MA.K.G.2.1) 4. Mark an X on the truck that does not belong. (MA.K.G.2.1)

5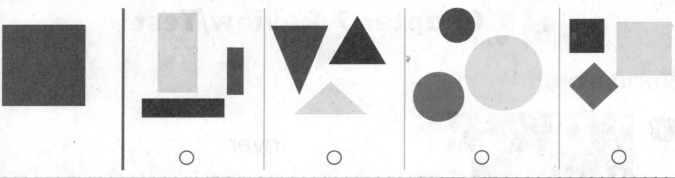

○   ○   ○   ○

6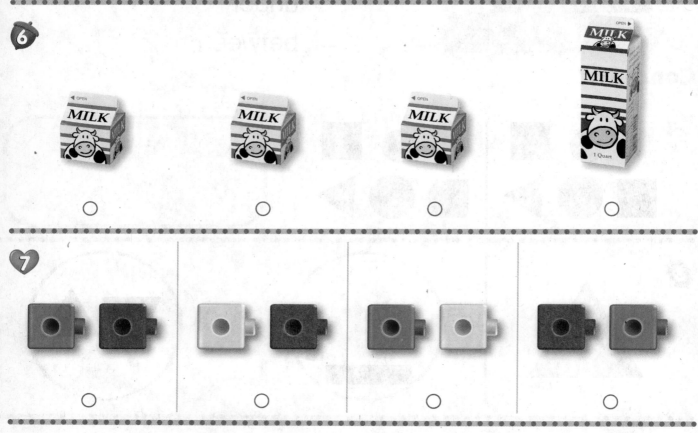

○   ○   ○   ○

7

○   ○   ○   ○

8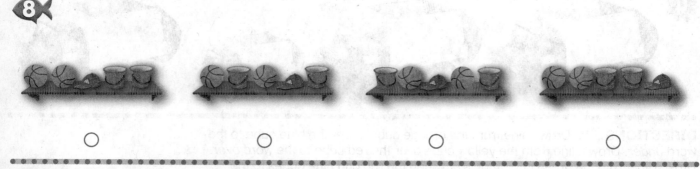

○   ○   ○   ○

DIRECTIONS **5.** Look at the shape at the beginning of the row. Mark under the group of shapes in which it belongs. (MA.K.G.2.1) **6.** Mark under the object that does not belong. (MA.K.G.2.1) **7.** Mark under the two cubes that show the red cube to the left of the blue cube. (MA.K.G.2.1) **8.** Mark under the picture that shows the bucket between the balls. (MA.K.G.2.1)

9

10

11

12

DIRECTIONS **9.** Mark under the picture that shows the bird above the tree. (MA.K.G.2.1) **10.** Mark under the picture that shows the apple inside the basket (MA.K.G.2.1) **11.** Mark under the picture that shows the bee to the right of the flower. (MA.K.G.2.1) **12.** Mark under the picture that shows a yellow cube next to a green cube. (MA.K.G.2.1)

Chapter 7

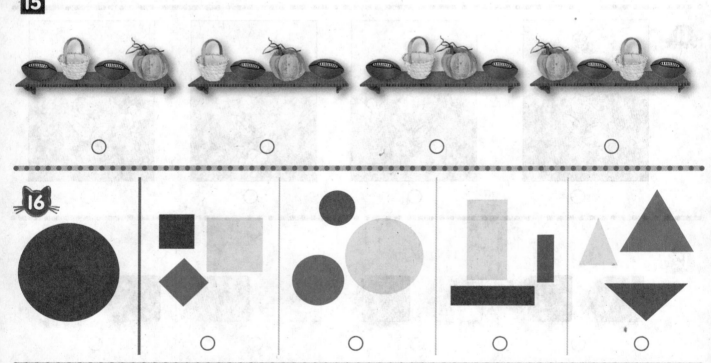

DIRECTIONS **13.** Mark under the object that does not belong. (MA.K.G.2.1)
14. Mark under the two cubes that show a blue cube above a red cube.
(MA.K.G.2.1)   **15.** Mark under the picture that shows the basket beside the
pumpkin. (MA.K.G.2.1)   **16.** Look at the shape at the beginning of the row.
Mark under the group of shapes in which it belongs. (MA.K.G.2.1)

324   three hundred twenty-four

Two-Dimensional Shapes

Name _____

Count Objects to 5

  |  |

_____   _____   _____

- - - - - - -   - - - - - - -   - - - - - - -

_____   _____   _____

Sort by Shape

  |

  |

Sort by Size

DIRECTIONS 1–3. Count and tell how many. Write the number. 4–5. Look at the shape at the beginning of the row. Mark an X on the group of shapes in which it belongs. 6. Mark an X on the object that does not belong.

FAMILY NOTE: This page checks your child's understanding of important skills needed for success in Chapter 8.

FLORIDA BENCHMARKS
Vocabulary Power

sort

DIRECTIONS Circle the box that is sorted by green vegetables. Mark an x on the box that is sorted by purple fruit.

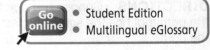

Student Edition
Multilingual eGlossary

Game

Follow the Shapes

DIRECTIONS Choose a shape from Start. Follow the path that has the same shapes. Draw a line to show the path.

Identify and Name Squares

Essential Question How can you identify squares?

MA.K.G.2.2 Identify, name, describe and sort basic two-dimensional shapes such as squares, triangles, circles, rectangles, hexagons, and trapezoids.

Listen and Draw

square	not a square

DIRECTIONS Place a handful of shapes on the page. Identify and name the squares. Trace and color the shapes on the sorting mat.

Share and Show

DIRECTIONS I. Mark an X on all the squares.

Name _____

DIRECTIONS 2. Color the squares in the picture.

Chapter 8 · Lesson 1

three hundred thirty-one **331**

PROBLEM SOLVING REAL WORLD

DIRECTIONS   I. Which shapes are squares? Mark an X on those shapes.
2. Draw shapes to show what you know about a square. Tell about your drawing.

HOME ACTIVITY • Have your child show you a household object that is shaped like a square.

FOR MORE PRACTICE:
Florida Benchmarks Practice Book, pp. P183–P184

Describe Squares

Essential Question How can you describe a square?

MA.K.G.2.2 Identify, name, describe and sort basic two-dimensional shapes such as squares, triangles, circles, rectangles, hexagons, and trapezoids.

Listen and Draw

vertex

side

DIRECTIONS Use your finger to trace around the square. Talk about the number of sides and the number of vertices. Draw an arrow pointing to another vertex. Trace around the sides.

Chapter 8 • Lesson 2

three hundred thirty-three **333**

square

 ✓

_____ **vertices**

 ✓

_____ **sides**

DIRECTIONS I. Place a counter on each corner, or vertex. Write how many corners, or vertices. 2. Place a counter on each side. Write how many sides.

Name _____

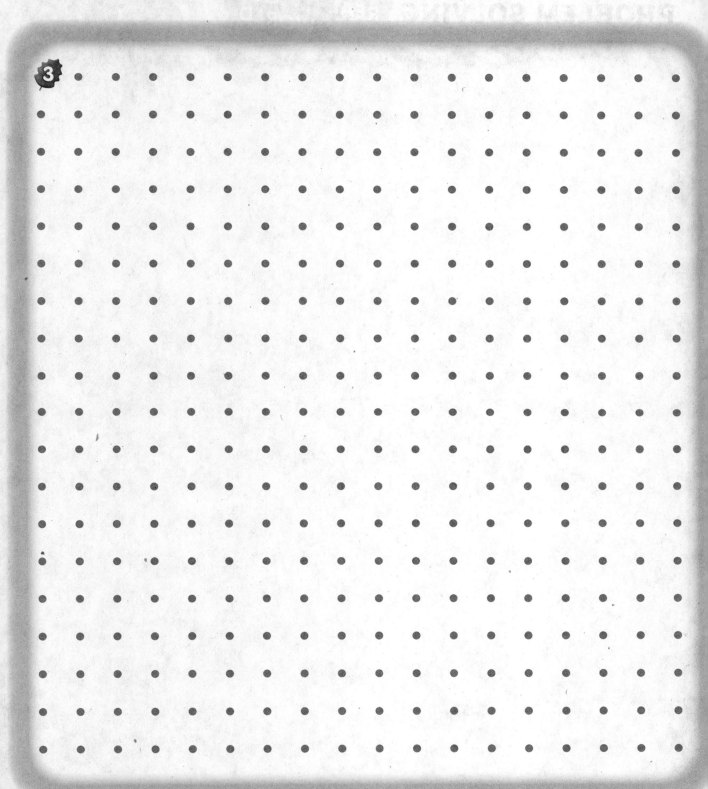

DIRECTIONS **3.** Draw and color a square.

Chapter 8 · Lesson 2

PROBLEM SOLVING REAL WORLD

DIRECTIONS I have 4 equal sides and 4 vertices. What shape am I? Draw the shape. Tell about your shape.

HOME ACTIVITY • Have your child describe a square.

336 three hundred thirty-six

FOR MORE PRACTICE:
Florida Benchmarks Practice Book, pp. P185–P186

Identify and Name Triangles

Essential Question How can you identify triangles?

MA.K.G.2.2 Identify, name, describe and sort basic two-dimensional shapes such as squares, triangles, circles, rectangles, hexagons, and trapezoids.

Listen and Draw REAL WORLD

triangle	not a triangle

DIRECTIONS Place a handful of shapes on the page. Identify and name the triangles. Trace and color the shapes on the sorting mat.

Share and Show

DIRECTIONS 1. Mark an X on all the triangles.

DIRECTIONS **2.** Color the triangles in the picture.

PROBLEM SOLVING REAL WORLD

1

2

DIRECTIONS **1.** Which shapes are triangles? Mark an X on those shapes. **2.** Draw shapes to show what you know about a triangle. Tell about your drawing.

HOME ACTIVITY • Have your child show you a household object that is shaped like a triangle.

FOR MORE PRACTICE:
Florida Benchmarks Practice Book, pp. P187–P188

Describe Triangles

Essential Question How can you describe a triangle?

MA.K.G.2.2 Identify, name, describe and sort basic two-dimensional shapes such as squares, triangles, circles, rectangles, hexagons, and trapezoids.

Listen and Draw

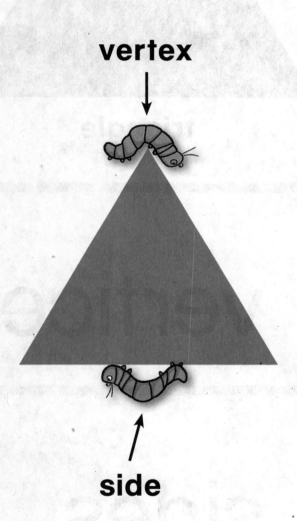

vertex

side

DIRECTIONS Use your finger to trace around the triangle. Talk about the number of sides and the number of vertices. Draw an arrow pointing to another vertex. Trace around the sides.

Share and Show

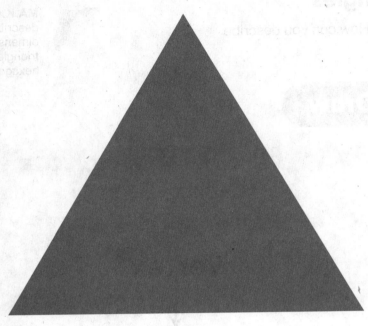

triangle

① ☑ ____ **vertices**

② ☑ ____ **sides**

DIRECTIONS **1.** Place a counter on each corner, or vertex. Write how many corners, or vertices. **2.** Place a counter on each side. Write how many sides.

Name _____

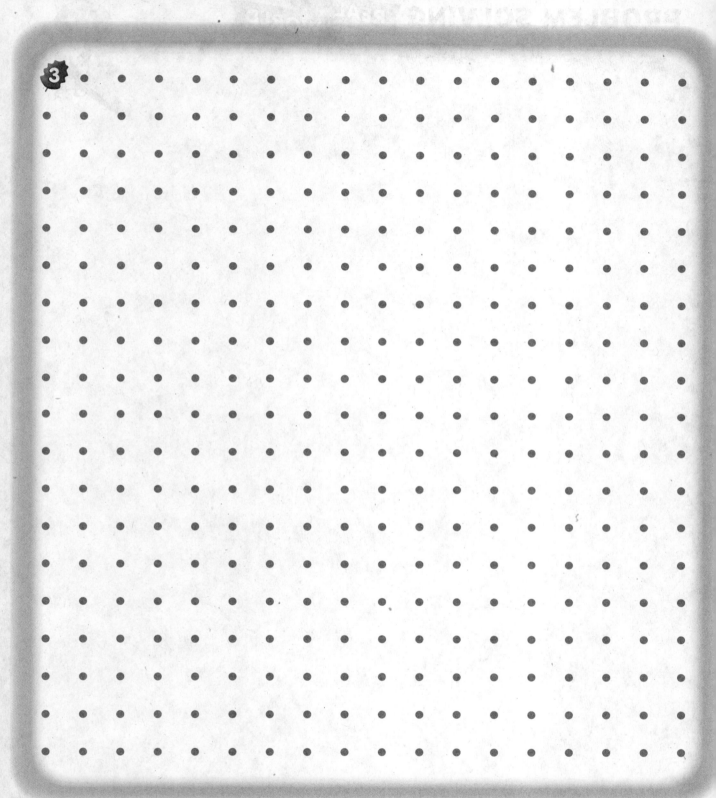

DIRECTIONS **3.** Draw and color a triangle.

PROBLEM SOLVING REAL WORLD

DIRECTIONS I have 3 sides and 3 vertices. What shape am I? Draw the shape. Tell about your shape.

HOME ACTIVITY • Have your child describe a triangle.

Identify and Name Circles

Essential Question How can you identify circles?

MA.K.G.2.2 Identify, name, describe and sort basic two-dimensional shapes such as squares, triangles, circles, rectangles, hexagons, and trapezoids.

Listen and Draw REAL WORLD

circle | not a circle

DIRECTIONS Place a handful of shapes on the page. Identify and name the circles. Trace and color the shapes on the sorting mat.

Share and Show

Name _____

DIRECTIONS 2. Color the circles in the picture.

Chapter 8 • Lesson 5

three hundred forty-seven **347**

PROBLEM SOLVING

REAL WORLD

 1

 2

DIRECTIONS **1.** Which shape is a circle? Mark an X on that shape. **2.** Draw to show what you know about a circle. Tell about your drawing.

HOME ACTIVITY • Have your child show you a household object that is shaped like a circle.

348 three hundred forty-eight

FOR MORE PRACTICE:
Florida Benchmarks Practice Book, pp. P191–P192

Describe Circles

Essential Question How can you describe a circle?

MA.K.G.2.2 Identify, name, describe and sort basic two-dimensional shapes such as squares, triangles, circles, rectangles, hexagons, and trapezoids.

Listen and Draw  REAL WORLD

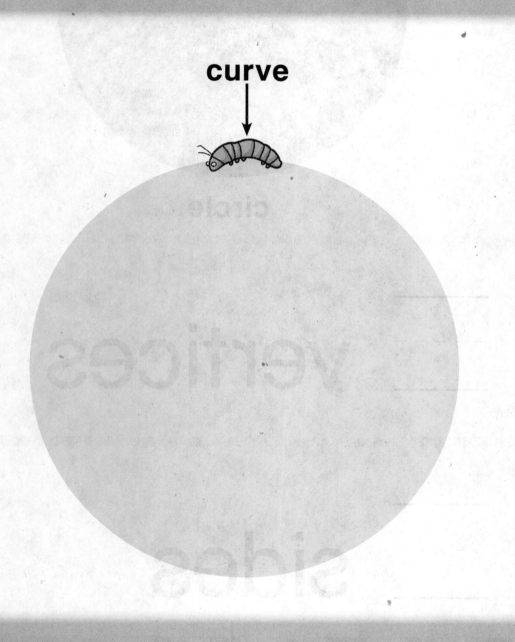

curve

DIRECTIONS Use your finger to trace around the circle. Talk about the number of straight sides and the number of vertices. Trace around the curve.

© Houghton Mifflin Harcourt

circle

1 ✓

_____ **vertices**

2 ✓

_____ **sides**

DIRECTIONS 1. Place a counter on each corner, or vertex. Write how many corners, or vertices. 2. Place a counter on each straight side. Write how many straight sides.

3

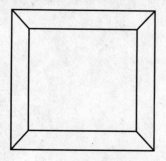  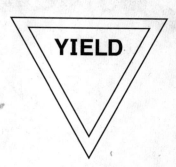

4

© Houghton Mifflin Harcourt

DIRECTIONS **3.** Color the object that is shaped like a circle. **4.** Look around the classroom for an object that is shaped like a circle. Draw and color that object.

PROBLEM SOLVING REAL WORLD

DIRECTIONS I have 0 vertices. What shape am I? Draw the shape. Tell about your shape.

HOME ACTIVITY • Have your child describe a circle.

352 three hundred fifty-two

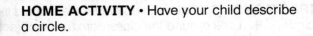

FOR MORE PRACTICE:
Florida Benchmarks Practice Book, pp. P193–P194

© Houghton Mifflin Harcourt

Identify and Name Rectangles

Essential Question How can you identify rectangles?

MA.K.G.2.2 Identify, name, describe and sort basic two-dimensional shapes such as squares, triangles, circles, rectangles, hexagons, and trapezoids.

Listen and Draw REAL WORLD

rectangle	not a rectangle

DIRECTIONS Place a handful of shapes on the page. Identify and name the rectangles. Trace and color the shapes on the sorting mat.

Share and Show

Name _____

PROBLEM SOLVING REAL WORLD

DIRECTIONS **1.** Which shapes are rectangles? Mark an X on those shapes. **2.** Draw shapes to show what you know about a rectangle. Tell about your drawing.

HOME ACTIVITY • Have your child show you a household object that is shaped like a rectangle.

FOR MORE PRACTICE:
Florida Benchmarks Practice Book, pp. P195–P196

Describe Rectangles

Essential Question How can you describe a rectangle?

MA.K.G.2.2 Identify, name, describe and sort basic two-dimensional shapes such as squares, triangles, circles, rectangles, hexagons, and trapezoids.

Listen and Draw

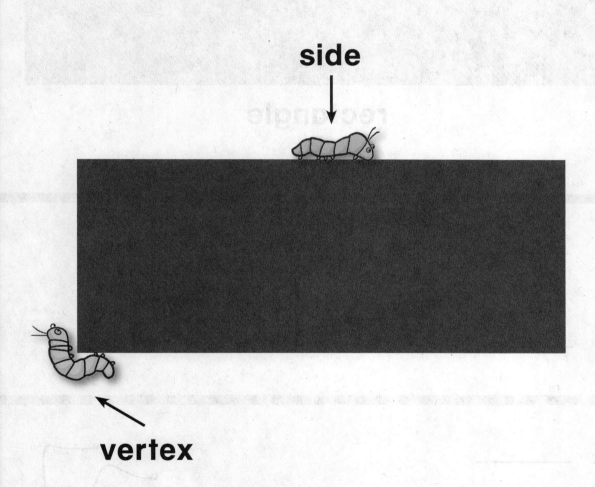

side

vertex

DIRECTIONS Use your finger to trace around the rectangle. Talk about the number of sides and the number of vertices. Draw an arrow pointing to another vertex. Trace around the sides.

Chapter 8 • Lesson 8

three hundred fifty-seven **357**

rectangle

 _____ vertices

 _____ sides

DIRECTIONS 1. Place a counter on each corner, or vertex. Write how many corners, or vertices. 2. Place a counter on each side. Write how many sides.

Name _____

3

DIRECTIONS 3. Draw and color a rectangle.

Chapter 8 • Lesson 8   **FOR MORE PRACTICE:**
Florida Benchmarks Practice Book, pp. P197–P198   three hundred fifty-nine **359**

© Houghton Mifflin Harcourt

Mid-Chapter Checkpoint

Concepts

_____

- - - - - - - sides

_____

_____

- - - - - - - vertices

_____

2

_____

- - - - - - - sides

_____

_____

- - - - - - - vertices

_____

3

4

Test Prep

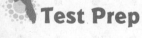

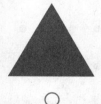   ○      ○      ○      ○

DIRECTIONS **I–2.** Place a counter on each corner or vertex. Write how many vertices. Place a counter on each side. Write how many sides. (MA.K.G.2.2) **3.** Mark an X on all of the circles. (MA.K.G.2.2) **4.** Mark an X on all of the rectangles. (MA.K.G.2.2) **5.** Mark under the shape that is a triangle. (MA.K.G.2.2)

360 three hundred sixty

Name _____

Sort Two-Dimensional Shapes

Essential Question How can you sort shapes?

MA.K.G.2.2 Identify, name, describe and sort basic two-dimensional shapes such as squares, triangles, circles, rectangles, hexagons, and trapezoids.

Listen and Draw

DIRECTIONS Place a handful of shapes on the page. Listen to the sorting rule. Sort the shapes by the number of vertices. Draw the shapes on the sorting mat.

Chapter 8 • Lesson 9

three hundred sixty-one **361**

Share and Show

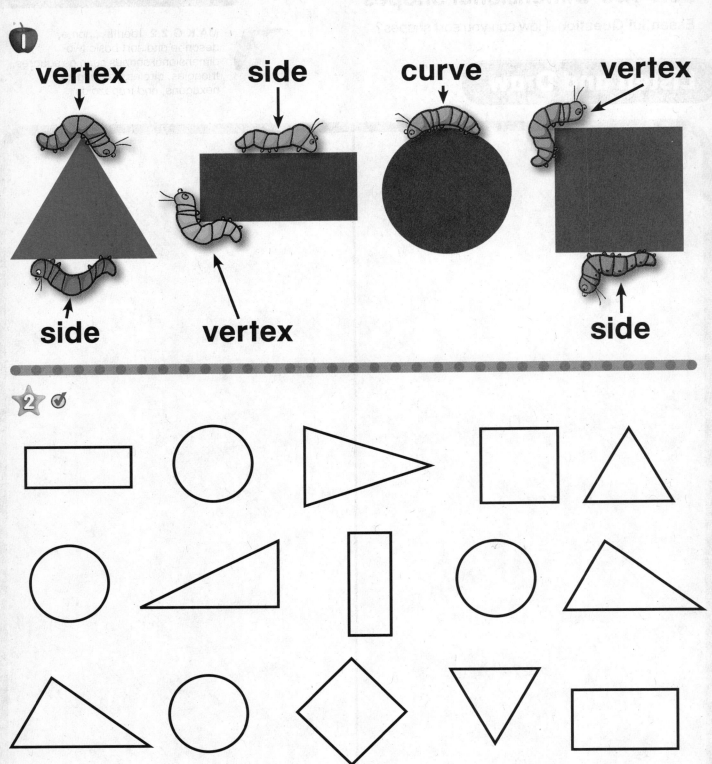

vertex

side

curve

vertex

side

vertex

side

DIRECTIONS 1. Look at the worms and the shapes. Use the words *vertex*, *curve*, and *side* to describe each shape. 2. Use green to color the shapes with four vertices and four sides. Use blue to color the shapes with curves. Use red to color the shapes with three vertices and three sides.

Name _____

3

DIRECTIONS **3.** Place a handful of shapes on the page. Listen to the sorting rule. Sort the shapes by the number of sides. Draw the shapes on the sorting mat.

Chapter 8 · Lesson 9

1

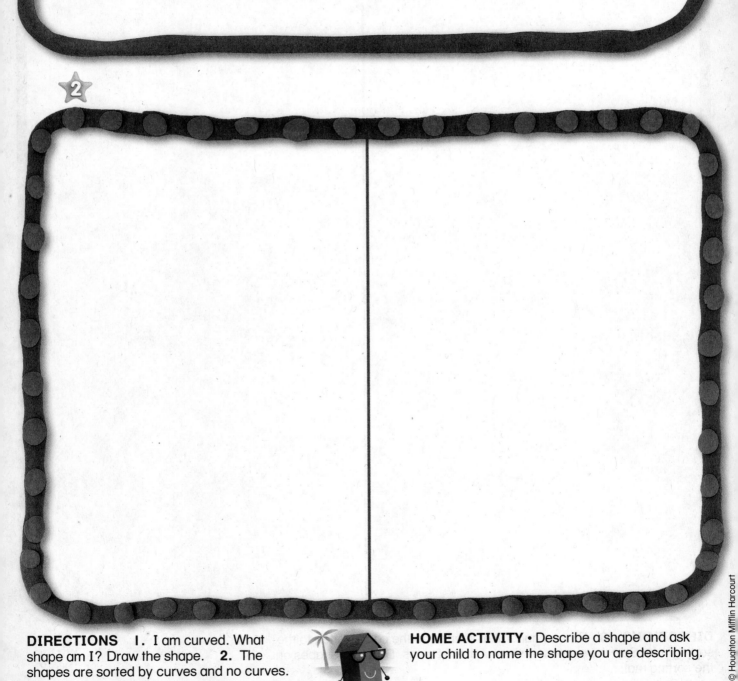

2

DIRECTIONS **1.** I am curved. What shape am I? Draw the shape. **2.** The shapes are sorted by curves and no curves. Draw to show the shapes.

HOME ACTIVITY • Describe a shape and ask your child to name the shape you are describing.

FOR MORE PRACTICE:
Florida Benchmarks Practice Book, pp. P199–P200

Name _____

Identify and Describe More Shapes

Essential Question How can you identify and describe other shapes?

MA.K.G.2.2 Identify, name, describe and sort basic two-dimensional shapes such as squares, triangles, circles, rectangles, hexagons, and trapezoids.

Listen

hexagon

trapezoid

rhombus

rhombus

DIRECTIONS Use your finger to trace around the shapes. Talk about the number of sides and the number of vertices. Talk about equal sides and parallel sides.

Chapter 8 • Lesson 10

three hundred sixty-five **365**

Share and Show

triangle

rhombus

trapezoid

DIRECTIONS 1–3. Place a shape that matches beside the shape. Draw and color the shape. Describe the shape. Tell the name of the shape.

366 three hundred sixty-six

Name _____

square

rhombus

hexagon

DIRECTIONS   4–6. Place a shape that matches beside the shape. Draw and color the shape. Describe the shape. Tell the name of the the shape.

Chapter 8 · Lesson 10   three hundred sixty-seven **367**

PROBLEM SOLVING REAL WORLD

❶

⭐2

DIRECTIONS **1.** I have 4 sides. Two pairs of sides are parallel. What shape am I? Draw the shape. **2.** I have 4 sides. One pair of sides is parallel. The other pair of sides is not. What shape am I? Draw the shape.

HOME ACTIVITY • Have your child find a household object that is shaped like one of the shapes in this lesson. Then have him or her name the shape.

368 three hundred sixty-eight

FOR MORE PRACTICE:
Florida Benchmarks Practice Book, pp. P201–P202

Name _____

Sort More Shapes

Essential Question How can you sort other shapes?

MA.K.G.2.2 Identify, name, describe and sort basic two-dimensional shapes such as squares, triangles, circles, rectangles, hexagons, and trapezoids.

Listen and Draw

DIRECTIONS Place a handful of shapes on the page. Talk about the different ways you could sort these shapes. Listen to the sorting rule. Draw the shapes on the sorting mat.

Chapter 8 • Lesson 11

three hundred sixty-nine **369**

Share and Show

1

3 sides	not 3 sides

2 ✓

4 sides	not 4 sides

DIRECTIONS 1–2. Place a handful of shapes on the page. Sort the shapes by the number of sides. Draw and color the shapes on the sorting mat.

Name _____

5 sides	not 5 sides

6 sides	not 6 sides

DIRECTIONS   3–4. Place a handful of shapes on the page.
Sort the shapes by the number of sides. Draw and color the
shapes on the sorting mat.

Chapter 8 • Lesson 11

three hundred seventy-one **371**

PROBLEM SOLVING REAL WORLD

DIRECTIONS I have more than 4 sides. I have more than 4 vertices. Draw to show what shape I am.

HOME ACTIVITY • Have your child describe some of the shapes in this lesson.

FOR MORE PRACTICE:
Florida Benchmarks Practice Book, pp. P203–P204

Name _____

Combine Shapes to Make New Shapes

Essential Question How can you use shapes to make new shapes?

MA.K.G.2.5 Use basic shapes, spatial reasoning, and manipulatives to model objects in the environment and to construct more complex shapes.

Listen and Draw

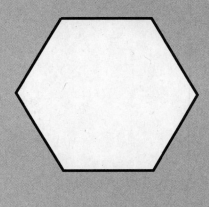

DIRECTIONS Use triangles to fill the outlines of the shapes. Draw and color the triangles you used.

Chapter 8 · Lesson 12

Share and Show

1

2 ✓

DIRECTIONS **1.** Use some or all of the shapes to make a larger square. Trace around the shapes to draw the square. **2.** Use some or all of the shapes to make a rectangle. Trace around the shapes to draw the rectangle.

374 three hundred seventy-four

© Houghton Mifflin Harcourt

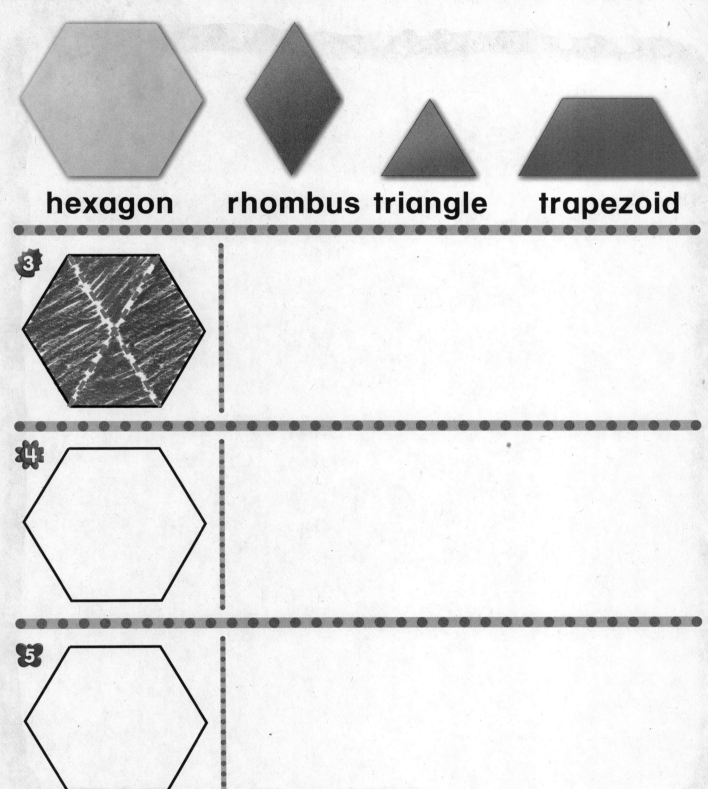

hexagon **rhombus** **triangle** **trapezoid**

3

4

5

DIRECTIONS **3.** Use 2 green and 2 blue shapes to cover the outline of the yellow shape. Draw and color the shapes. **4–5.** Draw other ways to use the shapes to cover the outline of the yellow shape.

Chapter 8 • Lesson 12   three hundred seventy-five **375**

PROBLEM SOLVING

DIRECTIONS **I.** Two of me can be put together to create a hexagon. What shape am I? Draw the shape.

HOME ACTIVITY • Have your child combine shapes to create another shape, and then tell you about the shape.

376 three hundred seventy-six

FOR MORE PRACTICE:
Florida Benchmarks Practice Book, pp. P205–P206

Name _____

Draw a Picture

Essential Question How can you draw
a picture using shapes?

MA.K.G.2.5 Use basic shapes,
spatial reasoning, and manipulatives
to model objects in the environment
and to construct more
complex shapes.

🔑 Unlock the Problem

DIRECTIONS Which shapes could fill the outline of the beach hut?
Draw and color the shapes you used.

Chapter 8 • Lesson 13

three hundred seventy-seven **377**

Share and Show

DIRECTIONS **1.** Which shapes could fill the outline of the flower? Draw and color the shapes you used.

378 three hundred seventy-eight

DIRECTIONS **2.** Which shapes could fill the outline of the dog? Draw and color the shapes you used.

Chapter 8 · Lesson 13

On Your Own

❶

②

DIRECTIONS **1.** I am 2 orange shapes with 1 red shape on top. What picture do I make? Draw the picture. **2.** Use the same shapes to make a different picture. Draw the picture.

HOME ACTIVITY • Have your child use shapes to draw a picture of something.

FOR MORE PRACTICE:
Florida Benchmarks Practice Book, pp. P207–P208

Chapter 8 Review/Test

Vocabulary

side

vertex

Concepts

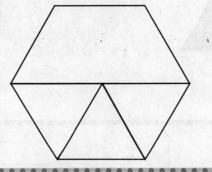

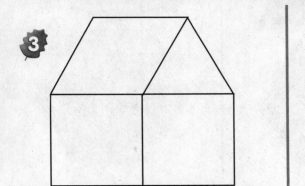

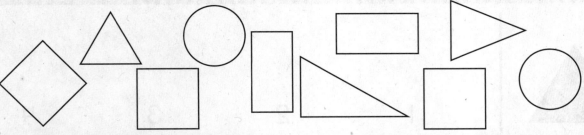

DIRECTIONS 1. Draw a line from the word *side* to a side of each shape. Draw a line from the word *vertex* to a vertex, or corner, of each shape. (MA.K.G.2.2) **2–3.** Use shapes to fill the outline of the shape. Draw and color the shapes you used. (MA.K.G.2.5) **4.** Use red to color the shapes with four vertices and four sides. Use green to color the shapes with curves. Use blue to color the shapes with three vertices and three sides. (MA.K.G.2.2)

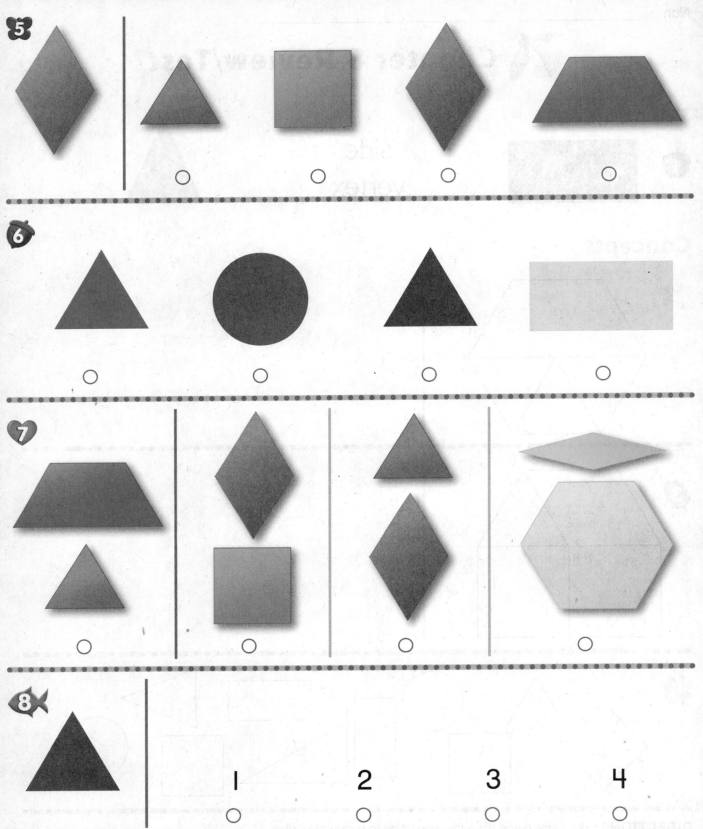

DIRECTIONS **5.** Mark under the shape that matches the one at the beginning of the row. (MA.K.G.2.2) **6.** Mark under the rectangle. (MA.K.G.2.2) **7.** Mark under the group of shapes that all have four sides. (MA.K.G.2.2) **8.** Mark under the number that shows how many sides the triangle has. (MA.K.G.2.2)

382 three hundred eighty-two

9 ○   ○   ○   ○

10 | 1   2   3   4

○   ○   ○   ○

11 ○   ○   ○   ○

12 ○   ○   ○   ○

DIRECTIONS 9. Mark under the shape that is a circle. **(MA.K.G.2.2)**
10. Mark under the number that shows how many vertices the rectangle has.
(MA.K.G.2.2) 11. Mark under the group that has all squares. **(MA.K.G.2.2)**
12. Mark under the shape that has zero vertices. **(MA.K.G.2.2)**

13

○   ○   ○   ○

14

○   ○   ○   ○

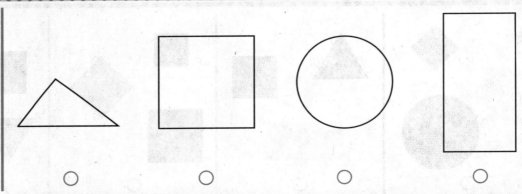

15

○   ○   ○   ○

16

○   ○   ○   ○

DIRECTIONS **13.** Mark under the shape that has four equal sides and four vertices. (MA.K.G.2.2) **14.** Mark under the shape that is a triangle. (MA.K.G.2.2) **15.** Mark under the shape that belongs with the shapes at the beginning of the row. (MA.K.G.2.2) **16.** Mark under the shape that matches the shape at the beginning of the row. (MA.K.G.2.2)

384 three hundred eighty-four

Three-Dimensional Shapes

Hallandale Beach

Name _____

Show What You Know

Identify Shapes

Describe Shapes

_____

- - - - - - - - - - -

_____ sides

- - - - - - - - - - -

_____ vertices

_____

- - - - - - - - - - -

_____ sides

- - - - - - - - - - -

_____ vertices

Sort Shapes

DIRECTIONS 1. Color the squares red. Color the triangles blue. 2-3. Look at the shape. Write how many sides. Write how many vertices. 4. Mark an X on the shapes with three sides.

FAMILY NOTE: This page checks your child's understanding of important skills needed for success in Chapter 9.

Name _____

rectangle

circle

square

triangle

DIRECTIONS Mark an X on the food shaped like a circle. Draw a line under the food shaped like a square. Circle the food shaped like a triangle.

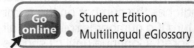

Go online • Student Edition
• Multilingual eGlossary

© Houghton Mifflin Harcourt

Game

Number Picture

DIRECTIONS Play with a partner. Decide who goes first. Toss the number cube. Color a shape in the picture that matches the number on the number cube. A player misses a turn if a number is rolled and all matching shapes are colored. Continue until all shapes in the picture are colored.

MATERIALS number cube (1–4), crayons

Identify and Describe Spheres

Essential Question How can you identify and describe spheres?

MA.K.G.2.3 Identify, name, describe, and sort three-dimensional shapes such as spheres, cubes and cylinders.

Listen and Draw REAL WORLD

sphere	not a sphere

DIRECTIONS Look at the shapes. Sort the shapes on the sorting mat. Draw the shapes. Describe the sphere.

Share and Show

1

sphere

flat surface

curved surface

  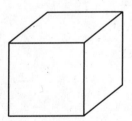

 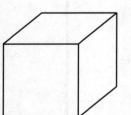 

DIRECTIONS 1. Look at the sphere. Circle the words that describe a sphere. 2. Color the spheres.

Name _____

DIRECTIONS **3.** Identify the objects that are shaped like a sphere. Mark an X on those objects.

Chapter 9 • Lesson 1

three hundred ninety-one **391**

PROBLEM SOLVING REAL WORLD

1

2

DIRECTIONS 1. I have a curved surface. Which shape am I? Mark an X on that shape. **2.** Draw to show what you know about a real object that is shaped like a sphere.

HOME ACTIVITY • Have your child identify and describe a household object that is shaped like a sphere.

392 three hundred ninety-two

FOR MORE PRACTICE:
Florida Benchmarks Practice Book, pp. P215–P216

Name _____

Identify and Describe Cubes

Essential Question How can you identify and describe cubes?

MA.K.G.2.3 Identify, name, describe, and sort three-dimensional shapes such as spheres, cubes and cylinders.

Listen and Draw

cube	not a cube

DIRECTIONS Look at the shapes. Sort the shapes on the sorting mat. Draw the shapes. Describe the cube.

Share and Show

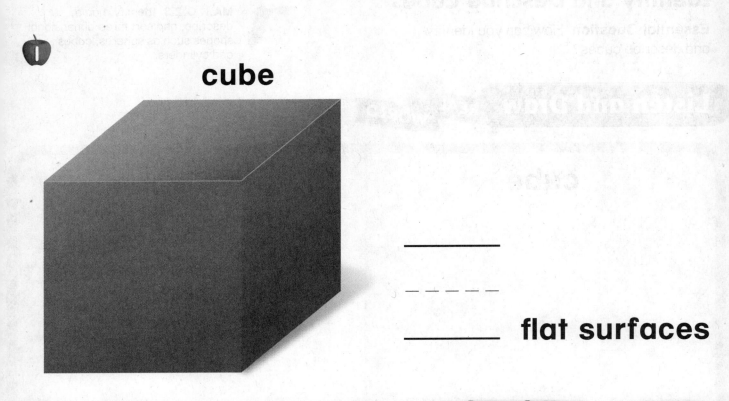

cube

_____

_ _ _ _ _ _ _ _ _

_____ **flat surfaces**

⭐2 ☑️

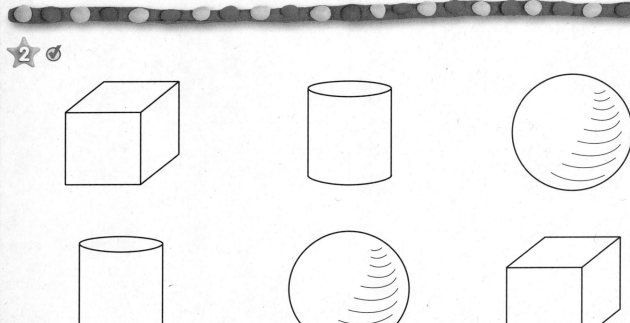

DIRECTIONS **1.** Look at the cube. Write how many flat surfaces. **2.** Color the cubes.

394 three hundred ninety-four

Name _____

DIRECTIONS **3.** Identify the objects that are shaped like a cube.
Mark an X on those objects.

DIRECTIONS 1. I have 6 flat surfaces. Which shape am I? Mark an X on that shape. 2. Draw to show what you know about a real object that is shaped like a cube.

HOME ACTIVITY • Have your child identify and describe a household object that is shaped like a cube.

FOR MORE PRACTICE:
Florida Benchmarks Practice Book, pp. P217–P218

Identify and Describe Cylinders

Essential Question How can you identify
and describe cylinders?

MA.K.G.2.3 Identify, name,
describe, and sort three-dimensional
shapes such as spheres, cubes
and cylinders.

Listen and Draw REAL WORLD

cylinder	not a cylinder

DIRECTIONS Look at the shapes. Sort the shapes on the
sorting mat. Draw the shapes. Describe the cylinder.

1

cylinder

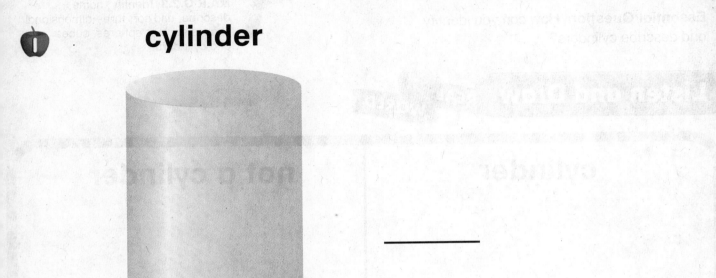

_____

- - - - - -

_____ **flat surfaces**

2 ✓

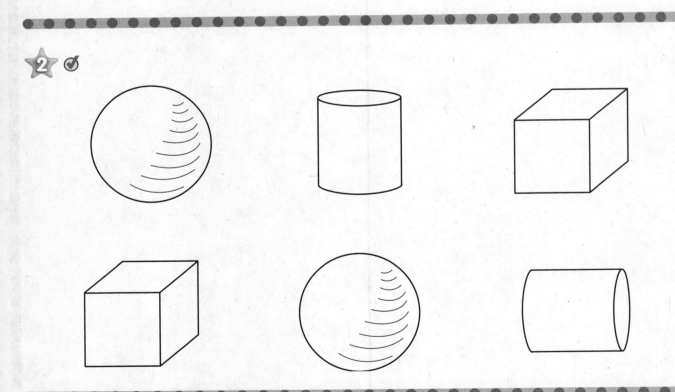

DIRECTIONS **I.** Look at the cylinder. Write how many flat surfaces. Tell about the curved surface. **2.** Color the cylinders.

Name _____

3

DIRECTIONS 3. Identify the objects that are shaped like a cylinder. Mark an X on those objects.

HOME ACTIVITY • Have your child identify and describe a household object that is shaped like a cylinder.

Chapter 9 • Lesson 3

FOR MORE PRACTICE:
Florida Benchmarks Practice Book, pp. P219–P220

three hundred ninety-nine **399**

Mid-Chapter Checkpoint

Concepts

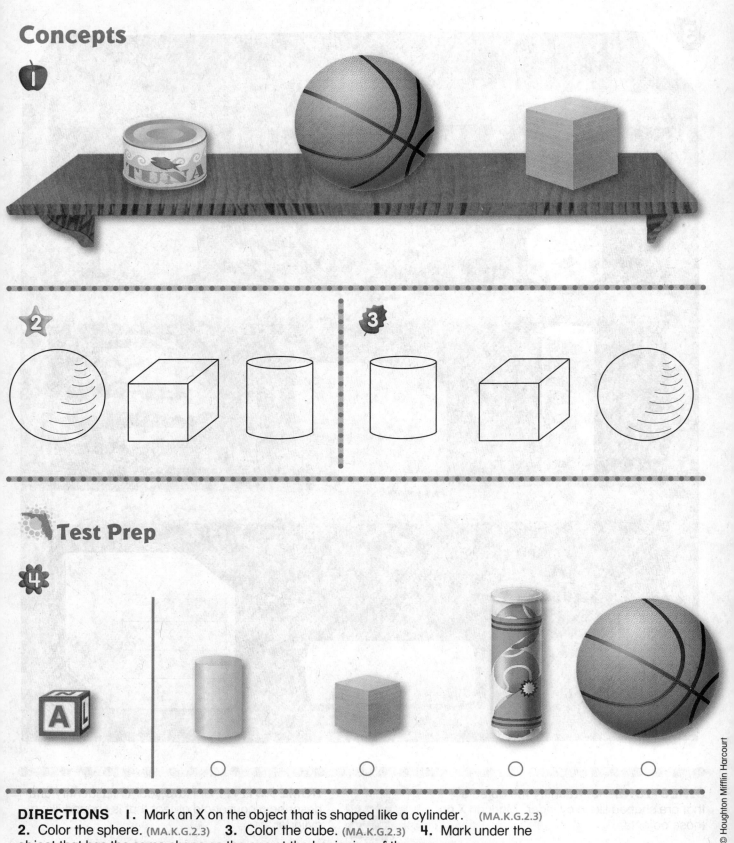

© Houghton Mifflin Harcourt

DIRECTIONS **1.** Mark an X on the object that is shaped like a cylinder. (MA.K.G.2.3)
2. Color the sphere. (MA.K.G.2.3) **3.** Color the cube. (MA.K.G.2.3) **4.** Mark under the
object that has the same shape as the one at the beginning of the row. (MA.K.G.2.4)

400 four hundred

Sort Three-Dimensional Shapes

Essential Question How can you sort three-dimensional shapes?

MA.K.G.2.3 Identify, name, describe, and sort three-dimensional shapes such as spheres, cubes and cylinders.

Listen and Draw REAL WORLD

does stack	does not stack

DIRECTIONS Look at the shapes. Sort the shapes on the sorting mat. Draw the shapes.

Share and Show

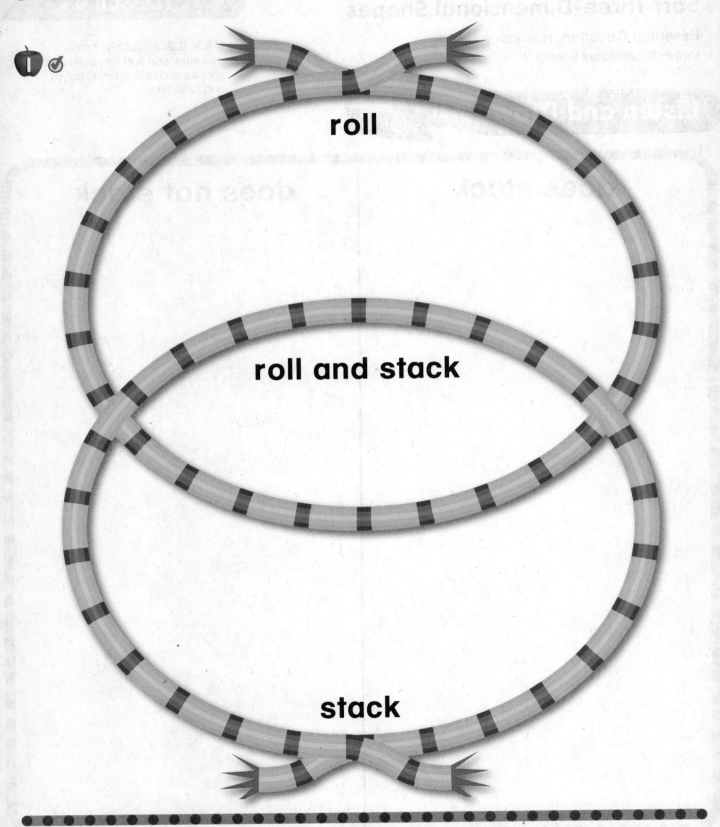

roll

roll and stack

stack

DIRECTIONS 1. Sort the shapes. Place the shape that rolls in the top section. Place the shape that stacks in the bottom section. Place the shape that rolls and stacks in the middle section. Draw the shapes.

402 four hundred two

2 roll

3  stack

4  slide

5  stack and slide

DIRECTIONS **2.** Mark an X on the shape that does not roll. **3.** Mark an X on the shape that does not stack. **4.** Mark an X on the shape that does not slide. **5.** Mark an X on the shape that does not stack and slide.

Chapter 9 • Lesson 4

PROBLEM SOLVING REAL WORLD

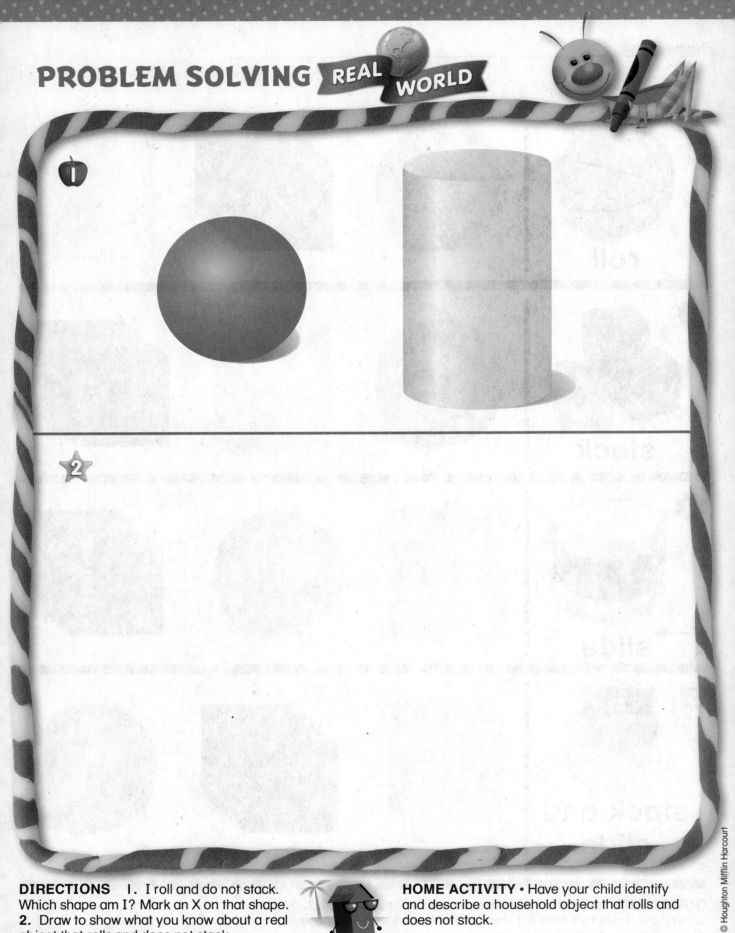

1.

2.

DIRECTIONS **1.** I roll and do not stack. Which shape am I? Mark an X on that shape. **2.** Draw to show what you know about a real object that rolls and does not stack.

HOME ACTIVITY • Have your child identify and describe a household object that rolls and does not stack.

404 four hundred four

FOR MORE PRACTICE:
Florida Benchmarks Practice Book, pp. P221–P222

© Houghton Mifflin Harcourt

Name _____

Sort by Attributes

Essential Question How can you solve problems by sorting?

MA.K.G.2.3 Identify, name, describe, and sort three-dimensional shapes such as spheres, cubes and cylinders.

🔑 Unlock the Problem

curved surface	no curved surface

DIRECTIONS Look at the shapes. Sort the shapes on the sorting mat. Draw the shapes.

Chapter 9 • Lesson 5

four hundred five **405**

Share and Show

Does It:	Stack?	Roll?	Slide?
sphere			
cube			
cylinder			

DIRECTIONS 1. Look at the shapes. Put a ✓ under Stack if the shape stacks. Put a ✓ under Roll if the shape rolls. Put a ✓ under Slide if the shape slides.

Name _____

Does It Have a:	Curved Surface?	Flat Surface?
sphere		
cube		
cylinder		

DIRECTIONS **2.** Look at the shapes. Put a ✓ under Curved Surface if the shape has a curved surface. Put a ✓ under Flat Surface if the shape has a flat surface.

Chapter 9 • Lesson 5

On Your Own

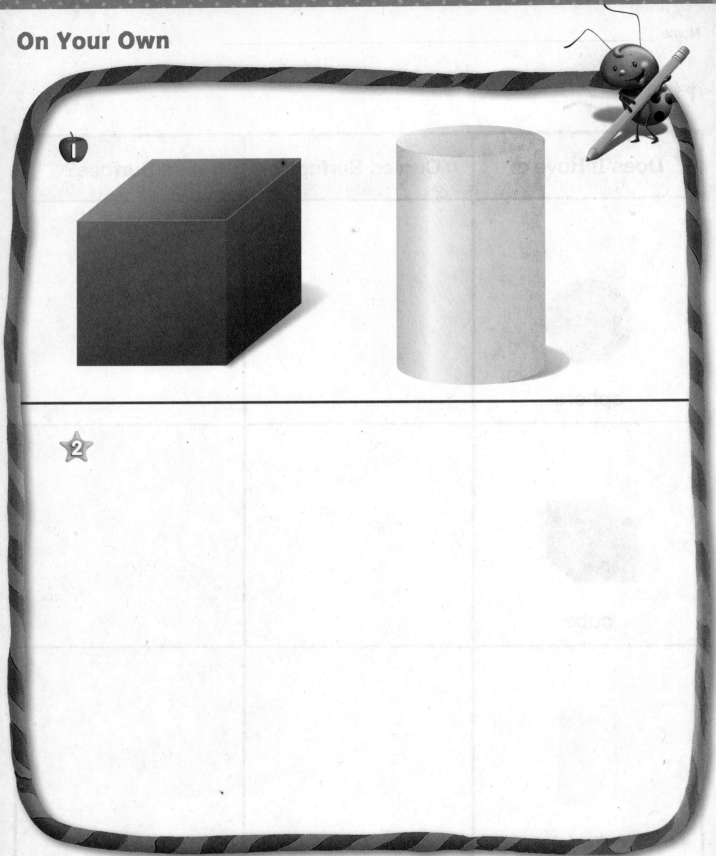

1

2

DIRECTIONS 1. I roll and stack. Which shape am I? Mark an X on that shape.
2. Draw to show what you know about a real object that rolls and stacks.

HOME ACTIVITY • Have your child identify and describe a household object that stacks and slides but does not roll.

FOR MORE PRACTICE:
Florida Benchmarks Practice Book, pp. P223–P224

Name _____

Describe Real World Geometric Shapes

Essential Question How can you describe geometric shapes in real world objects?

MA.K.G.2.4 Interpret the physical world with geometric shapes and describe it with corresponding vocabulary.

Listen REAL WORLD

DIRECTIONS Look at the picture. Tell about the shapes you see in the picture.

Share and Show

DIRECTIONS 1. Look at the picture. Describe the shape of the edge of the clock. Use blue to color the circle. Describe the shape of the edge of the bricks. Use brown to color the rectangles. Tell about any other shapes you see in the picture.

410 four hundred ten

DIRECTIONS **2.** Look at the picture. Describe the shapes in the rolling pin. Use red to color the spheres. Use yellow to color the cylinder. Tell about any other shapes you see in the picture.

DIRECTIONS **1.** I can stack and do not roll. What shape am I? Mark an X on that shape. **2.** Draw to show what you know about a real object that stacks and does not roll.

HOME ACTIVITY • Have your child find an object in your house and describe its shape.

412 four hundred twelve

FOR MORE PRACTICE:
Florida Benchmarks Practice Book, pp. P225–P226

Name _____

Use Shapes to Model Objects

Essential Question How can you use shapes to model objects?

MA.K.G.2.5 Use basic shapes, spatial reasoning, and manipulatives to model objects in the environment and to construct more complex shapes.

Listen and Draw REAL WORLD

DIRECTIONS Place the shapes on the page. Talk about the shapes, and the likeness to objects in the environment. Draw an object that looks like a shape.

Chapter 9 · Lesson 7

four hundred thirteen **413**

Share and Show

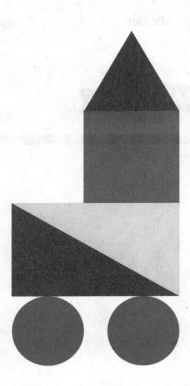

⭐2

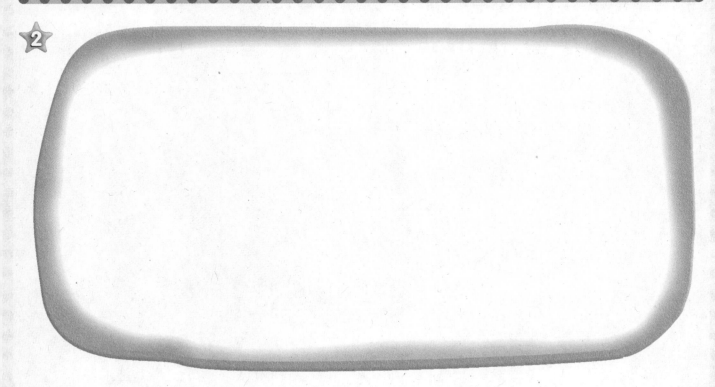

DIRECTIONS I. Place shapes as shown on the picture of a train.
2. Use those same shapes to model a picture of your own.

414 four hundred fourteen

Name _____

3

DIRECTIONS **3.** Use the shapes to show something in the real world.
Draw to show. Color the shapes you used. Tell about your drawing.

Chapter 9 • Lesson 7   four hundred fifteen **415**

PROBLEM SOLVING REAL WORLD

① ② ③

DIRECTIONS **1.** I am a ball. Which shape am I? Mark an X on that shape. **2.** I am a can of food. Which shape am I? Mark an X on that shape. **3.** Draw to show what you know about a box.

HOME ACTIVITY • Have your child find things around your house that are shaped like spheres, cubes, or cylinders. Have him or her describe the shape.

416 four hundred sixteen

FOR MORE PRACTICE:
Florida Benchmarks Practice Book, pp. P227–P228

Chapter 9 Review/Test

Vocabulary

 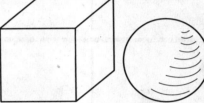

Concepts

DIRECTIONS 1. Color the spheres blue. Color the cylinders green. Color the cubes red. (MA.K.G.2.3) 2. A can of soup is shaped like this. Mark an X on that shape. (MA.K.G.2.4) 3. Look at the picture. Use blue to color the cubes. Use yellow to color the spheres. (MA.K.G.2.5) 4. Mark an X on the object that is shaped like a sphere. (MA.K.G.2.3)

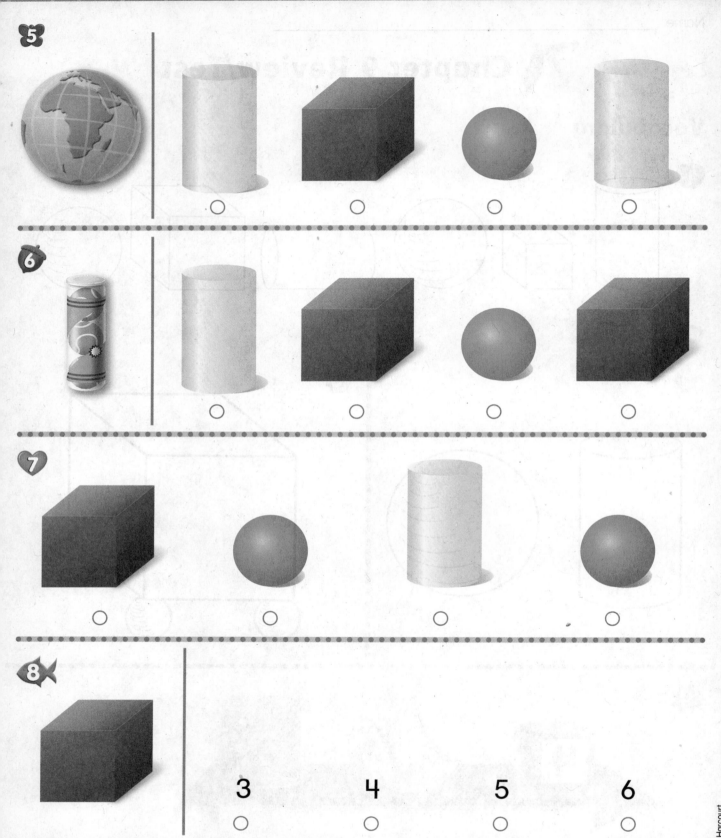

5

○ ○ ○ ○

6

○ ○ ○ ○

7

○ ○ ○ ○

8

3   4   5   6

○ ○ ○ ○

DIRECTIONS **5–6.** Mark under the shape that is the same shape as the object at the beginning of the row. (MA.K.G.2.3) **7.** Mark under the cube. (MA.K.G.2.3) **8.** Mark under the number that shows how many flat surfaces the cube has. (MA.K.G.2.3)

418 four hundred eighteen

9

○　　　○　　　○　　　○

10

| 2 | 3 | 4 | 5 |
| ○ | ○ | ○ | ○ |

11

○　　　○　　　○　　　○

12

○　　　○　　　○　　　○

DIRECTIONS **9.** Mark under the shape that stacks and rolls. (MA.K.G.2.3) **10.** Look at the picture. Mark under the number that tells how many cylinders are in the picture. (MA.K.G.2.5) **11.** Mark under the shape that does not roll. (MA.K.G.2.3) **12.** Mark under the object that is shaped like the cube at the beginning of the row. (MA.K.G.2.3)

Chapter 9

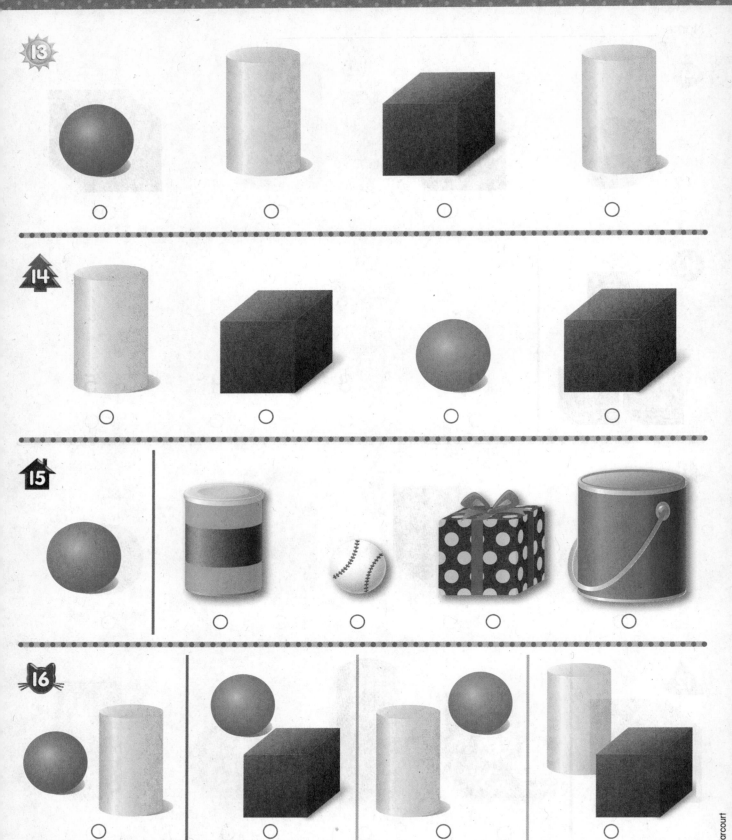

DIRECTIONS **13.** Mark under the shape that has curves and no flat surfaces.
(MA.K.G.2.3) **14.** A marble is shaped like this. Mark under that shape. (MA.K.G.2.4)
15. Mark under the object that is shaped like the sphere at the beginning of the row.
(MA.K.G.2.3) **16.** Mark under the group of shapes that slide. (MA.K.G.2.3)

420 four hundred twenty

Chapter 10

Patterns

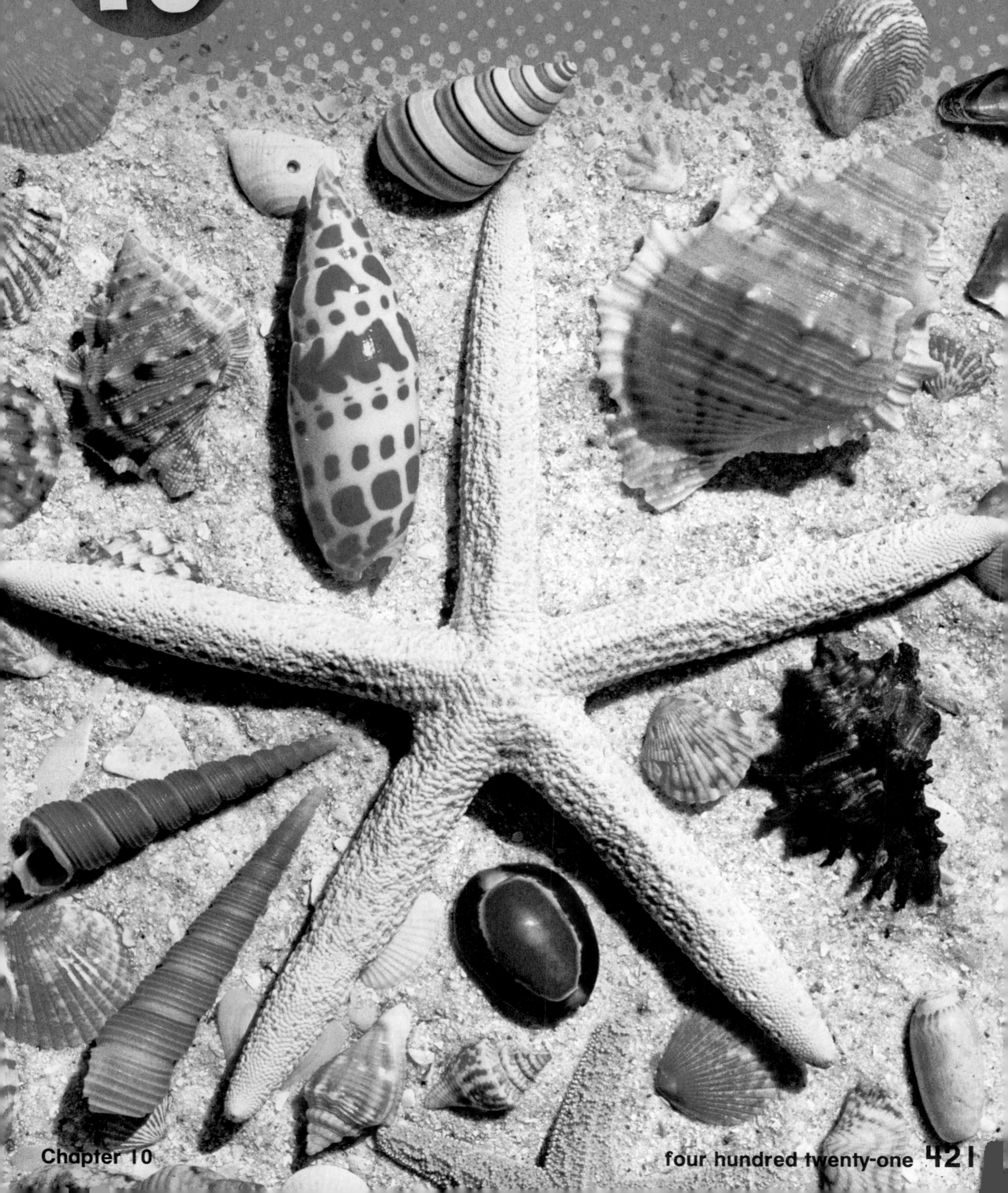

Show What You Know

Numbers to 10

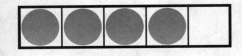  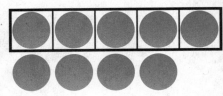

_____ _____ _____

\- \- \- \- \- \- \- \- \- \- \- \- \- \- \-

_____ _____ _____

Identify Shapes

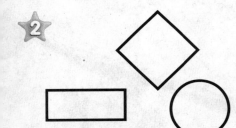 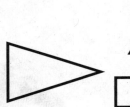 

Sort by Size

DIRECTIONS **1.** Count and write how many. **2.** Color the triangles red. Color the circles blue. Color the rectangles green. **3.** Mark an X on the object that does not belong.

FAMILY NOTE: This page checks your child's understanding of important skills needed for success in Chapter 10.

Name _____

pattern

DIRECTIONS Which color vegetable might belong in the last box? Draw the color.

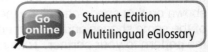

- Student Edition
- Multilingual eGlossary

Chapter 10

four hundred twenty-three **423**

Game Pattern Path

DIRECTIONS Play with a partner. Decide who goes first. Put your marker on Start. Toss the number cube. Move that number of spaces. Take the shapes shown on that space and place them in the workspace. Then take another set of the same shapes and place them in the same order in the workspace. Read the pattern to your partner. Take turns until both players reach the end.

MATERIALS game markers, number cube (1–6), plane shapes

424 four hundred twenty-four

Name _____

Identify and Copy a Color Pattern

Essential Question How can you identify and copy a color pattern?

MA.K.A.4.1 Identify and duplicate simple number and non-numeric repeating and growing patterns.

Listen and Draw

DIRECTIONS Point to each shirt as you identify the pattern. Color the shirts to copy the pattern.

Chapter 10 • Lesson 1

four hundred twenty-five **425**

© Houghton Mifflin Harcourt

Share and Show

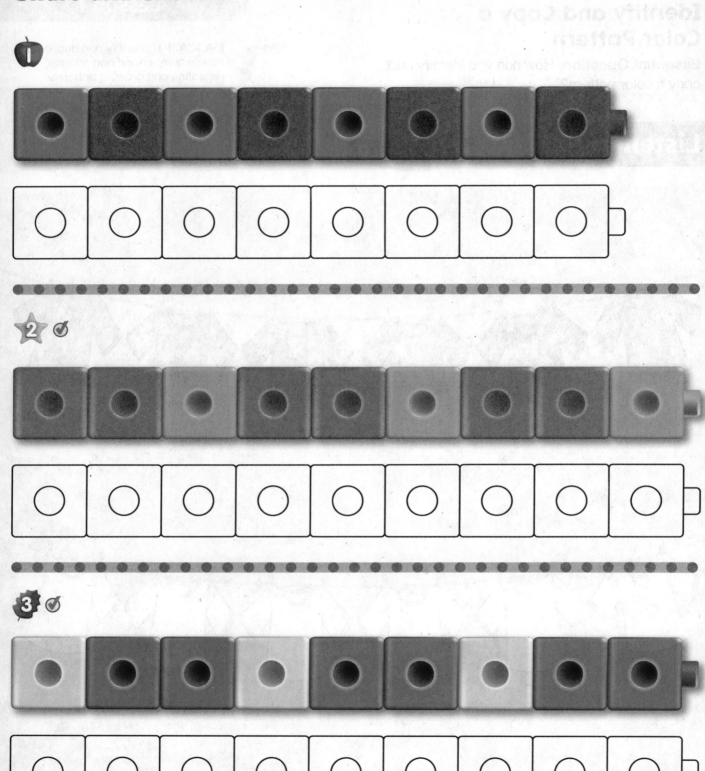

🍎 **1**

⭐ **2** ✓

🍁 **3** ✓

DIRECTIONS 1–3. Read to identify the pattern.
Place cubes to copy the pattern. Color the pattern.

Name _____

4

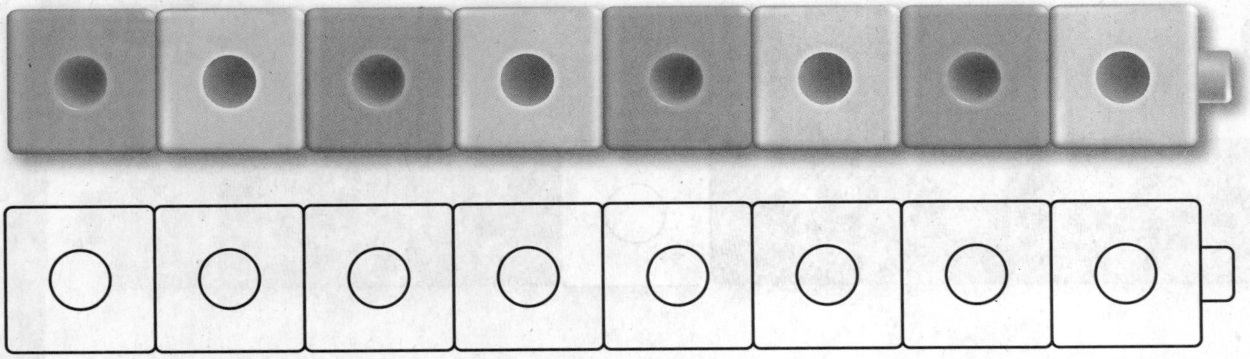

5

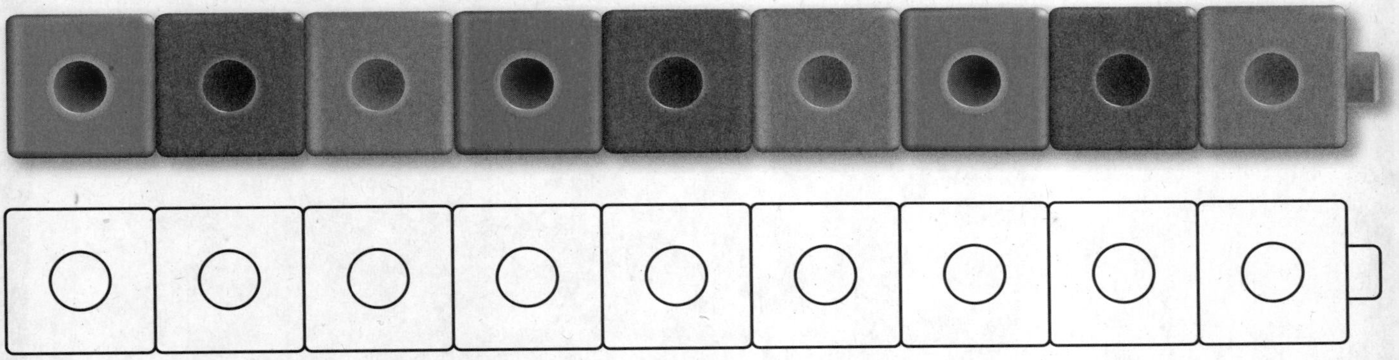

6

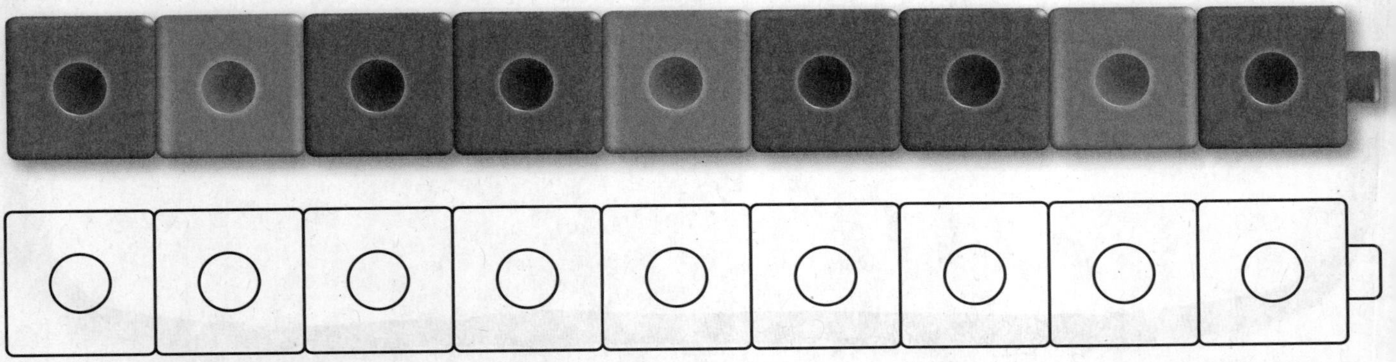

DIRECTIONS   4–6. Read to identify the pattern.
Place cubes to copy the pattern. Color the pattern.

Chapter 10 · Lesson 1

four hundred twenty-seven **427**

PROBLEM SOLVING

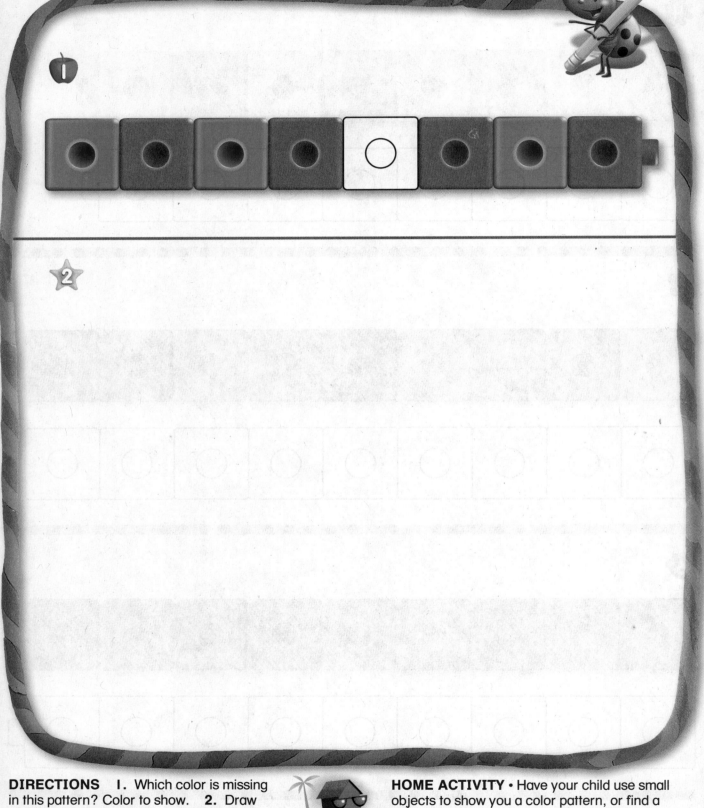

1

2

DIRECTIONS   1. Which color is missing in this pattern? Color to show.   **2.** Draw and color to show what you know about a color pattern.

HOME ACTIVITY • Have your child use small objects to show you a color pattern, or find a household object that has a color pattern.

FOR MORE PRACTICE:
Florida Benchmarks Practice Book, pp. P235–P236

Name _____

Identify and Copy a Size Pattern

Essential Question How can you identify and copy a size pattern?

MA.K.A.4.1 Identify and duplicate simple number and non-numeric repeating and growing patterns.

Listen and Draw REAL WORLD

DIRECTIONS Point to each shirt as you identify the pattern. Draw to copy the pattern.

Chapter 10 · Lesson 2

four hundred twenty-nine **429**

Share and Show

DIRECTIONS 1–3. Read to identify the pattern. Place shapes to copy the pattern. Draw and color the pattern.

© Houghton Mifflin Harcourt

4.

5.

6.

DIRECTIONS   4–6. Read to identify the pattern. Place shapes to copy the pattern. Draw and color the pattern.

PROBLEM SOLVING

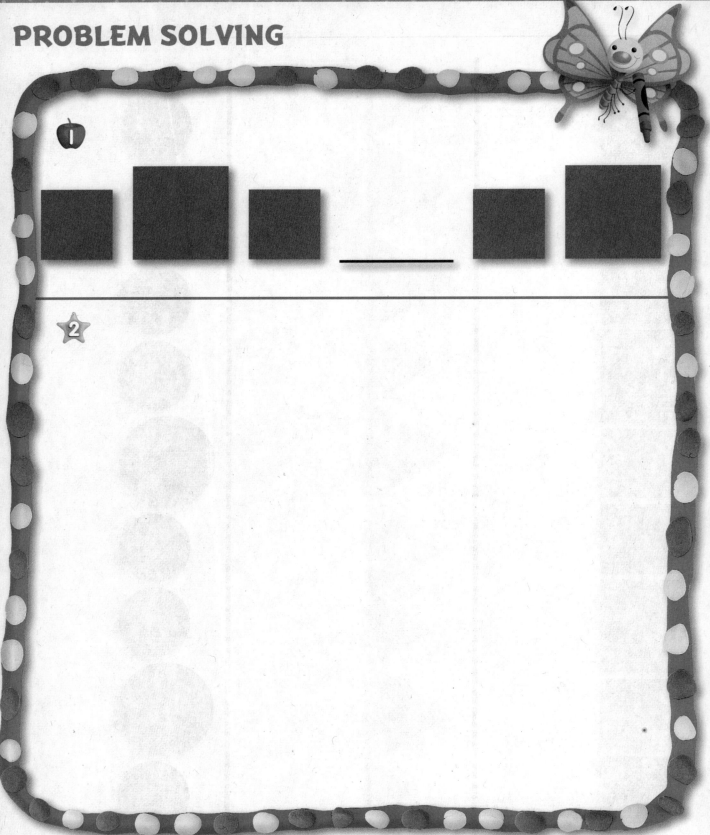

1

2

DIRECTIONS **1.** Which shape is missing in this size pattern? Draw and color the missing shape where it belongs.
2. Draw and color to show what you know about a size pattern.

HOME ACTIVITY • Have your child use household objects to show you a size pattern.

Name _____

Identify and Copy a Shape Pattern

Essential Question How can you identify and copy a shape pattern?

MA.K.A.4.1 Identify and duplicate simple number and non-numeric repeating and growing patterns.

Listen and Draw · REAL WORLD

DIRECTIONS Point to each shape as you identify the pattern. Use shapes to copy the pattern. Draw the shapes.

Chapter 10 · Lesson 3

four hundred thirty-three **433**

Share and Show

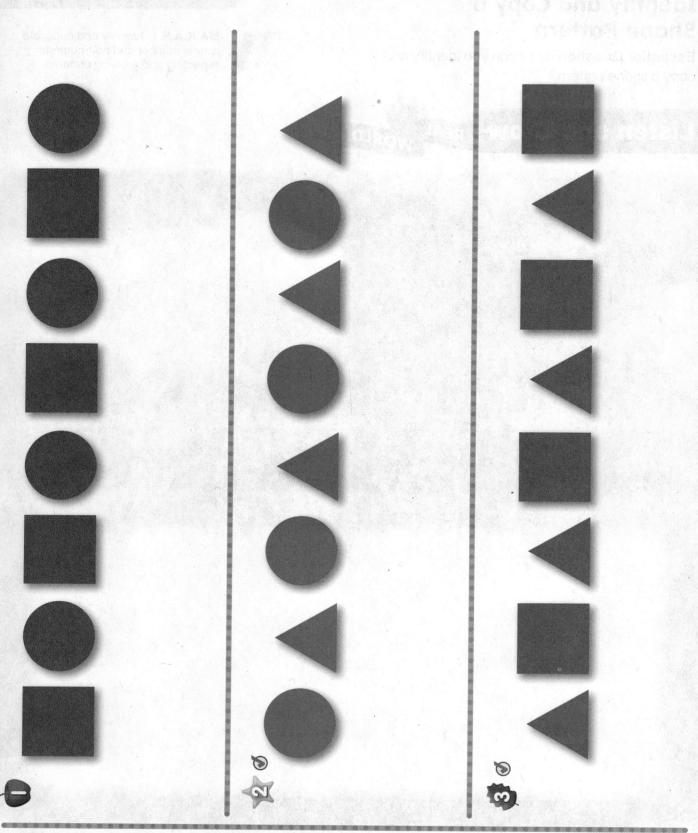

DIRECTIONS   1–3. Read to identify the pattern. Place shapes to copy the pattern. Draw and color the pattern.

Name _____

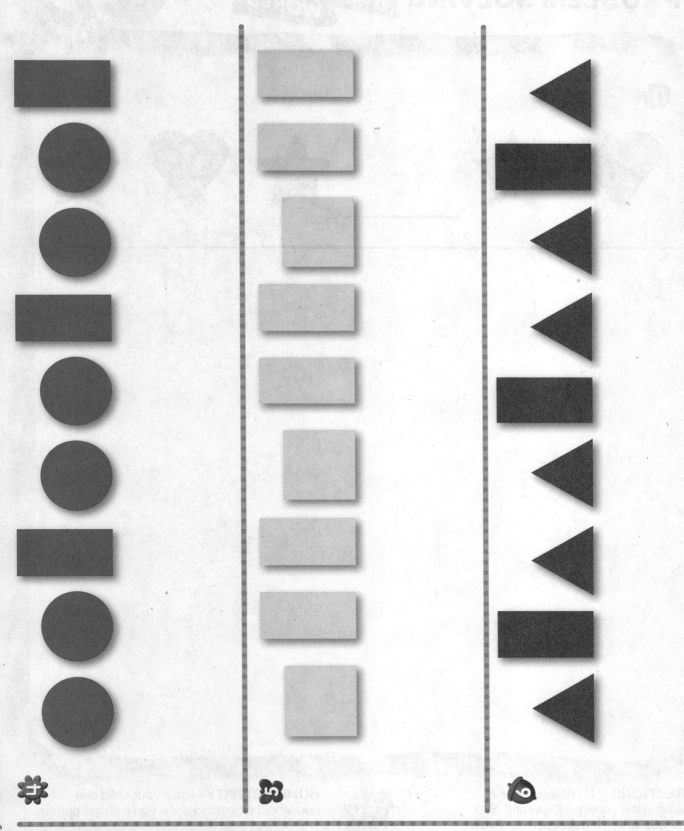

DIRECTIONS   4–6. Read to identify the pattern. Place
shapes to copy the pattern. Draw and color the pattern.

Chapter 10 • Lesson 3

four hundred thirty-five **435**

PROBLEM SOLVING REAL WORLD

1

♥ ★ _____ ★ ♥ ★

2

DIRECTIONS **1.** Which shape is missing in the pattern? Draw and color the shape where it belongs. **2.** Draw and color to show what you know about a shape pattern.

HOME ACTIVITY • Have your child use household objects to show you a shape pattern.

436 four hundred thirty-six

FOR MORE PRACTICE:
Florida Benchmarks Practice Book, pp. P239–P240

Identify and Copy a Number Pattern

Essential Question How can you identify and copy a number pattern?

MA.K.A.4.1 Identify and duplicate simple number and non-numeric repeating and growing patterns.

Listen and Draw REAL WORLD

DIRECTIONS Identify the number of dots on each card. Say the pattern. Write the pattern.

Share and Show

❶ 1 2 1 2 1 2 1 2

_____

- - - - - - - - - - - - - - - -

_____

⭐2 ✓ 1 1 2 1 1 2 1 1 2

_____

- - - - - - - - - - - - - - - -

_____

❸ ✓ 1 2 2 1 2 2 1 2 2

_____

- - - - - - - - - - - - - - - -

_____

DIRECTIONS 1–3. Read to identify the pattern. Write to copy the pattern.

4 2 2 3 2 2 2 3 2 2 3

5 1 2 3 1 2 3 1 2 3

6 1 2 1 1 2 1 1 2 1

DIRECTIONS   4–6. Read to identify the pattern. Write to copy the pattern.

HOME ACTIVITY Have your child show you a number pattern.

Chapter 10 • Lesson 4

FOR MORE PRACTICE:
Florida Benchmarks Practice Book, pp. P241–P242

four hundred thirty-nine **439**

Concepts

1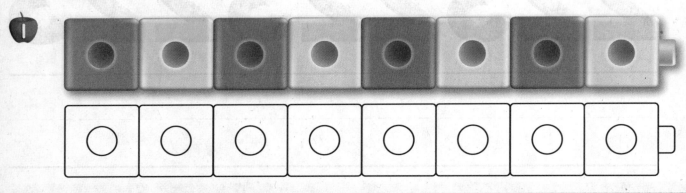

2

Test Prep

3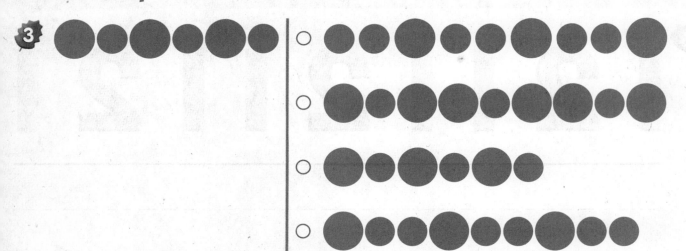

DIRECTIONS **1.** Identify the pattern. Place cubes to copy the pattern. Color the pattern. (MA.K.A.4.1) **2.** Identify the pattern. Place shapes to copy the pattern. Draw and color the pattern. (MA.K.A.4.1) **3.** Identify the pattern. Mark beside the pattern that is the same. (MA.K.A.4.1)

440 four hundred forty

Identify and Copy a Growing Pattern

Essential Question How can you identify and copy a growing pattern?

MA.K.A.4.1 Identify and duplicate simple number and non-numeric repeating and growing patterns.

Listen and Draw

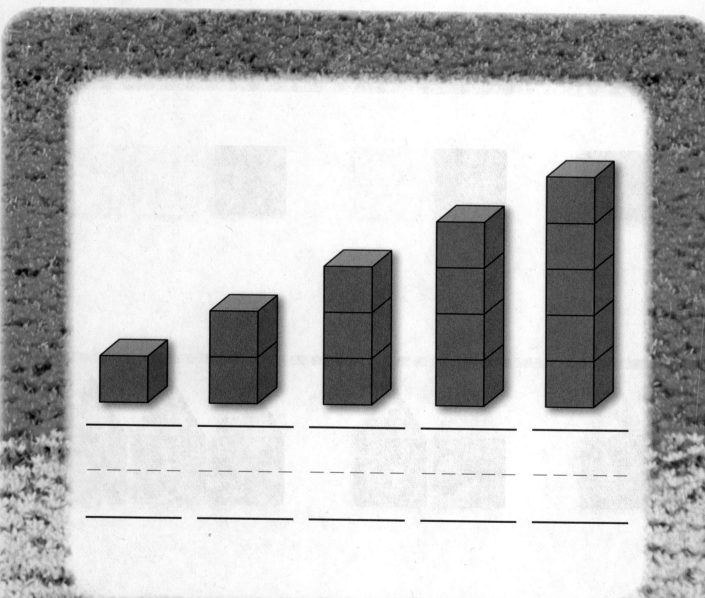

DIRECTIONS Point to the block towers, starting with the block on the left. Write how many blocks in each tower. Tell how the towers change each time.

Share and Show

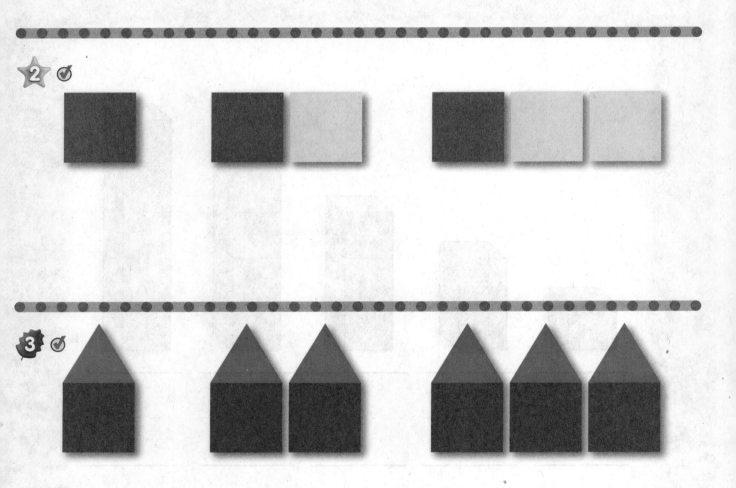

DIRECTIONS **1–3.** Read to identify the pattern. Place
shapes to copy the pattern. Draw and color the pattern.

442 four hundred forty-two

1 2 2 3 3 3 4 4 4 4 4

5

DIRECTIONS 4. Read to identify the pattern. Write to copy the pattern.
5. Write how many cubes in each train. Read to identify the growing number pattern.

PROBLEM SOLVING

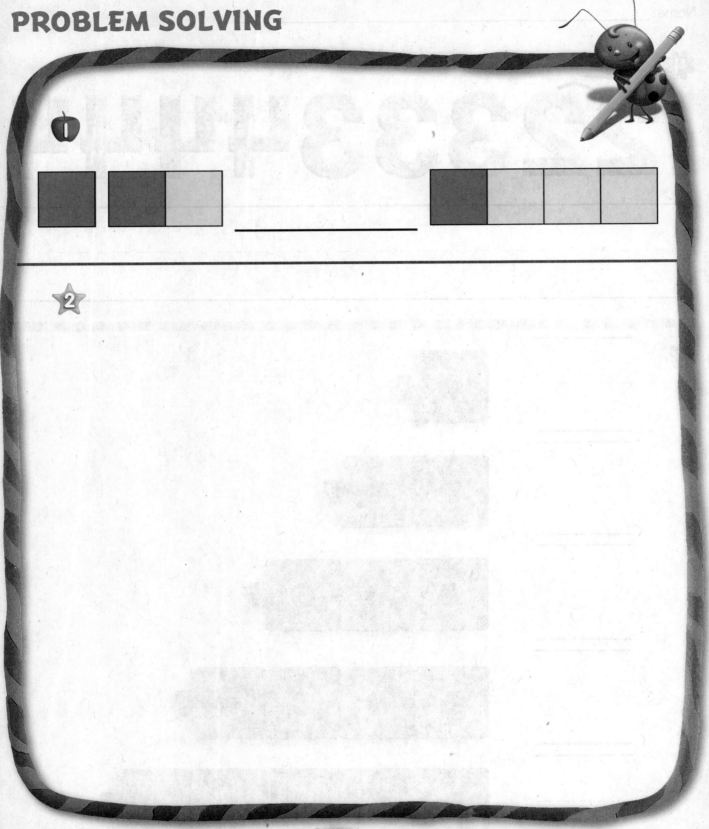

①

②

© Houghton Mifflin Harcourt

DIRECTIONS **1.** What is missing in this growing pattern? Draw and color to show what is missing. **2.** Draw and color to show what you know about a growing pattern.

HOME ACTIVITY • Have your child show you a household object that has a pattern.

444 four hundred forty-four

FOR MORE PRACTICE:
Florida Benchmarks Practice Book, pp. P243–P244

Find a Pattern

Essential Question How can you identify the pattern?

MA.K.A.4.1 Identify and duplicate simple number and non-numeric repeating and growing patterns.

Unlock the Problem

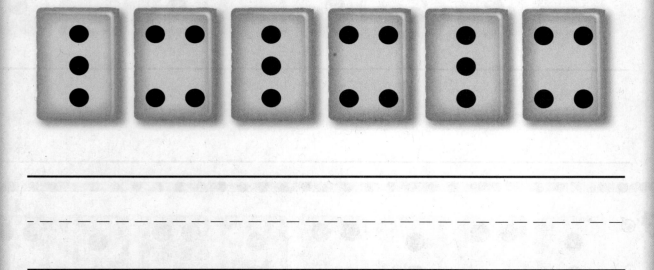

_____

- - - - - - - - - - - - - - - - - - - -

_____

DIRECTIONS Listen to the problem. This pattern repeats. Write the number pattern. Which part repeats again and again? Circle one of those parts.

Share and Show

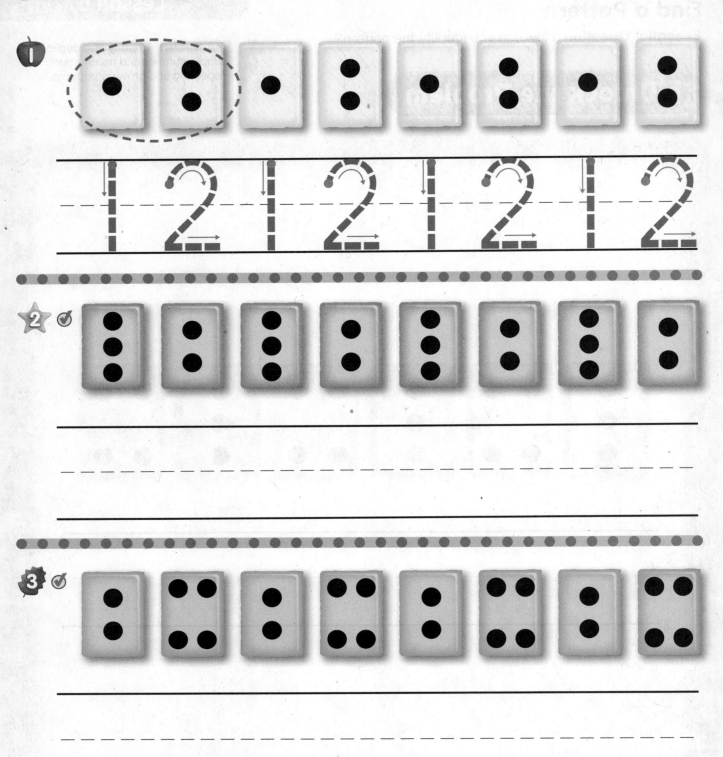

❶

1 2 1 2 1 2 1 2

❷ ✓

❸ ✓

DIRECTIONS 1–3. Look at the pattern. Write the numbers below the dot cards. Circle the part that repeats again and again.

446 four hundred forty-six

Name _____

4

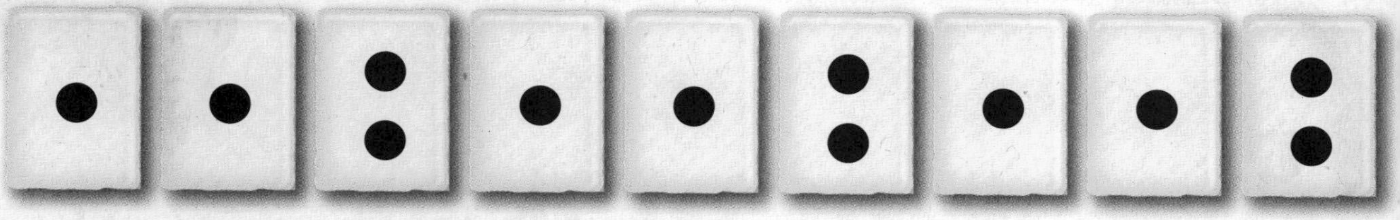

_____

- - - - - - - - - - - - - - - - - - -

_____

5

_____

- - - - - - - - - - - - - - - - - - -

_____

6

_____

- - - - - - - - - - - - - - - - - - -

_____

DIRECTIONS   4–6. Look at the pattern. Write
the numbers below the dot cards. Circle the part
that repeats again and again.

On Your Own

1

2

© Houghton Mifflin Harcourt

DIRECTIONS **1.** The part of the pattern that repeats is 4, 4, 2. Draw to show the dots on the dot cards. **2.** Draw to show what you know about a number pattern that repeats.

HOME ACTIVITY • Cut shapes from paper to make a circle/square/triangle pattern. Repeat the pattern three times. Have your child tell which part of the pattern repeats again and again.

448 four hundred forty-eight

FOR MORE PRACTICE:
Florida Benchmarks Practice Book, pp. P245–P246

Name _____

Identify and Copy a Pattern with Two Attributes

Essential Question How can you identify and copy a pattern with two attributes?

MA.K.A.4.1 Identify and duplicate simple number and non-numeric repeating and growing patterns.

Listen and Draw

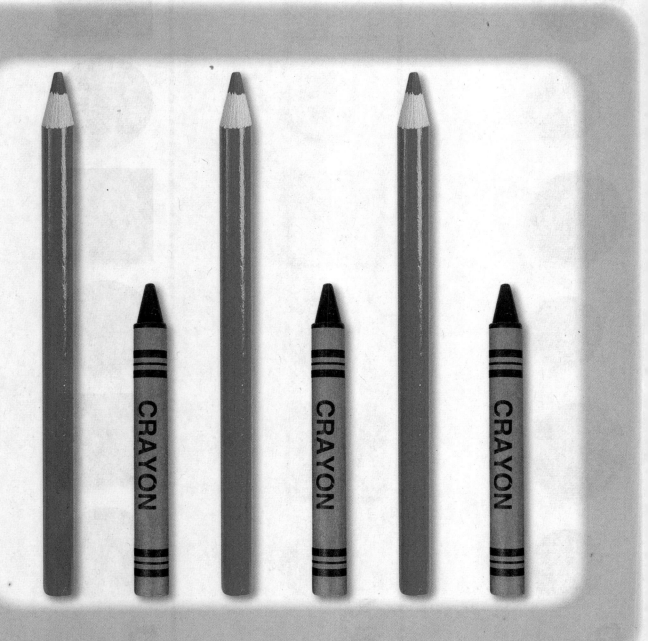

DIRECTIONS Place pencils and crayons on the page to show the pattern. Tell what you know about the pattern. Circle the part that repeats again and again.

Chapter 10 · Lesson 7

Share and Show

DIRECTIONS 1–3. Read to identify the pattern. Place shapes to copy the pattern. Draw and color the pattern.

450 four hundred fifty

Name _____

4.

5.

6.

DIRECTIONS 4–6. Read to identify the pattern. Place
shapes to copy the pattern. Draw and color the pattern.

Chapter 10 · Lesson 7

four hundred fifty-one **451**

PROBLEM SOLVING

1

2

DIRECTIONS **1.** Which shape is missing from this pattern? Draw and color the shape where it goes. **2.** Draw to show what you know about the patterns in this lesson.

HOME ACTIVITY • Have your child tell you the two attributes in one of the patterns in this lesson.

452 four hundred fifty-two

FOR MORE PRACTICE:
Florida Benchmarks Practice Book, pp. P247–P248

✓ Chapter 10 Review/Test

Vocabulary

Concepts

   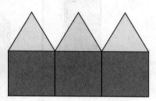

DIRECTIONS **1.** Look at the pattern. Write the numbers below the dot cards. Circle the part that repeats again and again. (MA.K.A.4.1) **2.** Identify the pattern. Place shapes to copy the pattern. Draw and color the pattern. (MA.K.A.4.1) **3.** Identify the pattern. Place shapes to copy the pattern. Draw and color the pattern. (MA.K.A.4.1)

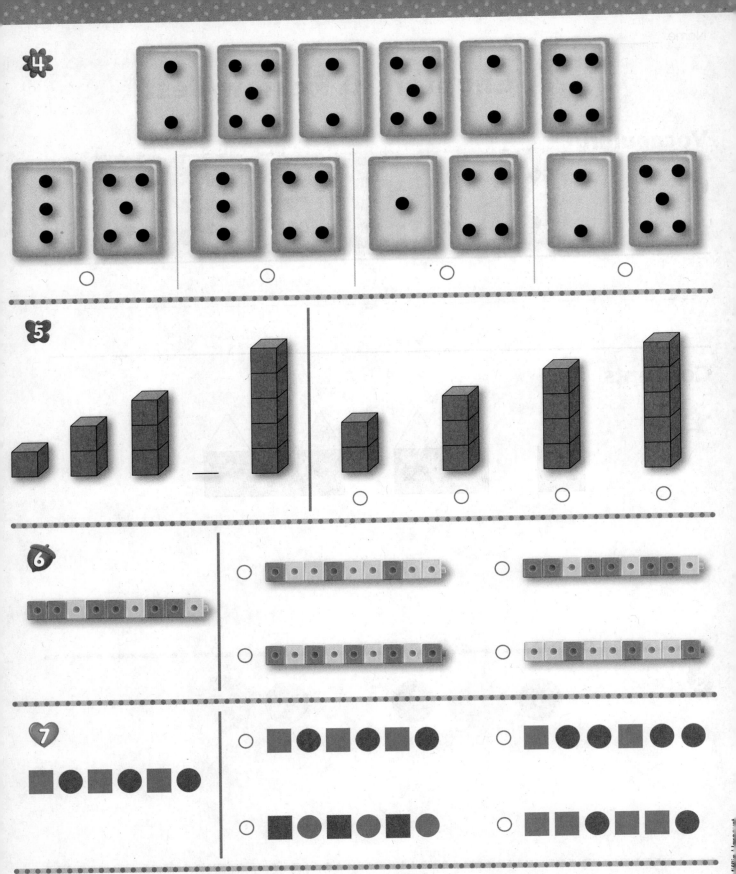

5

6

7

DIRECTIONS **4.** Mark under the dot cards that show the same part that repeats again and again. (MA.K.A.4.1) **5.** Mark under the cube train that belongs in this growing pattern. (MA.K.A.4.1) **6–7.** Identify the pattern. Mark beside the pattern that is the same. (MA.K.A.4.1)

Name _____

○ 112112112   ○ 123123123

123123123

○ 122122122   ○ 223223223

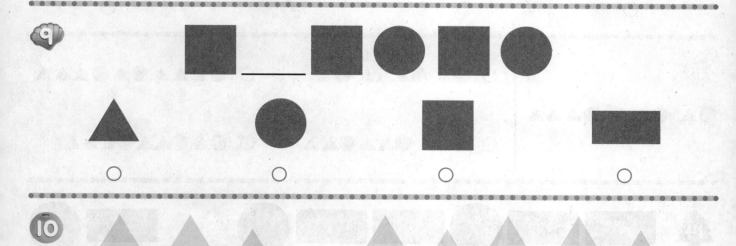

9

10

11

DIRECTIONS 8. Identify the pattern. Mark beside the pattern that is the same. (MA.K.A.4.1) **9–10.** Mark under the shape that is missing in the pattern. (MA.K.A.4.1) **11.** Mark under the dot cards that show the same part that repeats again and again. (MA.K.A.4.1)

Chapter 10   four hundred fifty-five **455**

12

○   ○   ○   ○

13

14

○   ○   ○   ○

15

○   ○   ○   ○

DIRECTIONS **12.** Mark under the shape that is missing in this
pattern. (MA.K.A.4.1) **13.** Identify the pattern. Mark beside the same
growing pattern. (MA.K.A.4.1) **14–15.** Mark under the shape that is
missing in this pattern. (MA.K.A.4.1)

456 four hundred fifty-six

Plants all Around

written by Tami Morton

BIG IDEA

Order objects
by measurable attributes.

A

Two leaves fall from a tree.

Circle the leaf that is longer.

Why do plants have leaves?

B

Two flowers grow near a wall.

Circle the flower that is shorter.

 Science

Why do plants have flowers?

These carrots grow under the ground.

Circle the carrot that is longest.

Why do plants have roots?

D

Cattails can be short or tall.

Circle the two cattails that are the same length.

Why do plants have stems?

One leaf is long. One leaf is short.

Draw a leaf to show the shortest.

Science

How are all these plants the same?

Name _____

Write About the Story

Draw a purple flower. Make it shorter than the orange flower and taller than the yellow flower.

Vocabulary Review

longer	longest
shorter	shortest
taller	tallest
same	

G

Longer and Shorter

1. Look at the roots. Draw a shorter carrot on the left.
Draw a longer carrot on the right.

2. Look at the leaf.
Draw a longer leaf above it.
Draw a shorter leaf below it.

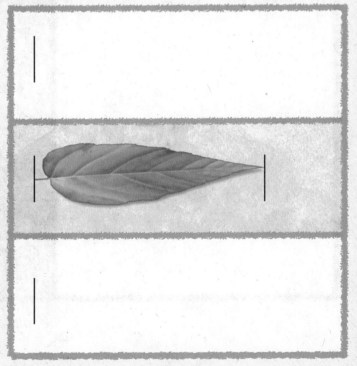

Name _____

More and Fewer

_____   _____

- - - - - - - - - - - - -   - - - - - - - - - - - - -

_____   _____

Compare Numbers

_____

- - - - - - - - - - - - -

_____

- - - - - - - - - - - - -

_____

Order Numbers

14 _____ _____ 17 _____ 19

- - - - - -   - - - - - -   - - - - - -

_____ _____

DIRECTIONS 1. Write how many in each set. Circle the set with fewer objects. 2. Write how many cubes in each set. Circle the set with more cubes. 3. Write the missing numbers on the number line.

FAMILY NOTE: This page checks your child's understanding of important skills needed for success in Chapter 11.

Name _____

bigger

smaller

DIRECTIONS Draw to show a bigger picture on the wall.

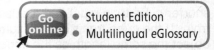

Student Edition
Multilingual eGlossary

Chapter 11 Game
Connecting Cube Challenge

DIRECTIONS Take turns with a partner tossing the number cube. Move your marker that number of spaces. If a player lands on a cube, he or she takes a cube and makes a cube train. At the end of the game, players compare cube trains. The player with the longer cube train must find a classroom object longer than his or her cube train. The player with the shorter cube train must find a classroom object shorter than his or her cube train. If the cube trains are the same length, players must find a classroom object the same length as the cube trains.

MATERIALS game markers, number cube (1–6), connecting cubes

Name _____

Compare Lengths

Essential Question How can you compare the lengths of objects?

MA.K.G.3.1 Compare and order objects indirectly or directly using measurable attributes such as length, height, and weight.

Listen and Draw REAL WORLD

DIRECTIONS Line up two pencils against the line on the left. Compare the lengths of the pencils. Use the words *longer than*, *shorter than*, or *about the same length*. Trace the pencils.

Chapter 11 · Lesson 1

Share and Show

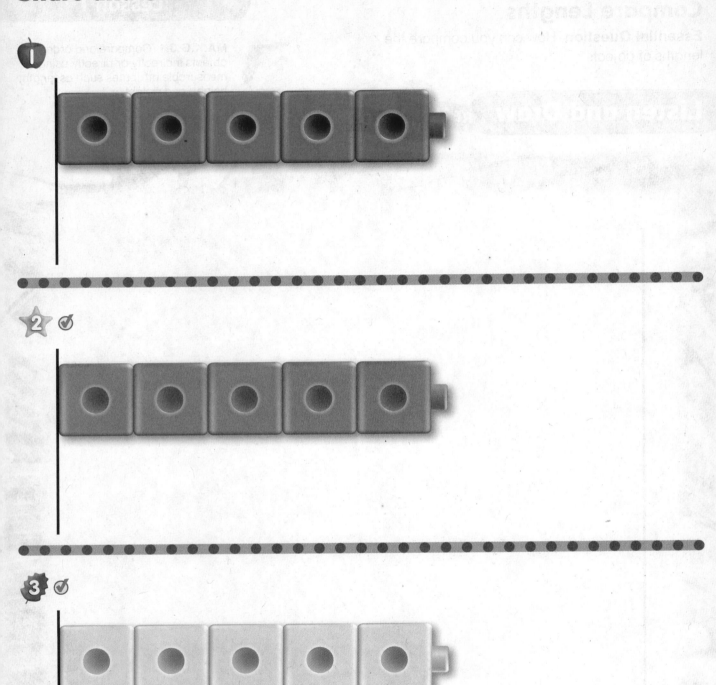

1

2 ✓

3 ✓

DIRECTIONS **1.** Make a cube train that is about the same length. Draw the cube train. **2.** Make a cube train that is shorter. Draw the cube train. **3.** Make a cube train that is longer. Draw the cube train.

462 four hundred sixty-two

© Houghton Mifflin Harcourt

Name _____

4

5

6

DIRECTIONS **4.** Make a cube train that is shorter. Draw the cube train. **5.** Make a cube train that is longer. Draw the cube train. **6.** Make a cube train that is about the same length. Draw the cube train.

PROBLEM SOLVING REAL WORLD

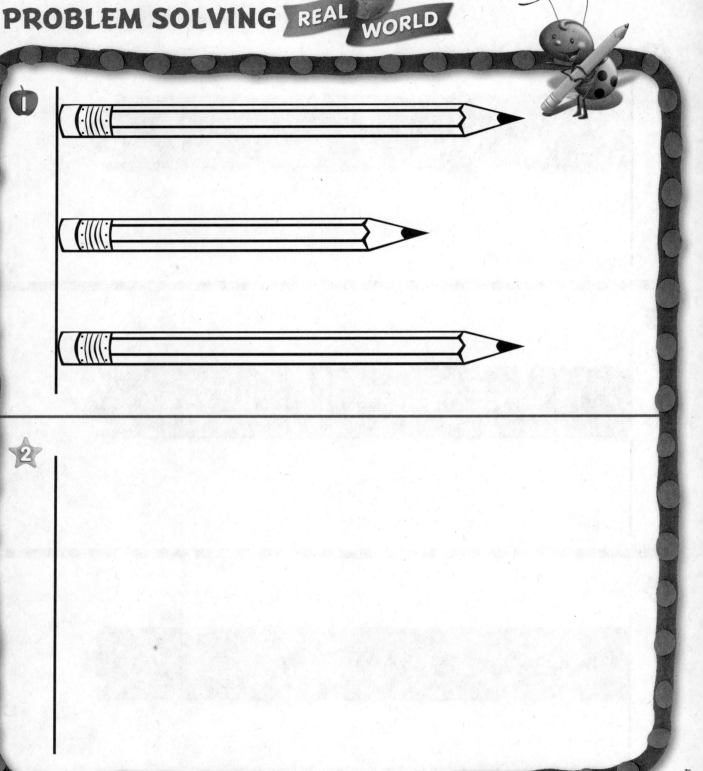

①

②

DIRECTIONS **1.** Two of these pencils are about the same length. Color those pencils. **2.** Draw to show what you know about objects being *longer than* and *shorter than*. Tell about your drawing.

HOME ACTIVITY • Show your child a pencil and ask him or her to find an object that is longer than the pencil. Repeat with an object that is shorter than the pencil.

464 four hundred sixty-four

FOR MORE PRACTICE:
Florida Benchmarks Practice Book, pp. P257–P258

Name _____

Indirect Comparison of Lengths

Essential Question How can you compare the lengths of curved and straight lines?

MA.K.G.3.1 Compare and order objects indirectly or directly using measurable attributes such as length, height, and weight.

Listen and Draw REAL WORLD

DIRECTIONS Is one line longer or shorter, or are the two lines about the same length? Talk about how you can measure these lengths. Mark an X on the longer line. Circle the shorter line.

1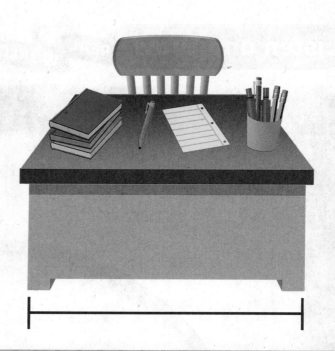

2 ✓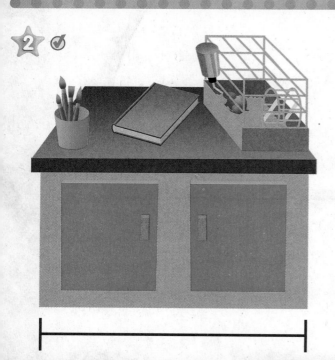

DIRECTIONS Go on a measurement walk. **1.** Use string to measure the length of a bookcase and the length of the teacher's desk. Compare the lengths of string. Circle the picture of the longer object. **2.** Use string to measure the length of a cabinet and the length of a doorway. Compare the lengths of string. Circle the picture of the shorter object.

Name _____

DIRECTIONS   3. Use string to measure the lengths of
the paths. Compare the lengths of string. Circle the longer
path.   **4.** Use string to measure the lengths of the vines.
Compare the lengths of string. Circle the shorter vine.

PROBLEM SOLVING REAL WORLD

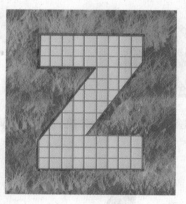

DIRECTIONS **1.** This string shows the length around a paint jar. Draw a string that might show the length around a smaller paint jar. Draw a string that might show the length around a larger paint jar. Draw the strings in order from shortest to longest. **2.** Use string to measure the length of each path. Draw the strings. Compare the strings.

HOME ACTIVITY • Have your child use string to measure the lengths of two objects in your home. Have him or her compare the lengths of string and tell you which object is longer.

468 four hundred sixty-eight

FOR MORE PRACTICE:
Florida Benchmarks Practice Book, pp. P259–P260

Name _____

Order Lengths

Essential Question How can you order objects by length?

MA.K.G.3.1 Compare and order objects indirectly or directly using measurable attributes such as length, height, and weight.

Listen and Draw REAL WORLD

DIRECTIONS Build three cube trains of different lengths. Place one end of each cube train on the line. Place the cube trains in order by length with the shortest at the top. Draw the cube trains.

Chapter 11 • Lesson 3

four hundred sixty-nine **469**

Share and Show

DIRECTIONS 1. Find a classroom object that is shorter than the crayon and an object that is longer than the crayon. Draw the objects in order from shortest to longest.

Name _____

Mid-Chapter Checkpoint

⭐ 2 ✓

3

🍁 3 ✓

🌼 4

5

DIRECTIONS 2–5. Write the numbers *1*, *2*, and *3* to order the objects from shortest to longest.

HOME ACTIVITY • Give your child three shoes of different lengths. Have him or her trace around each shoe on paper and write *1*, *2*, and *3* in the shoe shapes to order them from shortest to longest.

Chapter 11 • Lesson 3

FOR MORE PRACTICE:
Florida Benchmarks Practice Book, pp. P261–P262

four hundred seventy-one **471**

Concepts

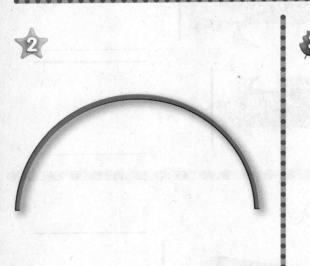

DIRECTIONS **1.** Make a cube train that is shorter. Draw the cube train. (MA.K.G.3.1) **2.** Use string to measure the lines. Circle the longer one. (MA.K.G.3.1) **3.** Write the numbers *1*, *2*, and *3* to order the objects from shortest to longest. (MA.K.G.3.1) **4.** Mark under the pencils that are the same length. (MA.K.G.3.1)

Name _____

Compare Heights

Essential Question How can you compare the heights of objects?

MA.K.G.3.1 Compare and order objects indirectly or directly using measurable attributes such as length, height, and weight.

Listen and Draw REAL WORLD

DIRECTIONS Look at the chairs. Compare the heights of the two chairs. Use the words *taller than*, *shorter than*, or *about the same height*. Circle the taller chair. Mark an X on the shorter chair.

Chapter 11 · Lesson 4

four hundred seventy-three **473**

Share and Show

DIRECTIONS 1. Build two cube trains of different heights. Place the cube trains on the line and compare the heights. Draw the cube trains. Circle the taller cube train. Mark an X on the shorter cube train.

Name _____

DIRECTIONS 2. Find two pencils of different heights. Place the pencils on the line and compare the heights. Draw the pencils. Circle the taller pencil. Mark an X on the shorter pencil.

PROBLEM SOLVING REAL WORLD

1

2

© Houghton Mifflin Harcourt

DIRECTIONS **1.** Jake's tree is taller than Austin's tree. Mark an X on Jake's tree. Circle Austin's tree. **2.** Draw to show what you know about comparing heights. Tell about your drawing.

HOME ACTIVITY • Have your child find two objects such as plastic toys or stuffed animals. Have him or her place the objects side by side to compare their heights. Ask your child which object is taller and which object is shorter.

476 four hundred seventy-six

FOR MORE PRACTICE:
Florida Benchmarks Practice Book, pp. 263–264

Indirect Comparison of Heights

Essential Question How can you compare the heights of objects by using string?

MA.K.G.3.1 Compare and order objects indirectly or directly using measurable attributes such as length, height, and weight.

Listen and Draw REAL WORLD

Height

Cynthia

Braeden

DIRECTIONS Look at the marks on the chart. Talk about which child is taller and which child is shorter. Circle the mark that shows who is shorter. Mark an X on the mark that shows who is taller.

© Houghton Mifflin Harcourt

Share and Show

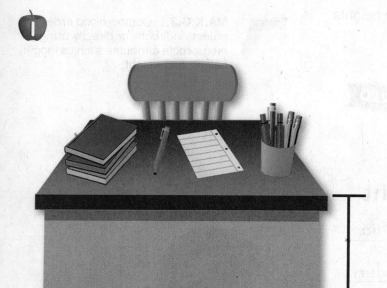

DIRECTIONS Go on a measurement walk. **1.** Use string to measure the height of the teacher's desk and the height of an easel. Compare the pieces of string. Circle the picture of the taller object. **2.** Use string to measure the height of a bulletin board and the height of a bookcase. Compare the pieces of string. Circle the picture of the shorter object.

478 four hundred seventy-eight

Name _____

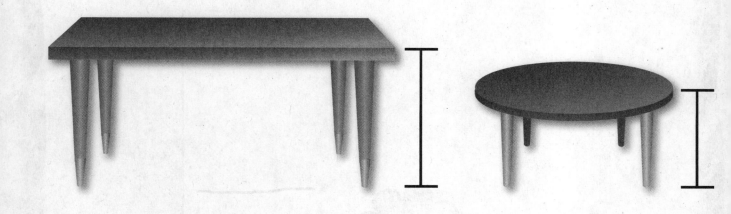

DIRECTIONS Go on a measurement walk. **3.** Use string to measure the height of a table in the cafeteria and the height of a classroom table. Compare the pieces of string. Circle the picture of the taller object. **4.** Use string to measure the height of the teacher's chair and the height of a child's chair. Compare the pieces of string. Circle the picture of the shorter object.

Chapter 11 · Lesson 5

four hundred seventy-nine **479**

PROBLEM SOLVING REAL WORLD

Height

___

DIRECTIONS Travis brought his plant to school. He placed a mark on a chart to show how tall the plant is. Tyler's plant is shorter. Use blue to mark how tall Tyler's plant might be. Brent's plant is the tallest plant. Use red to mark how tall Brent's plant might be.

HOME ACTIVITY • Have your child use string to measure the heights of two objects in your home. Have him or her compare the pieces of string and tell you which object is taller.

FOR MORE PRACTICE:
Florida Benchmarks Practice Book, pp. P265–P266

© Houghton Mifflin Harcourt

Name _____

Order Heights

Essential Question How can you order objects by height?

MA.K.G.3.1 Compare and order objects indirectly or directly using measurable attributes such as length, height, and weight.

Listen and Draw REAL WORLD

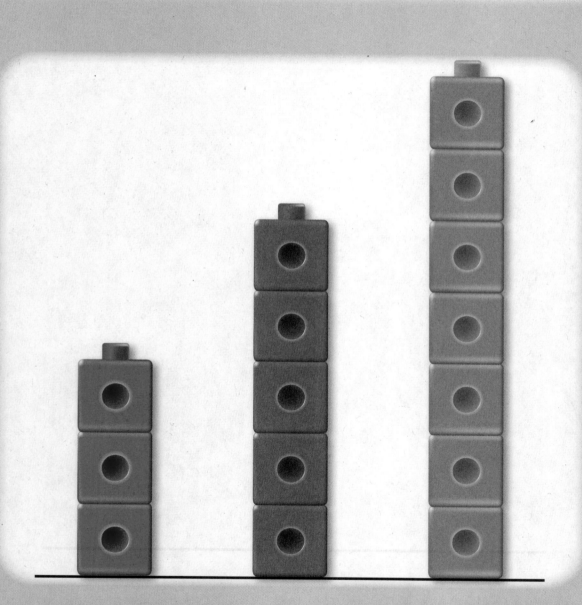

DIRECTIONS Build cube trains like these. Which cube train is the shortest? Mark an X on that cube train. Which cube train is the tallest? Circle that cube train. Draw a cube train that is about the same height as one of these cube trains.

Chapter 11 • Lesson 6

four hundred eighty-one **481**

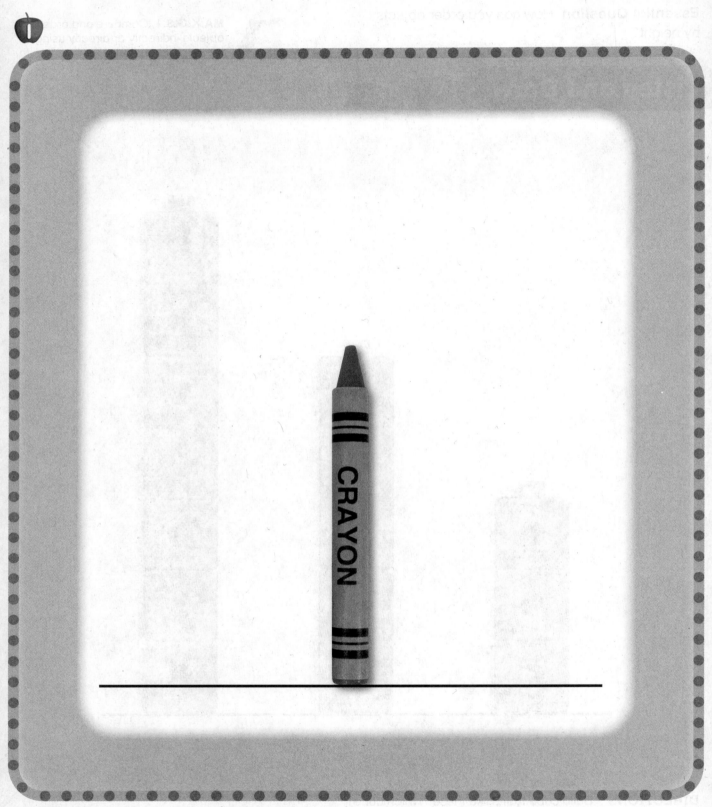

DIRECTIONS **1.** Find a classroom object that is shorter than the crayon. Find an object that is taller than the crayon. Draw the objects in order from shortest to tallest.

Name _____

⭐2 ✓

3

4

5

DIRECTIONS **2–5.** Write the numbers *1*, *2*, and *3* to order the objects from shortest to tallest.

PROBLEM SOLVING REAL WORLD

❶

 A  B  C

❷

DIRECTIONS **1.** Draw Flower A taller than Flower B and Flower C taller than Flower A. Circle the shortest flower. **2.** Draw to show what you know about ordering objects by height. Tell about your drawing.

HOME ACTIVITY • Have your child find three toys of different heights. Have him or her place the toys in order from shortest to tallest.

FOR MORE PRACTICE:
Florida Benchmarks Practice Book, pp. P265–P266

Name _____

Compare Weights

Essential Question How can you compare the weights of objects?

MA.K.G.3.1 Compare and order objects indirectly or directly using measurable attributes such as length, height, and weight.

Listen and Draw REAL WORLD

DIRECTIONS Look at the picture. Talk about which object you think is heavier and which object you think is lighter. Circle the heavier object. Mark an X on the lighter object.

Chapter 11 • Lesson 7

Share and Show

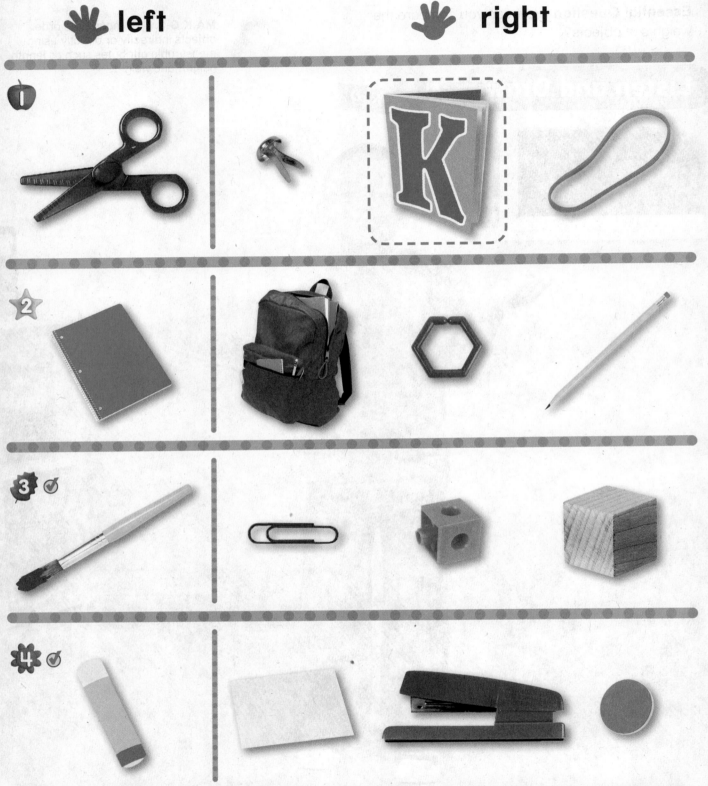

left   right

DIRECTIONS   **1–4.** Find the first object in the row, and hold it in your left hand. Find the rest of the objects in the row, and hold each object in your right hand. Circle the object that is heavier than the object in your left hand.

 **left**    **right**

5
 |

6
 |

7
 |

8
 |

DIRECTIONS **5–8.** Find the first object in the row, and hold it in your left hand. Find the rest of the objects in the row, and hold each object in your right hand. Circle the object that is lighter than the object in your left hand.

Chapter 11 • Lesson 7   four hundred eighty-seven **487**

PROBLEM SOLVING REAL WORLD

DIRECTIONS Draw to show what you know about comparing weights. Tell about your drawing.

HOME ACTIVITY • Give your child one household object to hold in his or her left hand. Have your child find another household object that is heavier to hold in his or her right hand. Then ask him or her to find a lighter object.

FOR MORE PRACTICE:
Florida Benchmarks Practice Book, pp. P269–P270

Name _____

Indirect Comparison of Weights

Essential Question How can you use marks to compare the weights of objects?

MA.K.G.3.1 Compare and order objects indirectly or directly using measurable attributes such as length, height, and weight.

Listen REAL WORLD

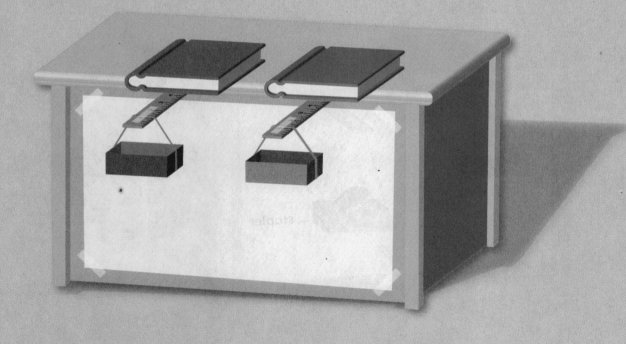

DIRECTIONS Look at the picture. Talk about classroom objects you might place in the boxes to compare the weights of the objects. Tell what you think might happen to the boxes.

Chapter 11 · Lesson 8

four hundred eighty-nine **489**

Share and Show

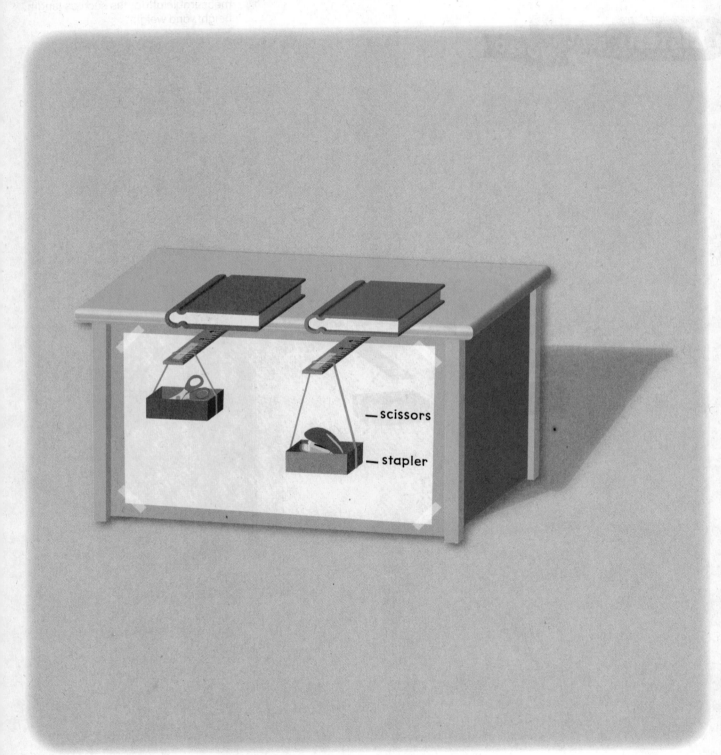

— scissors

— stapler

DIRECTIONS **1.** Look at the marks that show the different weights. Circle the mark that shows the heavier object.

Name _____

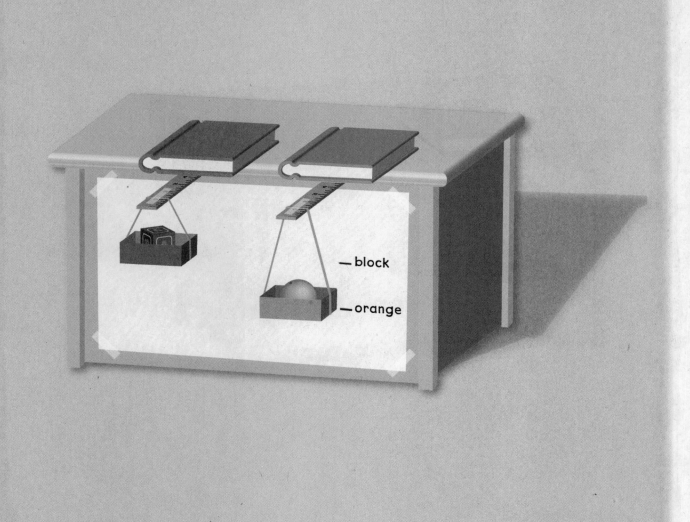

— block

— orange

DIRECTIONS **2.** Look at the marks that show
the different weights. Circle the mark that shows the
lighter object.

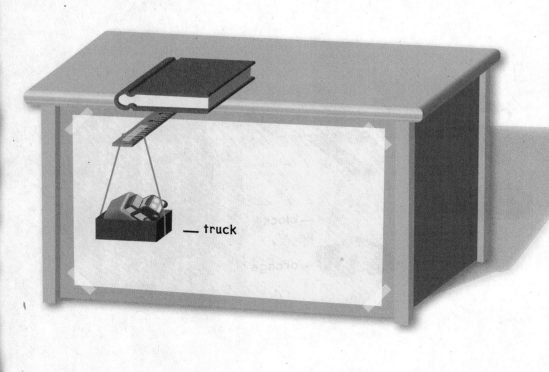

— truck

DIRECTIONS I. Use blue to mark a line for an object lighter than the truck. Use red to mark a line for an object heavier than the truck.

HOME ACTIVITY • Have your child hold an object in each hand and tell you which object is heavier and which object is lighter.

492 four hundred ninety-two

FOR MORE PRACTICE:
Florida Benchmarks Practice Book, pp. P271–P272

Name _____

Order Weights

Essential Question How can you order the weights of objects?

 Unlock the Problem

 MA.K.G.3.1 Compare and order objects indirectly or directly using measurable attributes such as length, height, and weight.

DIRECTIONS Look at the objects. Talk about which of these objects might be the lightest and which might be the heaviest. Mark an X on the lightest object. Circle the heaviest object.

Chapter 11 • Lesson 9

Share and Show

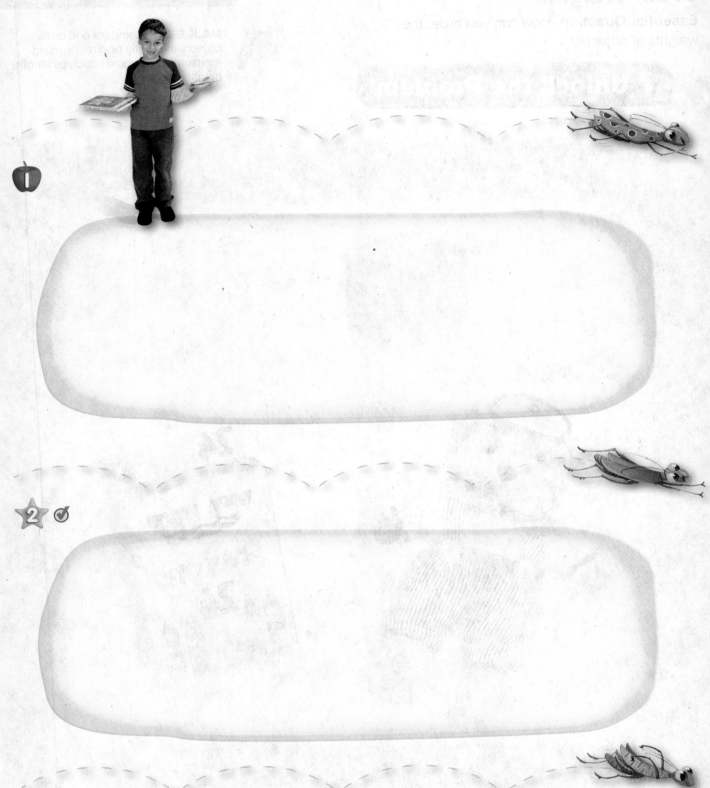

1

2 ✓

DIRECTIONS Find a book in the classroom. **1.** Find a classroom object that is lighter than the book. Draw it in the work space. **2.** Find a classroom object that is heavier than the book. Draw it in the work space.

Name _____

DIRECTIONS **3.** Find three classroom objects that have different weights. Draw the objects in order from lightest to heaviest.

On Your Own

DIRECTIONS Draw to show what you know about ordering objects by weight. Tell about your drawing.

HOME ACTIVITY • Have your child place three household objects in order by weight from the lightest to the heaviest.

496 four hundred ninety-six

FOR MORE PRACTICE:
Florida Benchmarks Practice Book, pp. P273–P274

Name _____

Vocabulary

1

taller   shorter

2

heavier   lighter

Concepts

 3

_____   _____   _____

- -

_____   _____   _____

4

DIRECTIONS **1–2.** Draw lines to match the words to the objects
(MA.K.G.3.1) **3.** Write the numbers 1, 2, and 3 to order the objects
from shortest to tallest. (MA.K.G.3.1) **4.** Look at the objects. Mark an
X on the lightest object. Circle the heaviest object. (MA.K.G.3.1)

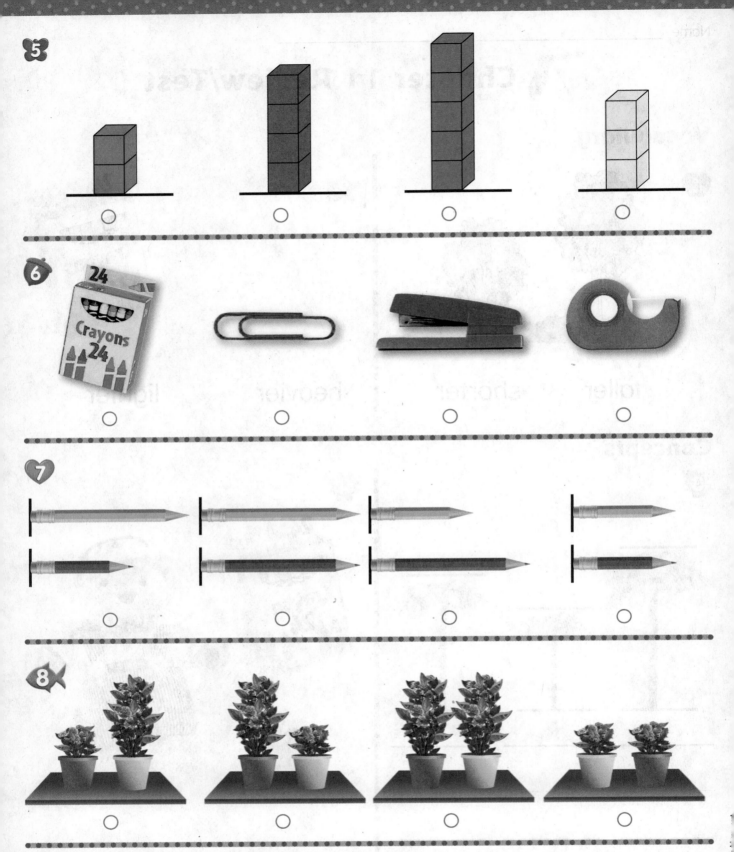

5

○ ○ ○ ○

6

24
Crayons
24

○ ○ ○ ○

7

○ ○ ○ ○

8

○ ○ ○ ○

DIRECTIONS **5.** Mark under the block tower that is the tallest.
(MA.K.G.3.1) **6.** Mark under the object that is the lightest (MA.K.G.3.1)
7. Mark under the picture that shows the orange pencil is shorter than the
green pencil. (MA.K.G.3.1) **8.** Mark under the picture that shows the plant
in the yellow planter is taller than the plant in the blue planter. (MA.K.G.3.1)

Name _____

9

○   ○   ○   ○

10

○   ○   ○   ○

11

○   ○   ○   ○

12

○   ○   ○   ○

DIRECTIONS **9.** Mark under the picture that shows the crayons in order from shortest to longest. (MA.K.G.3.1) **10.** The red flower is shorter than the orange flower but taller than the yellow flower. Mark under the picture that shows the flowers. (MA.K.G.3.1) **11.** Mark under the object that is the heaviest. (MA.K.G.3.1) **12.** Mark under the block tower that is the shortest. (MA.K.G.3.1)

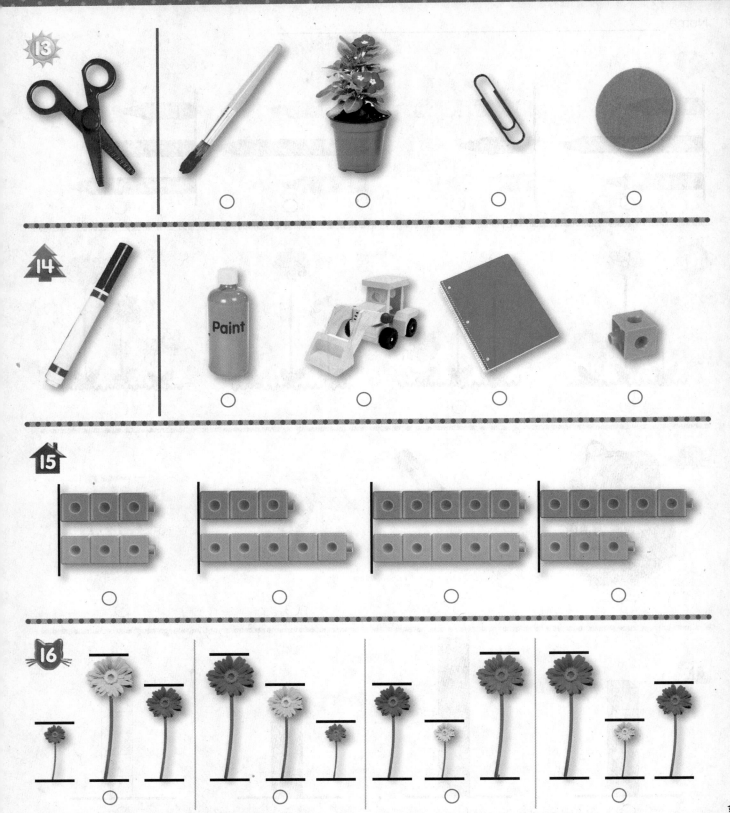

DIRECTIONS **13.** Mark under the object that is heavier than the one at the beginning of the row. (MA.K.G.3.1) **14.** Mark under the object that is lighter than the one at the beginning of the row. (MA.K.G.3.1) **15.** Mark under the picture that shows the orange cube train is longer than the green cube train. (MA.K.G.3.1) **16.** Mark under the picture that shows the red flower is shorter than the yellow flower. (MA.K.G.3.1)

500 five hundred

Name _____

Show What You Know

Order Numbers

1 13 _____

 2 _____ 6

3 _____ 10 _____

Comparing

4

5

_____   _____

DIRECTIONS **1.** Write the number that comes after thirteen. **2.** Write the number that comes before six. **3.** Write the numbers that come before and after ten. **4.** Circle the pencil that is longer. **5.** Count the objects in each set. Write how many. Circle the set with more.

FAMILY NOTE: This page checks your child's understanding of important skills needed for success in Chapter 12.

Name _____

before

after

DIRECTIONS Circle to show what the rabbit did before watering the seeds. Matk an X to show what the rabbit did after watering the seeds.

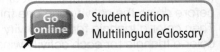

Go online • Student Edition
• Multilingual eGlossary

Chapter 12

Game

Before and After

DIRECTIONS Play with a partner. Decide who goes first. Take turns spinning the spinner. Look at the picture. Tell one thing you do before doing the activity and one thing you do after doing the activity. Then color a triangle for the activity you landed on. The first player to color a triangle for each activity wins the game.

MATERIALS paper clip, pencil, crayons

Name _____

Morning and Afternoon

Essential Question How can you understand time words such as *morning* and *afternoon*?

MA.K.G.5.I Demonstrate an understanding of the concept of time using identifiers such as morning, afternoon, day, week, month, year, before/after, and shorter/longer.

Listen and Draw — REAL WORLD

morning

afternoon

morning

afternoon

DIRECTIONS Look at the pictures. Talk about what is happening in the pictures. Circle the time of day when this activity may take place.

© Houghton Mifflin Harcourt

Chapter 12 · Lesson 1

Share and Show

DIRECTIONS **I.** Listen to the teacher. Circle the picture that shows the morning. **2.** Circle the picture that shows the afternoon.

Name _____

DIRECTIONS **3.** Listen to the teacher. Circle the picture that shows the morning. **4.** Circle the picture that shows the afternoon.

Chapter 12 • Lesson 1

PROBLEM SOLVING REAL WORLD

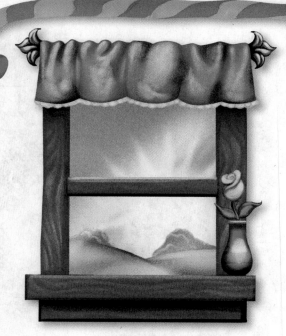

morning

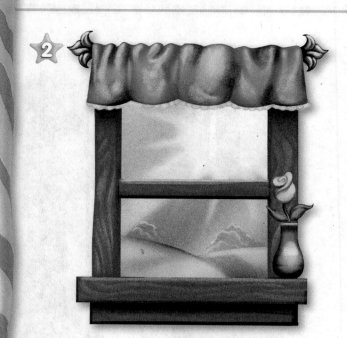

afternoon

DIRECTIONS 1-2. Draw to show what you know about morning and afternoon.

HOME ACTIVITY · Have your child draw two pictures, showing things he or she does in the morning and in the afternoon.

FOR MORE PRACTICE:
Florida Benchmarks Practice Book, pp. P281-P282

Name _____

Days in a Week

Essential Question How can you understand the days in a week?

MA.K.G.5.1 Demonstrate an understanding of the concept of time using identifiers such as morning, afternoon, day, week, month, year, before/after, and shorter/longer.

Listen and Draw

Sunday Monday Tuesday Wednesday Thursday Friday Saturday

DIRECTIONS Point to each day name as you say them in order. Circle the name for today. Draw something you would like to do today.

Share and Show

| Sunday | Monday | Tuesday | Wednesday | Thursday | Friday | Saturday |

⭐ 2 ✓

Tuesday

Friday

Sunday

Wednesday

Saturday

Monday

Thursday

DIRECTIONS **1.** Point to and say each day of the week. Circle the name for today. **2.** Number the days in order, beginning with Sunday.

510 five hundred ten

Name _____

Sunday	Monday	Tuesday	Wednesday	Thursday	Friday	Saturday
🎣	⚽	🎹	🥽	⚽	🍕	🚗

 3

1   2   3

 4

fishing   **swimming**   **soccer**

5

Monday   **Tuesday**   **Friday**

DIRECTIONS Circle your answer. **3.** On how many days is soccer played?
4. Which sport is played on Wednesday? **5.** On which day is the piano lesson?

Chapter 12 · Lesson 2

PROBLEM SOLVING REAL WORLD

Sunday Monday Tuesday Wednesday Thursday Friday Saturday

1

5   6   7   days in a week

2

Monday   Wednesday   Friday

3

Thursday   Saturday   Tuesday

DIRECTIONS   Circle your answer.
1. How many days are in a week?
2. Which day is two days after Wednesday?
3. Which day is one week from Saturday?

HOME ACTIVITY • Have your child say the days of the week in order beginning with Sunday.

512   five hundred twelve

FOR MORE PRACTICE:
Florida Benchmarks Practice Book, pp. P283–P284

Sequence Events: Before and After

Essential Question How can you understand time words such as *before* and *after*?

MA.K.G.5.1 Demonstrate an understanding of the concept of time using identifiers such as morning, afternoon, day, week, month, year, before/after, and shorter/longer.

Listen and Draw REAL WORLD

Morning

Afternoon

Yesterday	Today	Tomorrow

Sunday	Monday	Tuesday	Wednesday	Thursday	Friday	Saturday

DIRECTIONS Look at the charts. Use the words *before* and *after* to tell about order. Circle what you know about today.

Share and Show

yesterday

today

tomorrow

Sunday

Monday

Tuesday

Wednesday

Thursday

Friday

Saturday

DIRECTIONS **1.** Find the name of the day it is today. Trace the name. Draw a line to the word *today*. Do the same for the name of the day before today and the word *yesterday*. Do the same for the name of the day after today and the word *tomorrow*.

2

yesterday

3

today

4

tomorrow

DIRECTIONS   2. Draw something that happened yesterday.   **3.** Draw something that is happening today.   **4.** Draw something that may happen tomorrow.

HOME ACTIVITY • Have your child tell you what day it was yesterday.

Concepts and Skills

Sunday   Monday   Tuesday   Wednesday   Thursday   Friday   Saturday

---

2

| Today is Monday | Sunday | Tuesday | Wednesday |

3

Go home   Go to school

🌸 Test Prep

4

Monday	Tuesday	Wednesday	Thursday
🎹	🎣	⚽	🥽

Monday   Tuesday   Wednesday   Thursday
○   ○   ○   ○

DIRECTIONS **1.** What is the first day of the week? Circle the day. (MA.K.G.5.1)
2. If today is Monday, what day is tomorrow? Circle the day. (MA.K.G.5.1)
3. Circle the picture that shows the afternoon. (MA.K.G.5.1)   **4.** Mark under the
day that has swimming practice. (MA.K.G.5.1)

Name _____

Weeks in a Month

Essential Question How can you understand the weeks in a month?

MA.K.G.5.1 Demonstrate an understanding of the concept of time using identifiers such as morning, afternoon, day, week, month, year, before/after, and shorter/longer.

Listen and Draw REAL WORLD

May

Sunday	Monday	Tuesday	Wednesday	Thursday	Friday	Saturday
1	2	3	4	5	6	7
8	9	10	11	12	13	14
15	16	17	18	19	20	21
22	23	24	25	26	27	28
29	30	31				

DIRECTIONS Look at the calendar. Point to each date as you count. Talk about the days in a week and the full weeks in this month. Color the second week of this month.

Chapter 12 • Lesson 4

Share and Show

August

Sunday	Monday	Tuesday	Wednesday	Thursday	Friday	Saturday
	1	2	3	4	5	6
7	8	9	10	11	12	13
14	15	16	17	18	19	20
21	22	23	24	25	26	27
28	29	30	31			

1 4
5
6

2 4
5
6

3 ✓ Sunday
Monday
Tuesday

4 ✓ August 13
August 16
August 19

DIRECTIONS Look at the calendar. Circle your answer. **1.** How many Mondays are in this month? **2.** How many Fridays are in this month? **3.** What day of the week is August 9? **4.** What date is one week after August 9?

Name _____

November

Sunday	Monday	Tuesday	Wednesday	Thursday	Friday	Saturday
		1	2	3	4	5
6	7	8	9	10	11	12
13	14	15	16	17	18	19
20	21	22	23	24	25	26
27	28	29	30			

DIRECTIONS 5. Use red to color the name of the month. Use yellow to color the names of the days of the week. Use green to color the third week of the month. Use blue to color the fourth week of the month.

Chapter 12 · Lesson 4

PROBLEM SOLVING REAL WORLD

1

November						
Sunday	Monday	Tuesday	Wednesday	Thursday	Friday	Saturday
		1	2	3	4	5
6	7	8	9	10	11	12
13	14	15	16	17	18	19
20	21	22	23	24	25	26
27	28	29	30			

December						
Sunday	Monday	Tuesday	Wednesday	Tuesday	Friday	Saturday
				1	2	3
4	5	6	7	8	9	10
11	12	13	14	15	16	17
18	19	20	21	22	23	24
25	26	27	28	29	30	31

Sunday   Monday   Tuesday   Wednesday
Thursday   Friday   Saturday

 2

DIRECTIONS   1. If the last day of the month is Wednesday, what will be the first day of the next month? Circle that day.   **2.** Draw to show an activity you like to do in one of these months.

HOME ACTIVITY • Have your child tell you what day of the week it will be one week from today.

FOR MORE PRACTICE:
Florida Benchmarks Practice Book, pp. P287–P288

Name _____

Months in a Year

Essential Question How can you understand the months in a year?

MA.K.G.5.1 Demonstrate an understanding of the concept of time using identifiers such as morning, afternoon, day, week, month, year, before/after, and shorter/longer.

Listen and Draw REAL WORLD

January

Sunday	Monday	Tuesday	Wednesday	Thursday	Friday	Saturday
						1
2	3	4	5	6	7	8
9	10	11	12	13	14	15
16	17	18	19	20	21	22
23	24	25	26	27	28	29
30	31					

February

Sunday	Monday	Tuesday	Wednesday	Thursday	Friday	Saturday
		1	2	3	4	5
6	7	8	9	10	11	12
13	14	15	16	17	18	19
20	21	22	23	24	25	26
27	28					

March

Sunday	Monday	Tuesday	Wednesday	Thursday	Friday	Saturday
		1	2	3	4	5
6	7	8	9	10	11	12
13	14	15	16	17	18	19
20	21	22	23	24	25	26
27	28	29	30	31		

April

Sunday	Monday	Tuesday	Wednesday	Thursday	Friday	Saturday
					1	2
3	4	5	6	7	8	9
10	11	12	13	14	15	16
17	18	19	20	21	22	23
24	25	26	27	28	29	30

May

Sunday	Monday	Tuesday	Wednesday	Thursday	Friday	Saturday
1	2	3	4	5	6	7
8	9	10	11	12	13	14
15	16	17	18	19	20	21
22	23	24	25	26	27	28
29	30	31				

June

Sunday	Monday	Tuesday	Wednesday	Thursday	Friday	Saturday
			1	2	3	4
5	6	7	8	9	10	11
12	13	14	15	16	17	18
19	20	21	22	23	24	25
26	27	28	29	30		

July

Sunday	Monday	Tuesday	Wednesday	Thursday	Friday	Saturday
					1	2
3	4	5	6	7	8	9
10	11	12	13	14	15	16
17	18	19	20	21	22	23
24	25	26	27	28	29	30
31						

August

Sunday	Monday	Tuesday	Wednesday	Thursday	Friday	Saturday
	1	2	3	4	5	6
7	8	9	10	11	12	13
14	15	16	17	18	19	20
21	22	23	24	25	26	27
28	29	30	31			

September

Sunday	Monday	Tuesday	Wednesday	Thursday	Friday	Saturday
				1	2	3
4	5	6	7	8	9	10
11	12	13	14	15	16	17
18	19	20	21	22	23	24
25	26	27	28	29	30	

October

Sunday	Monday	Tuesday	Wednesday	Thursday	Friday	Saturday
						1
2	3	4	5	6	7	8
9	10	11	12	13	14	15
16	17	18	19	20	21	22
23	24	25	26	27	28	29
30	31					

November

Sunday	Monday	Tuesday	Wednesday	Thursday	Friday	Saturday
		1	2	3	4	5
6	7	8	9	10	11	12
13	14	15	16	17	18	19
20	21	22	23	24	25	26
27	28	29	30			

December

Sunday	Monday	Tuesday	Wednesday	Thursday	Friday	Saturday
					1	2	3
4	5	6	7	8	9	10
11	12	13	14	15	16	17
18	19	20	21	22	23	24
25	26	27	28	29	30	31

DIRECTIONS Point to the months as you say them in order. Count to find out how many months are in one year. Circle the month it is now.

Share and Show

| January | February | March | April | May | June |

January

February

March

April

May

June

DIRECTIONS **1.** Circle the month that comes between January and March. **2.** Circle the month that comes after May.

522 five hundred twenty-two

July	August	September	October	November	December

July

August

September

October

November

December

DIRECTIONS **3.** Circle the month that comes between July and September. **4.** Circle the month that comes before November.

PROBLEM SOLVING REAL WORLD

January	
February	
March	
April	
May	
June	
July	
August	
September	
October	
November	
December	

1
February
March
May

2
July
November
January

3
12
10
14

4
April
June
July

DIRECTIONS Circle your answer. **1.** What month comes right before April? **2.** What is the first month of the year? **3.** How many months are in one year? **4.** What month comes right after May?

HOME ACTIVITY • Show your child a year calendar. Have your child name the months of the year as he or she points to them.

524 five hundred twenty-four

FOR MORE PRACTICE:
Florida Benchmarks Practice Book, pp. P289–P290

More Time, Less Time

Essential Question How can you understand activities that are shorter or longer?

MA.K.G.5.1 Demonstrate an understanding of the concept of time using identifiers such as morning, afternoon, day, week, month, year, before/after, and shorter/longer.

Listen and Draw

DIRECTIONS Look at the pictures. Talk about whether it would take more time or less time to squeeze orange juice or to pour it from the carton. Circle the activity that would usually take more time.

Share and Show

DIRECTIONS 1–4. Circle the activity that would usually take more time.

5

6

7

8

DIRECTIONS 5–8. Circle the activity that would usually take less time.

PROBLEM SOLVING REAL WORLD

DIRECTIONS Draw two pictures to show what you know about activities that would usually take more time and less time.

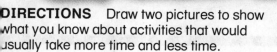

HOME ACTIVITY • Ask your child which of two chores, such as making the bed or setting the table, would take more time. Have your child do both chores while you time them, and then compare which chore actually took more time.

FOR MORE PRACTICE:
Florida Benchmarks Practice Book, pp. P291–P292

Act It Out

Essential Question How can you act out
activities that take shorter and longer times?

MA.K.G.5.1 Demonstrate an
understanding of the concept of time
using identifiers such as morning,
afternoon, day, week, month, year,
before/after, and shorter/longer.

🔑 Unlock the Problem

DIRECTIONS Look at the pictures. Talk about whether it would
take longer to make the shape with a cookie cutter or make the cat.
Act out the two activities. Circle the activity that took a longer time.

Chapter 12 • Lesson 7

five hundred twenty-nine **529**

Share and Show

DIRECTIONS 1–3. Mark an X beside the activity you think will take a longer time. Act out the two activities. Circle the one that took a longer time.

Name _____

DIRECTIONS 4–6. Mark an X beside the activity you think will take a shorter time. Act out the two activities. Circle the one that took a shorter time.

On Your Own

DIRECTIONS Which activity would usually take a longer time? Act out the two activities. Circle the one that took a longer time. Tell why it took a longer time.

HOME ACTIVITY • Ask your child to tell about two things he or she could do to help out at home. Have your child tell which activity would take a shorter time. Have him or her act out the chores to verify which chore took a shorter time.

FOR MORE PRACTICE:
Florida Benchmarks Practice Book, pp. P293–P294

Chapter 12 Review/Test

Vocabulary

January February March
April May June
July August September
October November December

Concepts

May

Sunday	Monday	Tuesday	Wednesday	Thursday	Friday	Saturday
1	2	3	4	5	6	7
8	9	10	11	12	13	14
15	16	17	18	19	20	21
22	23	24	25	26	27	28
29	30	31				

_____

- - - - - - - - - - -

DIRECTIONS 1. Circle the month that comes after August. (MA.K.G.5.1)
2. Circle the activity that would take longer to make. (MA.K.G.5.1) **3.** How many
Fridays this month? Write your answer. (MA.K.G.5.1) **4.** Look at the pictures. Circle
the activity that takes more time. (MA.K.G.5.1)

○   ○   ○   ○

August						
Sunday	Monday	Tuesday	Wednesday	Thursday	Friday	Saturday
	1	2	3	4	5	6
7	8	9	10	11	12	13
14	15	16	17	18	19	20

Sunday   Monday   Tuesday   Wednesday

○   ○   ○   ○

Sunday
Monday
Tuesday
Wednesday
Thursday
Friday
Saturday

Sunday   Wednesday   Saturday   Tuesday

○   ○   ○   ○

Monday	Tuesday	Wednesday	Thursday	Friday
(soccer ball)	(piano)	(goggles/flippers)	(soccer ball)	(paintbrush)

○   ○   ○   ○

DIRECTIONS   **5.** Mark the picture that shows something that usually happens early in the morning. (MA.K.G.5.1)   **6.** What day is August fifteenth? Mark under that day. (MA.K.G.5.1)   **7.** If today is Thursday, what day was yesterday? Mark under that day. (MA.K.G.5.1)   **8.** Mark under the picture that shows the activity on Friday. (MA.K.G.5.1)

9

January   August   June   November

○   ○   ○   ○

10

○   ○   ○   ○

11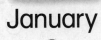

January   April   May   October

○   ○   ○   ○

12

Sunday	Monday	Tuesday	Wednesday	Thursday	Friday	Saturday
	5		6	7	8	
	○		○	○	○	

DIRECTIONS 9. Mark under the word that tells the name of the month. (MA.K.G.5.1) 10. Mark under the picture that shows something that usually happens in the afternoon. (MA.K.G.5.1) 11. Mark under the month that comes between September and November. (MA.K.G.5.1) 12. Mark under the number that tells how many days are in a week. (MA.K.G.5.1)

13

Monday	Tuesday	Wednesday	Thursday	Friday
🎹	⚾	〰	⚾	🥽

0 ○ 1 ○ 2 ○ 3 ○

14

Sunday
Monday
Tuesday
Wednesday
Thursday
Friday
Saturday

Tuesday ○   Monday ○   Saturday ○   Wednesday ○

15

September						
Sunday	Monday	Tuesday	Wednesday	Thursday	Friday	Saturday
				1	2	3
4	5	6	7	8	9	10
11	12	13	14	15	16	17

Saturday ○   Sunday ○   Monday ○   Tuesday ○

16

December ○   February ○   May ○   August ○

DIRECTIONS **13.** Mark under the number that tells how many days a week is baseball practice. (MA.K.G.5.1) **14.** Mark under the day that comes right after Tuesday. (MA.K.G.5.1) **15.** Which day is September 11th? Mark under that day. (MA.K.G.5.1) **16.** Mark under the month that comes after April. (MA.K.G.5.1)

536 five hundred thirty-six

Picture Glossary

above [sobre]

The kite is **above** the rabbit.

add [sumar]

$3 + 2 = 5$

after [después]

48 is just **after** 47.

afternoon [tarde]

are left [quedan]

2  **are left**

before [antes]

46 is just **before** 47.

below [debajo]

The rabbit is **below** the kite.

beside [al lado]

The tree is **beside** the bush.

between [entre]

47 is **between** 46 and 48.

big [grande]

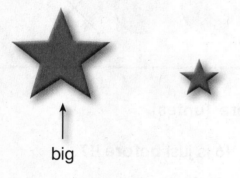

big

circle [círculo]

color [color]

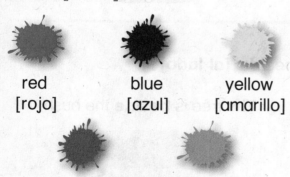

red
[rojo]

blue
[azul]

yellow
[amarillo]

green
[verde]

orange
[anaranjado]

corner [esquina]

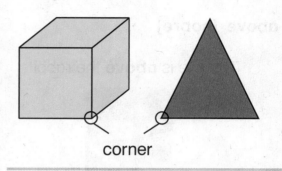

corner

cube [cubo]

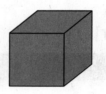

curved surface
[superficie curva]

Some solids have
a **curved surface**.

cylinder [cilindro]

days of the week
[días de la semana]

equal sides [lados iguales]

eight [ocho]

fewer [menos]

3 **fewer** birds

eighteen [dieciocho]

fifteen [quince]

eleven [once]

five [cinco]

flat surface [superficie plana]

Some solids have **flat surfaces**.

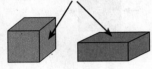

four [cuatro]

fourteen [catorce]

greater [mayor]

9 is **greater** than 6.

heavier [más pesado]

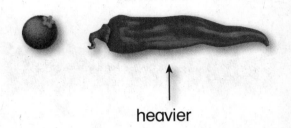

heavier

heaviest [el más pesado]

heaviest

hexagon [hexágono]

in all [en total]

2 plus 1 is equal to 3.
There are 3 **in all**.

inside [dentro]

inside the box

join [unirse]

left [izquierda]

The kite is to the **left** of the bird.

less [menor]

9 is **less** than 11.

9

11

less time [menos tiempo]

lighter [más liviano]

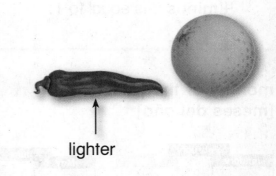

lighter

lightest [el más liviano]

lightest

longer [más largo]

longer

longest [el más largo]

minus − [menos]

$$4 - 3 = 1$$

4 **minus** 3 is equal to 1.

months of the year
[meses del año]

more [más]

2 **more** leaves

more time [más tiempo]

morning [mañana]

next to [al lado de]

The bush is **next to** the tree.

nine [nueve]

nineteen [diecinueve]

---

one [uno]

---

one fewer [uno menos]

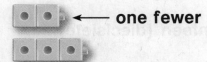

one fewer

---

one more [uno más]

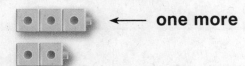

one more

---

outside [fuera]

outside
the box

---

over [encima]

The kite is **over** the rabbit.

---

pattern [patrón]

You can use a **pattern** to show ways to make 7.

---

plus + [más]

2 **plus** 1 is equal to 3.
2 + 1 = 3

---

rectangle [rectángulo]

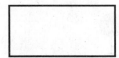

rhombus [rombo]

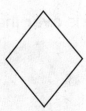

right [derecha]

The bird is to the **right** of the kite.

roll [rodar]

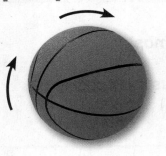

same number
[el mismo número]

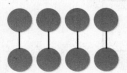

separate [separarse]

seven [siete]

seventeen [diecisiete]

shorter [más corto]

shorter

shortest [el más corto]

shortest

side [lado]

side

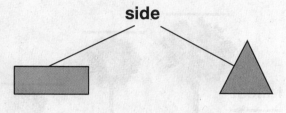

six [seis]

sixteen [dieciséis]

slide [deslizar]

small [pequeño]

sort [clasificar]

You can **sort** these bears.

sphere [esfera]

square [cuadrado]

stack [apilar]

subtract [restar]

Subtract to find out how many are left.

taller [más alto]

taller

tallest [el más alto]

tallest

ten [diez]

thirteen [trece]

three [tres]

today [hoy]

the day it is now

Sunday	Monday	Tuesday	W...
1	②↑	3	

yesterday   today   tomorrow

tomorrow [mañana]

the day after today

Sunday	Monday	Tuesday	W...
1	2	③↑	

yesterday   today   tomorrow

trapezoid [trapecio]

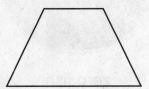

triangle [triángulo]

 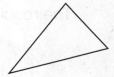

twelve [doce]

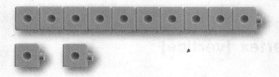

twenty [veinte]

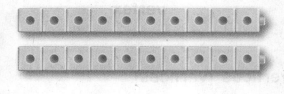

two [dos]

under [debajo]

The rabbit is **under** the kite.

vertex [vértice]

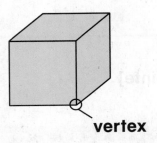

vertex

vertices [vértices]

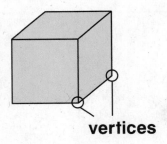

vertices

week [semana]

year [año]

yesterday [ayer]

the day before today

Sunday	Monday	Tuesday	
①	2	3	

yesterday　today　tomorrow

zero, none [cero]

zero fish

Photo Credits